From Dumyat to Mont Blanc

Ian McNeish

Other Books by
Ian McNeish

The Fearn Bobby

FROM DUMYAT
TO MONT BLANC

Being Alive with Mountains

Ian McNeish

From Dumyat to Mont Blanc: Being Alive with Mountains by Ian McNeish.

First published in Great Britain in 2020 by Extremis Publishing Ltd.,
Suite 218, Castle House, 1 Baker Street, Stirling, FK8 1AL, United Kingdom.
www.extremispublishing.com

Extremis Publishing is a Private Limited Company registered in Scotland (SC509983) whose Registered Office is Suite 218, Castle House, 1 Baker Street, Stirling, FK8 1AL, United Kingdom.

Typeset in Goudy Bookletter 1911, designed by The League of Moveable Type.

Printed and bound in Great Britain by IngramSpark, Chapter House, Pitfield, Kiln Farm, Milton Keynes, MK11 3LW, United Kingdom.

Cover photograph of Beinn Alligin is Copyright © Keith Yates, all rights reserved, and appears by kind permission of the photographer.
Cover design and book design is Copyright © Thomas A. Christie.
Author images are Copyright © Ian McNeish, all rights reserved, and appear from the author's personal photographic collection with permission.
Incidental interior illustrations by Mohamed Hassan at Pixabay.

Stac Polly by Cliff Wedgbury is Copyright © Cliff Wedgbury, all rights reserved, and is reproduced in this text by kind permission of the poet.

Internal photographic illustrations are Copyright © Ian McNeish, all rights reserved, unless otherwise indicated. While every reasonable effort has been made to contact copyright holders and secure permission for all images reproduced in this work, we offer apologies for any instances in which this was not possible and for any inadvertent omissions.

To
Catherine O'Hara
and
Thomas Barbour McNeish

Two of the bravest, most non-judgmental and decent people it was my privilege to know. Both tragically taken when so young. One from the ravages of serious illness and one from the ravages of war.
Thank you, mum and dad.

FROM DUMYAT TO MONT BLANC

Being Alive with Mountains

Ian McNeish

Misinformation

'The outlook is fair', the weather woman said;
her studio a cocoon of truth.
I ascend the ridge through stinging rain and hail, soon to
be a white hell.
Sweat, or sleet, nipping my eyes, a partnership?
I bend double, negotiating gale blown snow; a blizzard,
in truth.

Introduction

MY rucksack and tent, still unpacked, lay alone and unattended in the middle of a hinterland of peat hags in a less-travelled corner of the country I love. To be correct, this was not a corner of Scotland: this was smack bang in the centre. I was carefully manoeuvring myself through said peat-hagged hinterland, bottle of water in one pocket and some chocolate and nuts in the other, as I made my way to a remote hill that was on my Corbett 'bagging' list. Beinn Bhreac, the Speckled Hill. It is described in one journal as 'an exceptionally remote hill in an empty wilderness be-tween the Cairngorms to the north and Atholl to the south' – suffixed by the quaint comment: 'One for the real enthusiast'. I can attest to that. Cackling grouse, the occasional meadow pipit and winter-garbed mountain hares were my closest com-panions that day. That is, until I met a Mackem.

I had set out early from Blair Atholl and walked north, along Glen Tilt to Gilbert's Bridge, where I crossed the River to the west bank. I continued north, following another track that led me away from the river, over another two perfectly-shaped old, stone-arched bridges, into Gleann Mhairc, on the east flank of of Beinn Mheadhonach – the 'Middle Hill' – a distinctive, perfectly shaped, narrow wedge, lying directly to the north of Blair Castle. It is easily recognisable from the A9 trunk road to the south, where it appears as a distinctive, and impressive, narrow whaleback. Not long after entering the narrow steep-sided glen I encounter another shapely, arched stone bridge, taking me over Allt Mhairc onto the east flank and my first steep ascent of the day. Carrying a tent and cooker, and all else that goes with a plan to stay out on the hill overnight, adds to the fun. I sweat up the steep sided gleann, through knee-deep heather, onto the spine of 'Middle Hill'. After that it is simply about pace and rhythm as I ease myself up onto the summit, at 901 metres; not much below Munro status. It has a second and lower top, a bit to the north, Carn a' Chiaraidh. I choose the latter for my lunch stop and, as I munch fruitcake with tomatoes and cheese washed over with simple burn water, I gaze north into the huge expanse of upland moor towards the distinctive and impressive Munro duo of Carn an Fhidhlier and An Sgarsoch,

Bivouac in hinterland near Beinn Bhreac

4

guardians of The Feshie and The Geldie and southern outliers of the huge Cairngorm plateau. Lunch and gazing north finished, it is time to tackle said boggy hinterland and find a suitable camp site. I had walked about nine miles, some of the latter over difficult, ankle-breaking ground, when I found the perfect spot for my overnight bivouac. I dump my rucksack and tent on a reasonably flat area, right beside a burn that meandered – and still does – through the hag, on its gurgling journey to Loch Mairc, some distance to the north east. *No likelihood of a flash flood*, I muse?

I had been through this part some years before, when Munro bagging. High point of that day was lying by the sun-kissed bank of Feith an Lochain, the steam that flows south from Loch Mhairc before changing its name to Allt Mhairc, as it flows into Gleann Mhairc, having some lunch and watching a lizard scooting and flitting about, totally oblivious of our presence. Mind you, I had nearly trampled on it earlier, as I had a red deer fawn. The latter stayed low and did not stir, and I quickly moved away, hoping I had not spooked its mother. The lizard had no such qualms, and played about for a while as we dined and looked on. How lucky we are.

That was then. Back to the now, and my solo hinterland trip and serendipity. Having temporarily ditched all my gear and after some grub, I head off to the Speckled Hill. Beinn Bhreac is guarded to the south by the upper reaches of the Tarf Water. No way round, so I plunge across; not too wet. It was just after six o'clock that evening, and about three miles from my campsite, when I crested the final rise leading to the summit. Was I in for a surprise: there was a lone figure sitting by the cairn. This place really is off the beaten track, and two 'real enthusiasts' finding themselves at the summit of an exceptionally remote hill, virtually simultaneously, is a bit of happenstance. We chat for a while. His first concern is for my welfare, as he notices I am innocent of rucksack. He asks where it is, knowing I cannot be heading back to the bright lights of Blair Atholl at that time. I point back from whence I came, the hinterland of bog, and said, 'about three miles back that way'. He cannot understand how I will find it, even after I assure him I will. I ask him where he is bound, and what he said over the next few minutes had me in awe of him. He is from Sunderland, a Mackem. He had suffered from cancer and was assured it was in remission. A recent routine test tragically overturned that earlier prognosis. His cancer was back, and had spread – to quote him, 'with a vengeance'. He had only received that news about two weeks before. He spoke to his family and they agreed to his plan. He was desperate to get back into the mountains of Scotland, perhaps for the last time. So a few days before our meeting, he packed his tent and gear, including chemotherapy tablets and other medication, and headed for the hills. A train from Sunderland to Newcastle, then on to Edinburgh. He alighted from the Inverness train at Blair Atholl. He had been two days camping in the area, and he planned another day or two before reversing the journey back to his family.

We chatted on a while and, as we shook hands and parted, he said, 'This is the best part'.

'The best part of what?' I asked.

'Being alive,' he answered.

We did not exchange names; it seemed irrelevant and unnecessary. We knew who we were. As I descended and looked back, he was still sitting by the summit cairn, staring north and deep in thought. I have never forgotten Mackem, and will not forget him. I still see him sitting with his back to the summit cairn, gazing north, contemplating mountains and glens, dreaming of days past and wondering about days to come, my approach interrupting his moment of reflection.

Serendipity? My earnest wish is that he beat his illness and maybe, one day, will read this and maybe get in touch. My second wish, is that I will do Mackem justice and evidence to the reader what he meant when he said, 'Being Alive'.

Obiter Dictum, I found my tent.

Chapter 1

THIS is not a guide book. Mind you, as I recount my experiences, I will leave plenty of clues as to my chosen routes. It is simply and unashamedly an account of a small part of my life meandering, perhaps *stravaiging* describes it best, through and over huge tracts of Scotland, with and without tent – not always on foot, as a bike occasionally features. I will also include some 'furth of Scotland' experiences, and I will deviate a bit more to have a look at a few hill and place names and muse over the English translations. A smattering of geology will emerge. It is a crucial element in the shaping of our country, the scenery: the mountains, the lochs and rivers, the flowers, the animals. What lies below in so many ways determines what lies above. So, because you will be traipsing about amongst its influences, I include a few references; not a lot. It is pretty much out of my comfort zone. I did seek expert advice. If you have a burning desire to do well in the next pub quiz and you think a question on shielings is sure to appear, I will say a bit about them. So stick with me, you might find something of interest.

I was, still am, a dedicated amateur, like the vast majority of others who venture out most weekends. And yes, I did manage some quite big challenges and I did ascend Mont

Blanc – but any fit person, with a bit of experience, the right guidance and the desire, can manage what I achieved. It is not, however, all about getting to the top of every mountain, although that is the aim of many and I can confess was a big part of my early drive. But the more time I shared with the rivers, glens and peaks, the more I appreciated simply being amongst them, watching and listening. I rejoiced in my fortune of being able to meander through what remained of Transhumance settlements, to follow in the tracks of the cloven footed Ruminantia and drovers – the creators of Scotland's economy for so many years – to wander through the glens of the Clans, to follow the Jacobites, to camp where perhaps proud Tinkers and Travellers had encamped in years gone by, and I was humbled to walk through the domains of the Clearance victims and to listen for their voices as their stories echoed through the mountains. Did they listen to the same whispering breezes, tinkling burns, cascading rivers, booming deer and birds in song that I did? Did these past travellers gaze in awe at it all; did they watch the water ouzel dip, did they jump back as the snipe upped from below their feet to twist and turn into the distance and were they startled by the grouse, clattering out of their heather nook, cackling and laughing, or perhaps warning of Red Coats? Did they look up when hearing the trilling and tew of a sacrifice of Snow Bunting, and watch as they melted away over a wintery ridge? Were they lucky enough to spy an eagle, majestically and effortlessly swinging along a mountain face, carving its shape in the air, leaving the observer with mouth agape? Did the glens and gulleys echo to the 'tac-tac' call of the ringed ouzel or its shriller, more urgent 'chrech-rech', as though startled by their passing. It's all out there, just waiting for you.

Whatever else the reader may take from this book, I hope that it will encourage some to pull over, park up, get out of the car and walk away from the tarmac onto a path or track – into a woodland, along a river, wherever; even just half a mile, it does not matter how far, it only matters that you take the steps. For that daft hour in your otherwise busy life, leave your telephone in the car, remove your ergonomically designed earpiece, then stand, sit, lie down, perhaps close your eyes and simply listen to the sound of nature. A near namesake, William Neish, was moved to say it better than I ever could, in this snatch of his poetry, taken from the 1893 publication, *The Harp of Perthshire*, by Robert Ford. From the poem 'The Braes Roun' Aboot Auchterairder':

I'm list'nin' again to the hum o' the bee
As it scans ilka flooer on the wet dewy lea;
Or list'nin' the laverock that sings blyth and free
'Bune the brae roun' aboot Auchterairder.

Scotland abounds with beauty. A beauty that is enhanced by being close to it, immersed in it. I have been fortunate enough to get close. I will not take you on a diary of chronological journeys, nor will I recount every step I took – because I took a lot. No; I will dip in and out of events, adventures perhaps, and I will do that in a randomness that suits my nature. I will employ, if I can, a *seanachaidh* way that takes you back to the days when families sat round the hearth, chatted and told stories, and – in following that style and tradition – it is my wish to keep you alert and hold your interest. You will be the judge of that. There will be encounters with characters who inspired me. I will be delighted if you now accompany me through the basement of its straths and glens, to the roof tops of its lofty ridges and peaks as I ramble and meander on my own very personal journey of discovery through Scotland. A journey that changed my life.

Before we head off, however, allow me a moment to explore my motivation. Why mountains? I can say for definite, I was not influenced by the mountains that surrounded me in my early, post-World War II childhood in Bonnybridge. The highest part of the village, Cowden Hill, at 180 feet might well be one of the lowest hills in Scotland to be adorned by an Ordinance Survey Trig Point. Bonnybridge offered a lot to my childhood and upbringing, but little – well, nothing, actually – by way of mountaineering. The talk amongst my school friends was of many things, but mountains never featured. Tensing and Hillary on Everest might have merited a mention; I cannot be sure. It was a different world. We simply made use of what we had, including sneaking down the clay mines in the vicinity. The Stein Brickworks head office and refractory were based in nearby Allandale. They had a few mines on the moorland to the south of Bonnybridge where they extracted the clay for brick making. These were drift mines with wheeled bogeys that ran on rails into the depths. Funny how the more adventurous of our group would be the ones to sneak down the ramp into the dark recesses. For the life of me, I have no memory of what we used to illuminate our trespass. I have no recollection of flashlights; were they even invented by then? Probably, but not a stock item in our household.

Antonine's Wall was very near our home and so provided us with a perfect play area, allowing our imagination to run free. Maybe the adventure gene could not be curtailed and, whether mountains or trespassing in drift mines, we were learning to explore and push boundaries. My dad's employment saw us move to Balloch, in the Vale of Leven – or as we knew it, The Vale. My parents had an old cabin cruiser on Loch Lomond, the *Seahawk*. It slept four with comfort, and we spent many weekends and our summer holidays touring the loch and sleeping on the islands. Favourites being Inchtavannach and Inchmoan. Topping up on provisions would see us anchored off Luss while dad or myself and Allister, my younger brother, would row ashore to access the village shop. They were great adventures, and Allister and I loved every minute of that part of our young lives.

To get from the *Seahawk* to land we had to use a pram dinghy. It was a particularly unstable and dangerous mode of transport and we had quickly to learn the art of rowing, balance and not capsizing it. A few soakings later, we were kind of getting the hang of it. I was only ten or eleven then and still could not swim. So I had to learn. Being able to swim was an advantage; no, it was essential. My method of learning was probably not conventional, although perhaps in these postwar days, it was as conventional as it gets. Like all young tatterdemalions I could not steer clear of danger, or perhaps just adventure.

One day after school, a group of us wandered up the road to the old decaying wooden pier at the foot of Loch Lomond. As I stood on the edge, the water – dark grey and foreboding – looked a long way down. 'How deep is it?' I heard myself ask, to no one in particular. Someone said, 'Aye, it will be fifty feet'. I am not sure what difference that made; I could not swim anyway. To add insult to injury, I was bloody chittering with the cold, frozen, and I was not even in the water.

I then asked: 'What do I do?'

'Just jump – and when you get in the water, keep your hands under and paddle like a dog. It's easy.'

Then I was on my own as the rest did just that; they jumped... well I think some dived. Having been suitably briefed, I jumped myself. To anyone who has never experienced this, trust me: you get a shock. First there is that feeling when your innards seem to be heading into the back of your throat, and there is the 'sploosh' as you hit the water with a violent impact. I had no idea how deep under the water I went. At first I hadn't a clue where 'up' was, not to mention the water in my nose. My next memory was thrashing my arms about and trying to get back to the surface. The impact followed by the thrashing must have been almost instantaneous, though it felt like an eternity. I did have the presence of mind to hold my breath, and that helped. Then my head was above the water and I was paddling like a mad dog (with due reverence to any dog having this read to them). My 'swimming' pals shouted encouraging words at me and, lo and behold, I was swimming – after a fashion. This turned into a regular adventure, and my confidence grew (and nobody drowned). Jumping off the deck of the *Seahawk* into the loch and swimming under the boat to

Seahawk and pram dinghy

14

come out on the other side was now easy. Rowing the pram dinghy was not so terrifying.

* * *

My time living in Balloch, at the southern end of Loch Lomond, certainly had me looking at mountains – if not actually ascending any. Ben Lomond dominated the view when looking north from Balloch, and still does. Its magnificent form, uniform shape and prominent shoulders formed the backcloth of my days there. A covering of snow in winter added to the stately, sentinel look, as though it was guarding the loch and observing all who ventured north. Setting my feet on it would take a few years, however, as my life in the interim would take me to many other places.

Was there a motivational person or an inspirational moment that pulled me to mountains? Not from my early days. My mum and dad were inspirational characters, but ascending mountains was not part of their experience. My dad had been a prisoner of war during the Second World War, and after it was over and he was home, he and mum were too busy earning a living and raising a family to indulge in much else. So where did the desire to climb and ramble amongst mountains come from? Perhaps the spirit of adventure is a genetic thing; perhaps one is born like that? The direction one takes is the bit that is developed by a variety of influences and opportunities, some scarcely recognised. There was not, as I recall, a particular *eureka* point that I can claim was 'the moment' mountains reached into my psyche; nothing like that. It was, certainly in my case, a gradual process and probably involved several unrelated experiences. One I recall came along from a completely unexpected source, in the shape of two of the most decent men it has ever been my privilege to know and to call friends: my father in law, Alex Goodsir, and his old pal Frank Wilson. Neither were mountaineers; they were just decent, lovable characters, full of enthusiasm for life and huge influences in my chosen mountain route, although they probably had no idea this was the case. They were hill fishermen and fanatical followers of Falkirk Football Club – hail, rain and shine. While finding hill lochs came second nature to them, I'm not sure navigation was a strong point. One wet, dark wintery evening in the late 1950s they were exiting the Morton Football Ground car park in Greenock, having just watched their beloved Falkirk Football Club beat Greenock Morton. They were in high spirits when they got into the car to drive home. Frank was driving. In the dark and horrible night they got slightly misplaced and were not sure of the road. Then fate lent a hand. They spied a car with a Stirlingshire number plate, WG. It was obviously heading their way, so they followed it. And follow it they did. In these days, vehicle registration numbers were issued locally and each area had its own unique identification. For example, West Lothian was SX and Stirlingshire was WG. They duked in and out of busy teatime traffic and, like a *Z-Cars* plot, they could not be shaken off. Like jam to a carpet, round bends, along straights, more bends, the only thoughts in their heads being the Falkirk win they had just witnessed, a warm supper and maybe an hour in the Black Bull Pub in Polmont to cap off a great day. After a few miles, the car had heated up, the windscreen cleared and life could not get any better. The road sign announcing their arrival in Largs hit them like a ton of bricks. *Largs? How the hell did we get tae Largs?* (Or words to that effect.)

Back to their inspirational intervention to my life. They always watched the game from the uncovered terracing at the railway end of old Brockville Park, the south terracing. No matter the weather, this hardy pair's support for the Bairns never wavered, nor could they be moved from their favourite perch – from whence, coincidently and importantly, they got a clear view of the distant Ochil Hills to the north. As I mentioned, they were enthusiastic hill fishermen and would travel the length and breadth of Scotland to fish remote rivers and even remoter hill lochs. They had years of experience tramping hills all over Scotland, although they had little idea which hills. They did, however, have perfect memories of the lochs. Many a hill and fishing discussion took place because of that view. One day, on that very terracing, Frank handed me a book and urged me to read it. I devoured it. One image seared itself on my consciousness. The Horns of Alligin. Not just the image, but the mystical name: like a Celtic warrior, or Norse God. As I would one day discover, it was neither named after a Norse God nor a mythical Celtic warrior. Mike Darton, in his book *The Dictionary of Scottish Place Names*, argues that because of the element *Ail* or *All* in the name, it means 'rocky' or perhaps 'rocky hill'. Others have a different take and suggest that it means 'the jewelled mountain'. The latter version is favoured by Pete Drummond in his book *Scottish Hill Names*. Alligin, certainly using that spelling, is not a Gaelic word. The nearest Gaelic word I find that approximates is *ailleagan*, or *alligean*. My Gaelic speaking friends on Harris are amused by my attempts to pin down a definitive translation, and explain it to me in this fashion: 'Gaelic is complicated in some ways, and in fact we can use the same word to describe different things, so not only is it a descriptive language – it is contextual. The nearest actual Gaelic word is probably *alligean*. However, that really does not strictly mean jewel – like a diamond, for instance. No, *alligean* is a kind of hybrid word, a made-up word, used as a term of endearment, usually to a child. When we say it, we are calling the child 'our small jewel'. I hope that helps'.

I consulted my friend's copy of *Dwelly*, one of the foremost Gaelic dictionaries, for the meaning of *All* and *Ail*. I found multiple meanings: 'foreign', 'horse', 'generation' and 'race' being just some. It can also mean 'cliff' or 'rock', as Mike Darton writes. The mountain has a huge visible scar – the black notch, Eag Dubh – running from top to bottom of the south flank, the result of a huge rock movement many thousands of years ago. Perhaps that is where the rock or rocky element of the name originated? So, you have choices. Both versions appear to have merit. I am sure a learned etymologist and Gaelic expert will tear my meanderings on the subject to pieces, but that will be okay. Is that not part of the fun? It is still fascinating to explore and, if nothing else, it evidences my earlier assertion that it is not always about getting to the top.

One thing is certain, however; whatever the mystery of its name, Beinn Alligin is a thing of beauty, and one thing is not in doubt – it played an important part in my motivation. I promised both Alex and Frank that one day I would climb that mysterious mountain and go over the 'mystical' Horns to the summit. I further promised that it would be my final big mountain – not knowing of Munros then – and if I did not get the others done, Alligin would stay innocent of my attentions, and remain a mystery. Oh, the book – it was called *The Scottish Peaks* by W.A. Poucher. I still have Frank's copy. It takes pride of place on my bookshelf. Unfortunately both these decent men died long before they would know if I kept my vow. If I could get a message to them, it would say: 'Trust me – I kept my promise'. To discover in which way, you will have to read on.

Another important motivation came a few years later. It was my second ever day out on a big hill – well, two, actually: Glas Maol and Creag Leacach in the eastern Cairngorms at Glenshee. I think that day was probably the clincher: the day my enthusiasm to get into mountains and move past dreaming was cast. I am sure many will question the motivational qualities of these two, but bear with me for a wee while (well, a few pages, anyway) and I will get back to explaining. Other things were happening about then; things like normal family life and earning a living, and things that took me around the country following employment. First to Essex, then to Aberdeen and to Dingwall, then back to the Central Belt of Scotland. Mix that with events that were much more important than any of these, and certainly hugely more important than whether or not I ever set foot on a hill again: marriage and three children. So exposure to hills during these years was a bit spasmodic.

I will return to motivations at this point, from a different angle, with a tale completely out of any chronological sequence but inserted here for a purpose. It raises the 'why bother at all?' question. It also demonstrates that Scotland's mountains are in control of how they receive you. A lesson one should learn early. The rewards they present – and trust me, there will be rewards – might be found in places, at times and in ways that perhaps did not always seem obvious when setting out. So stick with me, and perhaps I might be able to address both. I had been into mountains, in earnest, for a few years by this point. We were a bit tardy in setting out that autumn morning, and didn't get parked in Glen Etive until just before 11.00 am. Weather was good – cold but clear – as we meandered north out of the Central Belt on the belated commencement of our journey and our mountain adventure for that day. As we pass the north end of Annie's Straight, the beauty of Loch Lubnaig opened to our gaze. The morning water vapour clinging to the surface, just where it drains south into the Garbh Uisge, was stunning. Reminiscent of, perhaps, a classic *National Geographic* documentary, shot in some inaccessible, hidden, mystical, beautiful corner of the world. A corner most of us stare at in wide-mouthed wonder on our smart, flat-screen TVs, with little chance of ever getting there ourselves. This was none of these places. This was accessible Scotland, just a few short miles north of Callander, about an hour's drive north of Glasgow – well, maybe a tad longer on a sunny summer weekend. A grey heron, standing stately and statuesque amongst the reeds and rising mist, completed the scene. Scotland is like that: just round a bend and 'wow', a scene to take your breath away. Our busy lifestyles, however, driven by self-imposed time constraints, demand that we scurry on to meet our next schedule. The photograph will wait for another day. Or will it? We continue along the twisty road past the loch, through Strathyre then Lochearnhead and up Glen Ogle – a mountain rescue theatre that I will enlighten the reader about later. We are soon passing Lix Toll, with its tale of Roman influences. LIX, apparently being Roman for 59, seems to be the link. I have my doubts, particularly with the following contra-explanation to hand: it appears, as far as I can ascertain, the word might be *leac*, not 'lix', and pronounced 'leechk'. It means 'flagstone', or perhaps 'ledge'. So take your pick: Roman numerals or a flagstone.

Then we are past, on straighter roads and making up time. After merging with the A82 road at Crianlarich, we cover the few miles to Tyndrum in jig time and a decision is again facing us. Not much of a decision, really. Stopping for the ubiquitous coffee and a roll on crispy bacon. An extrava-gance? Probably, but irresistible nonetheless. We continue our journey and sweep north though the impressive deep glen our road shares with the West Highland Railway and an old mili-tary road, part of which was transformed in 1980 to the West Highland Way. The view on our right is dominated by the towering and impressive symmetrical, natural pyramid that is Beinn Dorain. We are soon through Bridge of Orchy and gain-ing height as we cross by the north-east end of Loch Tulla and head round a sweeping left hand bend before corkscrewing back on ourselves as we ascend the Black Mount. To our right, and then momentarily our left, the 1,039 metres of the Great Wall of Rannoch rears up, dominating the skyline; the magnificent Beinn Achaladair. Views onto its north face are stunning. It looks precipitously steep and is streaked by shal-low, vertical scars, giving it a curtain-like appearance, topped by a horizontal rock band cornice stretching the full length of that aspect, creating what looks like an impregnable fortress.

My thoughts drift back a few years to when I first as-cended the Great Wall, on a seriously cold winter day in Feb-ruary 1985. Our route that day was from Achaladair Farm. First over the railway, then following a bearing for the mid-point of the summit ridge, we set off straight up the said im-penetrable north flank. We were soon standing in calf-deep, wet, clinging snow. Thick clag – mountaineer's vernacular for cloud – hit us at about two thousand feet, and the day con-tinued with pretty limited visibility. (A euphemism for: 'we couldn't see a bloody thing'.) The ground was unrelentingly steep and did not ease off. We were picking our way up be-tween two of the shallow vertical scars: small gullies – well, hardly gullies, if I am honest; water run-offs might be a better description. To our left there was a gash that came nearer the 'gulley' description, but not quite. It was useful, however, as a left marker – a navigational aid – to keep us on track. Mind you, the stepth of the ground was a pretty reliable navigational aid in itself. (If depth works as a descriptive word, why not stepth? The book aims to show that conventional risk-averse living is not how a person learns. So be bold, take a risk, stay with stepth. You know it makes sense.) Underfoot conditions of unstable snow on top of frozen undersoil made for treacherous conditions, requiring care. It was seriously steep and, while 'grade three' frozen turf does not make for ideal ice axe conditions, we used them anyway. To our surprise – our relief – picking our way up and through the seemingly impregnable rock cornice, while pretty steep, was nonetheless easy. Visibility was still zero when the angle eased off and the snow got deeper. Then we were on the summit ridge where our friendly navigation gash petered out. After that it was a left turn along the roof ridge of the mountain, pushing through deep snow onto the summit – not before a couple of chest-deep plunges through snow-covered gaps between boulders. After a few minutes of rest and refreshment, staring into swirling grey mist, we vacated our lofty perch and continued along the ridge, before dropping to the *bealach*, the low point before the next top, Meall Buidhe – not on our schedule that day. Then it was left and down steep icy terrain into a sheltered, eerily still and quiet *coire*, a tranquil spot.

I am reminded of a similar calm a few years later, and a silly wee incident that I shall relate at this self-made author's interlude. My friend Brian and I were out in the Fannichs one wild winter day. We had parked at Loch a'Bhraoin and gone over Chailleach in a real hooley of a day, wild and blizzard-strewn. At the summit of our second Munro, Sgurr Breac, we stopped for a quick cup of tea and a biscuit. Just as we were setting off to head north-east, down a steep but shallow gulley bordered by two rock ridges into the valley, where we would catch the path back to Loch a'Bhraoin, the outer red cover of my Kit Kat biscuit was caught by a gust of wind and spun away into the air, never to be seen again. Or so I thought. Twenty minutes, four hundred metres lower and about a kilometre later, we were in an oasis of calm tranquillity: no wind, no blizzard – in fact, deep blue sky contrasting with pristine snow. One of these wonderful moments our mountains offer up, just to entice you back. Then, just as we were getting to the bottom of the gulley, a fantastic thing happened. I spotted something fluttering down towards us from high above. It was silhouetted against the high sun and difficult to identify. We stopped and stared up at the strange fluttering bird as it continued to drift towards us, before it landed on the snow, right at my feet. It was no bird: it was my Kit Kat wrapper. Now that is spooky. (Yes, I took it home.)

Anyway, enough of the eerie happenings and back to Achaladair. We played about for a while on the ice and hard neve. The latter word is Italian for snow, and adopted into mountaineering and skiing language to describe tightly compacted snow. Good climbing snow. After a while we sat and enjoyed the tranquillity of that spot before bailing out for the day and following the Allt na Crannaich down into the remains of an ancient Caledonian Pine forest, Crannoch Wood. Thereafter, a longish tramp back to Achaladair Farm along the railway. There was a bonus: the cloud had cleared to free the sun and, as we got back to the car, it was settling on a wonderful evening with the ruins of the sixteenth-century Castle looking splendid in the glow. It is not all about the mountain.

But that was then. While the memories of that day flooded back as I looked over, we were still a few miles short of today's destination in Glen Etive. Beetling black skies, and clouds were gathering. It is end of October 1988, nearly four years since our Achaladair adventure. I am a bit fitter today, having ascended over one hundred Munros in the intervening years, and having just come back from two weeks of climbing in the French and Swiss Alps. Today's mountains, Stob Coir'an Albannaich (at a reasonable 1,044 metres) and Glas Bheinn Mhor (997 metres), are not paired up in the guide books, and for the life of me I cannot remember why we were tackling them as a pair. I think maybe my partner for the day had climbed some in this area before and these two had been neglected. Who knows? Mountains do not get asked how they would like to paired up when guide books are compiled.

We are soon heading down Glen Etive into the rain that has been waiting to greet our arrival. Looks like a water-proof day. I hate donning waterproofs, particularly the leg-dragging trousers. We get parked and ready for the off, into a grey, glowering day of low cloud and precipitation. The River Etive is a lovely Highland river and, at the stretch where we cross the only bridge in the vicinity, it runs black and deep through steep rocky banks. We can admire it on the way back. I knew that bacon roll was an extravagance.

We are soon in a wet Glen Ceitlein, where we checked the map before striking up the north slopes of Beinn Choarach, the top between us and our first Munro of the day. The early ground is steep, wet and boggy, with rocky out-crops to pick through. We are soon deep in clag and a little snow, with occasional sleety showers. Visibility is down to a grey, fifty-or-so yards (if that). It is a serious navigation day. Coire Glas falls away, steep, bottomless and menacing into the

swirling, gloomy mist to our left. However, with careful foot-
fall it offers no threat and is a useful navigation aid. We pass
the first top, and more compass work is required as we swing
left round the head of the *coire* and onto a wider shoulder
before the ground rears up through rockier terrain towards
the summit of Stob Coire an Albannaich. It is well clagged in,
and we are not seeing a thing as we plod on through ankle-
deep snow.

Navigation to the summit is a bit tricky, involving
three changes of direction and careful pacing. After a short
break at the top we are off again into the unknown, on a
trusty compass bearing. Getting to the low point between our
two main tops for the day required another bearing change,
tricky in this visibility of limiting mist, yet not a problem on a
clear day. The pull up to the summit of Glas Bheinn Mhor
from that low point on the adjoining ridge was straightforward and enjoyable. We were soon tucked in beside the summit cairn, having another top-up of calories. Here is a wee
navigation tip. Leave a rucksack or a walking pole, or something, at the side of the summit cairn you approached from.
That gives you a directional clue when you head out again.
Just as we were about to leave, a party of half a dozen or so
appeared through the mist. They were coming up the same
ridge we had just ascended, and seemed a bit agitated as they
shouted a woman's name. I was in a mountain rescue team at
that time and remember thinking, should I say something?
That was a fleeting thought; of course I should 'say something'. I could not simply leave, so I approached. One of their
group had not appeared at the summit, and nobody had seen
her for some time. I narrowed the time down to about fifteen
minutes. Some were setting out to go back down the ridge. It
was more of a shoulder than a typical narrow ridge, so a bit

wider – in fact, wide enough in this mist for two people to walk past each other without seeing the other. I started to explain who I was, and that the first principle is their own safety and not to lose anyone else. I had a search plan in my head, involving warning them of the steepness of the terrain, of the distinct lack of visibility and – crucially – the need to, at all times, keep in visible contact with the persons on either side. Boy was I relieved when, before I could lay out my thoughts, the missing woman emerged safely out of the cloud and snow.

We left them to their enquiry and headed west from the summit to the first col, then north down steep, horrible ground to find and follow Allt Mheuran to where it runs into the River Etive. A tiring slog through wet and extremely boggy ground. Then we were out of the cloud and, lo and behold, our trusty chariot that would take us home was patiently waiting on our return, a few hundred feet below us. Always a strangely satisfying moment. Six hours or so in virtually zero visibility and out of the cloud we pop, right at the precise spot we planned. It is not as difficult as putting a man on the moon, but does require navigational skills, confidence and experience. Planning is important. Every trip I took or take, even today, I spend time poring over the relevant map or charts, getting the shape of the terrain, the topography and the route into my head.

The rain is still persistent when we get back to the car. Mountaineering involves many skills, of which the following is paramount. Getting changed out of wet, sweaty gear, in a downpour, requires speed and dexterity. Going through the soft shoe shuffle, whilst hopping about on one leg trying to swiftly extricate your other leg from the clammy grip of dripping wet gear, without falling over or putting your sock down on wet ground, is a bit of an art. Wet clothing and sweaty bodies soon steam up the car windows and it takes a minute or two of full-on, hot fan action to clear for take-off. Then it is on to the Bridge of Orchy Hotel and a welcome refreshment. When I am the non-driver, particularly on a winter trip, I tend to heat the cockles of my heart with a Whisky Mac. A whisky, spiced up with essence of green ginger: usually Crabbie's. Nectar is the only fitting description. Given today's 'healthy living' climate, supported by the diet police, it is probably best to ignore that last suggestion and stick to water.

So there you have it; a typical day in Scottish mountains. Well, two-and-a-bit for the price of one on this occasion. By the way, my reference to Scotland's mountains being in control of how they receive you was none more evident than that day. While we squelched and peered through thick clag, the rest of Scotland was bathed in glorious sunshine (as predicted by the weather experts, in their cocoon of a studio). Then the 'why bother?' question. Why subject yourself to hours of steep, knee-popping, thigh-straining mountains, plunging knee-deep in bog, then extricating your glaur-covered boot only to skite over a wet rocky slab, all in a wet, driech day with visibility no more than a hundred yards? I should point out at this juncture, for those unsure: 'skite', in this form, is a particularly Scottish descriptive word that defies direct translation to English, but I will try. It literally means to skitter, or to slip violently. That is where it markedly differs from the more genteel 'stumble' or 'slip', both of the latter implying the possibility of recovery. But no, 'skite' does not imply any chance of recovery, and involves a degree of instant and violent momentum, usually accompanied by a certain amount of gyration and muscle damage to the lower back – or, if lucky, the less-dangerous 'wet arse syndrome'. The latter involving an alarming moment or two airborne before landing on your aforementioned arse, deep in the bog. I have some experience of both, and I do not offer my hard-gained knowledge of the subject lightly.

Let me move on quickly to perhaps the most famous quote ever on the subject of climbing a mountain, given in response to a 'why bother?' type of question. It was in 1923, and George Mallory was preparing for an expedition to climb Mount Everest the following year. The question came from a *New York Times* reporter, and Mallory responded thus: 'Because it's there'. Mallory was an educated man, and perhaps his answer evidenced his irritation at the question. Perhaps it evidenced his education, in that his answer took the questioner straight to the purpose Everest served rather than deliberating on motivational causes. Who knows? Maybe he was just trying to be funny; perhaps even sarcastic. Whatever he intended, the answer has become one of the most iconic short answers in English history. Mallory and his summit bid partner in that ill-fated expedition of 1924, Andrew Irvine, never returned. Speculation has swung back and forward ever since about whether they died in the attempt to reach the summit or on their 'victorious' return from the summit. I do not suppose the question will ever be answered. The body of Mallory was discovered in May of 1999, some eight hundred feet from the summit. So who knows? I like to think he and Irvine were heading home, with grins on their faces. I doubt any answer I have on the subject of 'why bother?' or even 'what was your motivation?' will be so iconic.

I will attempt my explanation by trying to define my motivation. It is challenging. At times there can be an element of danger. It tests many things about your character. It involves a level of competitiveness. Not involving other people;

just you against yourself. Against the conditions, perhaps. But never against the mountain; you have to be as one with the mountain. Caress it, respect it. No, never against the mountain. It requires fitness and confidence, and it builds both. The feeling of intense satisfaction, when – on a day like I have just described – you get safely back to where you started, is outstanding. Also in my case was a secret motivation that I now air for the first time. My life has been blighted by a lack of confidence; a feeling that I was worthless. Mountaineering, for me – particularly when solo (and I did spend a lot of hours in mountains, winter and summer, alone) – was perhaps a subliminal attempt to prove people wrong, or perhaps prove myself wrong. Whatever my motivation, what was important was my promise to two decent men.

Chapter 2

TO repeat myself, I am a dedicated amateur, just like many who might read this book and like the vast majority of others who venture out most weekends. I really do not regard myself as an adventurer. I have never hung from the north face of the Eiger on a frayed rope, I have never been the first person to explore and conquer some unclimbed peak, nor have I gone down the deepest, longest, narrowest cave. I have never been to the moon. These are real adventurers. I meandered in mountains; some steep, some less so, some ice covered, some rain-soaked, some gale-blown and (believe it or not) sometimes sun-kissed. It did not matter. I was never the first. I was following well-worn paths, not always literally. I had a map. It is true there were times when the spot I was in perhaps carried an element of risk, but the risk was usually calculated and worth taking, if you can even call it that. Everything I did was in the knowledge that somebody had already done it, so it must be possible. Well, nearly always.

When asked to pen this book, the first problem was memory. How will I recall everything – or anything, for that matter? So a search was the order of the day. Many of my rambling days I had recorded in brief note form. Not really a regular diary; just a variety of notebooks, for periods enthusiastically penned, sometimes less so – and sometimes, maybe just the name of a mountain on a diary page. You must recognise the pattern. To write this account, therefore, I have raked about in my attic, shifting and opening dusty boxes, sometimes to find not a lot other than perhaps a dead spider or bee or a few mouse droppings. But I did not climb Mont Blanc without having at least a smidgeon of resilience, so I kept on my dusty search until old photographs and notebooks started to appear under 'old treasures', not all in the same box. I also searched my memory banks, crammed with worthless bric-a-brac, but not completely. I gathered material, spoke to some friends and slowly, a book emerged. Probably not like a rose blooming. Before I move into the fuller, perhaps more refined, versions of my meanderings. I will recount two short pieces, directly from my diary scribblings, word for word as I wrote them at the time:

> Fisherfield. Ruadh Stac Mor, 171, Alex. 18.4.91. Night of 18th at Dundonnall, slept in car. Walk into Shenavall with big packs on Fri 19.4.91, eat, then over two rivers (feet wet), straight up Gleann na Muice, up very steep E. Flank of R.S. Mor – snow, slab, ice c2,500 – very cold N. Wind. Reach top with no enthusiasm to continue – long slog back out to bothy – footsore, new plastic boots crippling.

> 20.4.91. Long slog back in to climb A'Mhaighdean – get to outfall of Lochan Feith Mhic'illean – both with bleeding blisters – sit down in snow, watch four red throated divers for sometime. On our way

back to bothy – watch goats on cliff face at junction of Gleann na Muice Beag and Glean ne Muice. Weather now closed in, only one Munro on trip. What a lovely – lonely place. I'll be back. Beann Dearg Mor is one of the best looking mountains in the country. Not a Munro.

Later in the book I refer to my trip back into Fisherfield and completing the round, including A'Mhaighdean. The lochan, referred to in my diary note – where we sat and watched the Red Throated Divers – is the same lochan we heard them calling from on that successful Fisherfield trip. The number 171 at the beginning of my notes refers to the number of Munros I had climbed.

My second diary scribbling:

Cluanie. 1992. A'Chralaig, Stob Coire na Cralaig, Mullach Fraoch-Choire. 206, 207.

Set out along An Caorran Mor then soon up w. flank of A'Chralaig – wet boggy start. Very steep unrelenting pull. Eventually to shoulder then in clag, wander up ever narrowing shoulder to ridge, rising to very large cairn. – Nice walking as descending beyond, before pull onto Stob Coire – clag opening a bit to reveal shapely curve of narrow arete between Stob Coire then curving gracefully up to left (N) shattered teeth on lovely ridge to summit of Mullach. Whilst attacking one of the teeth direct – handhold gives way and falls hundreds of feet into E. Coire – nearly go after it – teeter for what appears an eternity before regaining balance and hold – phew, that was a close shave. Great day.

It was from such notes and sometimes less, that I regained my memory of these lovely places and outstanding experiences. I also poured over my stack of OS maps to assist my memory.

My first actual big outing, however, was in 1972. I am 26 years old and I am persuaded to go up a hill. I am advised to get a waterproof jacket and boots. Seems stout shoes and my rugby gear will not do. I had no hill experience. Playing about on Cowden Hill in Bonnybridge and a couple of small hillocks near Luss, Loch Lomond when I was about eleven or twelve did not qualify. I worked in Aberdeen at the time of the fateful invitation. An invitation that would lead, eventually, to a significant change in my lifestyle. Not that I realised that then.

So a quick trip one lunchtime found me seeking advice in a climbing shop, somewhere in the city centre. I cannot be sure; however, Marshall's seems to ring a bell. Whatever it was called, I faced a barrage of questions about my intentions. Does the same inquisition takes place today? What did I intend to do? Would snow be involved? Camping? Rock climbing? Will you need an ice axe? I really had no idea. My weak, but truthful answer, 'I am just going up a hill with a friend,' seemed not to satisfy the helpful shop assistant and obvious mountaineering expert. 'Is your friend experienced? Where exactly are you going?' I have to assume my identical answer to both questions, 'I have no idea', had him in a quandary. His mind in a spin, he probably thought, *Should I just get a sale, or should I suggest he does more research?* He opted for the former, on what I had to assume was a slow midweek lunchtime. That is how I finished up with a pair of bendy but extremely comfortable boots, and a very safe 'Ventile' jacket. The latter weighed more than my bendy but extremely comfortable boots. I suspected 'Ventile' was bullet-proof, or perhaps only shotgun pellet proof. The hill I climbed that day was Beinn Chìochan.

It is the seventh day of October; a cold, clear day. We park at Spittal of Glenmuick. I have vague memories of a Royal shooting lodge, sweating up a rocky slope, Meikle Pap. What followed, however, was not in the least vague. My first view over the edge to the black water below, set against an awesome amphitheatre of broken crags and cliffs that seemed to touch the sky, will live with me forever. The black water is called Lochan na Gaire, from various accounts, meaning 'little loch of the noisy sound'.

However, searching *Dwelly* and discussing it with my Gaelic speaking friends leaves me a tad uncertain. *Gaire*, according to my search, means 'laugh'. *Toirmeach* seems to mean noisy. *Gair*, with no 'e', means 'short'. It is an adapted form of Brythonic Gaelic – 'caer', meaning fort or castle. Whatever it is called, and however it translates, I had never seen anything like it. I couldn't take my eyes off it.

Lochan na Gaire and the amphitheatre of broken crags

After a while of gazing into the lochan and up to the beetling cliffs, I continued ever upward and onto a plateau, then round the edge of the huge bowl to my right and onto the top. Beinn Chìochan, mountain of the breasts. An alternative name for the top is Cac Càrn Beag, 'little cairn of the faeces'. *Cac* being the interesting word. However, Peter Drummond of the Architectural Heritage Society of Scotland proffers a different view. He thinks the word is *Cadha*, which translates to slope, and that it has been corrupted to *Cac*. If he is correct, then it should be, Cahda Càrn Beag. So, slope or shit? Mind you, the nearby Loch Muick is 'Loch of the Pigs'. So perhaps *cac* is correct. I leave that to you. I do not know why it has alternative names. Perhaps a few hundred years ago, when transport and communication were not what they are today, the folks on one side looked up and called it what they saw; meanwhile, miles on the other side, folks called it as they saw it. Whatever name it attracted, it was my first Munro – albeit that I had never heard of a Munro then, and it would be a few years later before I became aware. The mapping of our country by the Ordinance Survey programme has played a big part in 'standardising' our historic hill and valley names and, in doing so, many names have vanished and the spelling of many a Gaelic name has been compromised. I fear they continue to disappear and get lost, and in that way our history is further diminished. The price of progress?

In terms of Cac Càrn Beag or Beinn Chìochan, these names and that of Lochan na Gaire, have been melded into the single, popularly-named Lochnagar. It was, certainly for me, a hard day, as my legs, unused to such prolonged activity, screamed at me. Mind you, despite my pain, every minute of it was worth the sore legs I dragged home that evening. A memorable day. I saw and heard booming deer and a few ptarmigan: a first for me in terms of the latter. Would it always be like this? Over the next forty years and more, I would learn; it would not always be like that. Sometimes it would be even better than that.

After three weeks rest, I am off again. This time to the second of my inspirational events – yes, the ones I warned you about a few pages ago: Glas Maol and Creag Leacach. Same 'hill gear', same companion. We leave the car at the Glenshee Ski Centre car park, and the journey begins through an assortment of skiing paraphernalia, diesel patches and broken ski lift equipment. There were hard-working attendants swarming about, readying for the forthcoming ski season. I did not find it an inspiring start to the day. We push on, and are soon hauling ourselves over Meall Odhar and up the ramp that leads to the 1,068 metre summit of Glas Maol. We take advantage of a wooden hut on the summit plateau and shelter from the strong cold winds that carried a fair amount of snow. I don't know why, but the snow was a surprise to me as I had not expected it in October. I would learn.

The views to the east over the impressive steep-sided Ceanlochan Glen were impressive. It looked like some mythical giant had scooped the glen out from the east side of the Glas Maol plateau using a giant ice cream scoop. The waters from that glen, and the adjoining Cannes Glen, drain into and form the headwaters of the south-flowing River Isla. It was then I saw the Land Rover and two small figures walking near it. For the sake of accuracy, the figures might have been strapping six-footers; they only looked small from my vantage point. They were on the far side of the glen, beyond the River Isla tributaries, in the wilderness I was looking into. How did they get there? There is no road for miles, and certainly no sign of tarmacadam anywhere. Thus I am introduced to the second part of my inspiration jigsaw. I will explain it in this way. I, like many I suppose, learned and understood the layout of my country from the road and rail transport networks. In this case, we had parked beside the A93 road that runs from Blairgowrie to Braemar and beyond. It has become the norm, when working out where places are, how to get to them and the distance between them, to use the transport networks as the ready reckoner. We are in a fixed dimension – or should I call it a paradigm? But here I was, staring at a vehicle with two people walking around it, seemingly in the 'middle of nowhere' and not obviously linked to a road network. Where were they from, and how did they get there? Reading the map was the key. They were at the top reaches of the River Isla, therefore they were at the top of Glen Isla, where a few miles south a minor road was located. That minor road led to other roads and to Alyth and beyond. But it was not the roads that fascinated me, it was the fact that on foot one could dispense with the road network and head directly overland and, in about three or four kilometres, could be at the head of Glen Isla. A few kilometres beyond that, maybe six or seven, one could be at the head of Glen Clova. A road journey to the latter being in the region of fifty miles, about eighty kilometres or thereby from where we were parked. It was a paradigm shift in my understanding; a parallel universe that fascinated and inspired me.

Despite the oily and scrapyard-type start, it turned into a really good day. The wind and snow tested us as we teetered along the rocky ridge to the summit of Creag Leacach. The steep descent to the Devil's Elbow also tested out my unfit thighs and knees. I saw grouse, mountain hares and red deer. By the time I got home, my head was spinning with the desire to get more maps and understand the topography of these mountains and work on my paradigm shift moment. Whether Topology or Paradigm Shift or Multi-Dimensional, one thing became crystal clear: as the years passed and I tested out all these on my feet, it was – first and foremost – all about hard work and perseverance. When struggling on through bog and sleet and gales, looking for a place to pitch a tent, fancy words and theories pale into insignificance. But you know, it was inspiring; it made me long to get out and off the main highways.

It was in the early spring of 1976, three years from my Glas Maol and Creag Leacach venture, before I seriously set foot on hills again. I had not planned things that way. Life sometimes moves you in different directions, and in the three intervening years I became a dad for the first and second time, moved jobs, joined the police service by way of the Ross and Sutherland Constabulary based in Dingwall, and moved home. I had been in the police for a year or so when I heard the Ross and Sutherland Police Mountain Rescue Team was on the lookout to recruit new talent. That will be me, I thought? What a cheek; who was I trying to kid? Undaunted, I enquired and was invited to join two of the leaders and one other guinea pig on a casual day out on the hill. Nothing too strenuous; just a bit of a plod. I cannot remember the sadist who used that pun. The day was to 'try out' prospective rescue team members. Sergeants Roddy Lovat and Donnie Smith were our guides and testers that day. I may have forgotten the pun sadist; I have not forgotten the 'casual' day in the hill. While I still possessed my hardly-used, extremely comfortable bendy boots and my 'bullet-proof' Ventile jacket, I still had not acquired suitable trousers. Jeans were definitely not *de rigueur*. I was living, at that time, in a farm cottage at Garguston on the Black Isle. One of my neighbours worked on the nearby estate. Many of these large estates supplied their staff with tweed jackets and trousers, all with the same pattern: the estate 'check'. My neighbour had an old pair of well-worn estate trousers that I could borrow. Perfect for the hill, he said. So on the big day I alighted the police transport sporting my natty pair of heavy duty, tweed 'plus fours'. Known quaintly by many as 'shit catchers'. Not to be mistaken for their slimmer and much more suitable cousin, 'plus twos'. I assume my neighbour was giggling somewhere.

Oh, the mountains used for the fitness test: Meall Gorm and An Coileachan in the Fannichs. It was a gloomy, wet and foreboding day when we parked at the top end of Loch Glascarnoch at the small space beside Abhainn an Tor-rain Duibh. We followed aforesaid stream to the Abhainn a' Ghiuthais Li, then through deep heather before a slow, but not too difficult, uphill plod to Loch Li. The ground behind the loch was more taxing, and we were soon hauling ourselves up a steep shoulder onto the main ridge of the Fannichs before turning left along to the summit of Meall Gorm, followed by a couple of kilometres of easy walking to An Coileachan. The summits by then had their heads in a swirling blanket of gloomy grey cloud. It was with some relief – well, to me and my aching leg muscles anyway – to realize we were at the outer reaches of our test, and getting back was next on the agenda. Our descent route was steep and rough, and soon had us dropping below the moving ceiling of swirling cloud to Loch Gorm, nestling in a hanging valley, just off the ridge. Then it was down less steep ground to meet the stream out falling Loch Li before plodding back to the transport. I had never experienced anything like that interminable trudge through deep, wet heather, my weary legs being dragged back by sodden, heavy-duty plus fours. Yes, the baggy, leg-dragging

Area of Fannichs where I failed my mountain rescue test

variety. My test was semi-successful. I did not get selected, and was told to get more time on the hill. Oh, the semi bit, I survived. A dram or two in the Aultguish Inn rounded off a memorable, if tiring, day in the West Highlands. Oh, and I had now ascended five Munros – and still had not acquainted myself with the term.

Despite my resolution to get more time in mountains, transferring from Northern Constabulary to police in the Central Belt, studies – and, more importantly, an addition to the family (three sons now) – all took priority in my life. The mountains, however, were never for from my thoughts, and – despite my stop/start, stuttering beginning – the opportunity to get into them in a bigger way came along about 1979, a few years after my failed test. My rugby-playing days had come to an abrupt end, brought on by cracked and bruised ribs, the rigors of age, and the realisation that my international aspirations had hit the buffers. Not that a single soul, other than me, suspected I was even on the track. So a new challenge awaited, and my suppressed desire to take to the hills re-emerged. Over the next third of a century and more, I was a regular. I did join a Mountain Rescue Team, did not fail the test the second time, and spent some happy years in that organisation where I had spells as training officer and secretary. Two crossings of Scotland in the 'Ultimate Challenge'; classic rock climbs like Agag's Grove and Savage Slit; ascent of Mont Blanc; bothy nights; crossing rivers at midnight; inversions; Brocken Spectres; wonderful companions and tall stories.

As I gained more experience and got fitter and more confident, something changed in me. I felt completely at one in a mountain environment; I felt I belonged, more than in any other environment before or since. I was often alone, and on some occasions in seriously difficult weather, but I never felt at risk, in danger, nor was I fazed. I loved every last minute of it and still do – even though, in my seventies and with an injury or two to annoy me, my time in them has lessened and I have slowed. The secret now is to carry a camera and make every day in mountains a photography day. No requirement to rush, calm pacing and photographic interludes make for a good day. My mountain and meandering story will settle down now and take you through some of my adventures. I hope you stick with me and hopefully be inspired enough to look at boots in a climbing shop, or get them down from the attic and think *you know, I could do that*. And do you want to know something? I know you can.

Chapter 3

TIME flies. Life flashes past. It is now July 1984 and I have been over a few mountains by now. 'Tis a fine day; a bit fresh early on, with clouds on the tops. I am with my family holidaying in Gairloch and I am setting out to traverse one of Scotland's finest mountains, An Teallach – 'The Anvil', or perhaps 'The Blacksmith's Forge'. It seems the latter is more popular amongst many as it seems to refer to the changing colour varieties of the mountain, brought about by differing light conditions. Whether the Anvil or Forge or even hearth, it still looks big and imposing. Viewed from Loch Toll an Lochain, which snuggles close in directly beneath its thousand feet-high crescent of towering sand stone terraces and gullies, topped by a craggy, pinnacled and shattered summit crest, I can attest to how fearsome it looks. Another impressive aspect of its beauty is from the Destitution Road when heading west and dropping down past the waterfalls at Fain Bridge – particularly in a grey, winter day, with snow clinging to the foreboding shelved ramparts. It looks fearsome. I cannot wait to set foot on it.

I am taking my ten year old son with me. I have been assured that doing such a thing today will bring the wrath of the 'risk-averse' brigade upon me. No matter; it is then and not now, and we are both looking forward to the day. This was my son Stuart's first exposure to one of Britain's foremost mountain challenges: the traverse of An Teallach and its two Munro-rated peaks, Sgurr Fiona having not long been elevated to that status. We park at Dundonnell Hotel and walk a few hundred yards along the road till we get to the Junior Mountaineering Club of Scotland's hut, distinctive with its blue and white Saltire-painted door. We locate the path that zig-zags behind it, up through some small crags and outcrops. We are soon above that and in boggy terrain as we strike a direct line, following a stream that passes the steep north flank of Glas Mheall Mor.

We had started at sea level, so every inch of ascent is real. The smaller top of Sron a Choire lies directly in our path. Getting a bit bored by our boggy, plodding approach, we decide – about the 650 metre mark – to swing left and strike out straight up the steep flank of Glas Mheall Mor. Hard work, but rewarding in more ways than we had anticipated. Gaining height quickly was the obvious bonus, although sweat inducing – certainly for me. Just short of the 979 metre ridge, we sit down on what looked like sandstone dinner plates. As we had some refreshment, we heard stones being dislodged and clattering down the steep ground over to our left. We could not see anything, but the skittering loose stones continued to clatter down the steep slope. Another party was approaching our position. They hove into view, and I felt vindicated. I was not the only parent exposing my child to the dangers of An Teallach that day. A family of goats was calmly clip clopping along at about our elevation and seemingly not paying a blind bit of notice to Stuart and I as they passed, a few yards below our perch. There were seven of them. The large male, who kept between us and his charges, had fearsome curving horns and a wild, piratical beard. It was a wonderful moment, even although we did catch a whiff of their underarm odour.

As we got up to set off, Stuart dislodged a flat, plate-size piece of sandstone. Or so I thought. It was about half an inch thick and was covered with small, white round marks, each going straight through the flat plane of the stone. I had initially thought each white mark was a fossilised worm, and that the stone itself was sandstone. I later discovered – thanks to Donald Fisher, a geologist – that they were not worms, but in fact the fossilised marks left by worms, called 'trace fossils'; to be more precise, the fossilised homes of the worms. The stone was not 1,000 million year old sandstone, but actually 530 million year old Cambrian Quartzite and called 'pipe rock', for obvious reasons. Oh, just that old? We took it home, and years later it featured in Stuart's Higher Grade geography exam.

An Teallach comprises mainly Torridonian Sandstone, pinkish brown in colour, about 1,000 million years old. It is capped by the much younger Cambrian Quartzite – the bit the worms lived in; the 530 million year old stuff. It is a whit-ish, light grey colour. Both rock types are sedimentary. The Torridonian Sandstone was deposited by fast-flowing rivers at a time when the land we now call Scotland formed a small part of a larger land mass, now known as North America. All part of a tectonic plate called Laurentia, at that time south of the equator, in what geologists call the Iapitus Ocean. The sandstone of An Teallach was originally river sediments from a hot desert environment laid down during a period of intense desert storms. The much younger Cambrian Quartzite origi-nated in a very shallow sea covering the continental shelf at the outer edge of Laurentia, 530 million years ago. When An Teallach emerged, it would have appeared as a bigger mountain than we see today. In time it will eventually, through the rock recycling process of weathering and decay, get even smaller. During the next ice age, it may well get ground back to base height. It is sobering to note that the country we live in, the land we walk on – Scotland – has been a desert, a tropical swamp, a mountainous landscape with volcanoes, and an ocean floor. It has also been covered with ice through several ice ages. Study of the rocks and fossils evidence this. Stuart and I, however, would not have to get too exercised by where An Teallach originated or what age it was; safely navigating its present form was enough of a challenge.

There is something humbling about being in these mountains. It is difficult to get one's head around how old they are. They make me feel so insignificant, yet at the same time so thrilled. The walk over to the first Munro, Bidein a' Ghlas Thuill, did not hold any difficulties. Traversing over the narrow adjoining ramp to Sgurr Fiona, our second Munro, looked scarier than the actual reality. It is precipitous on all sides, and – apart from the feelings of exposure some may experience – it is straightforward. The early cloud on the summits had burned off, leaving stupendous views. Innse Gall looked within touching distance as did the Fisherfield, Torridon and the northern hills. It has to be one of the best viewpoints in Scotland. It is again hard to imagine that during the last Ice Age, the Minch was a wide low basin, covered with ice and – certainly in theory – one could sled from An Teallach right over.

Enough dreaming. Less inviting was the view along the next kilometre of seriously exposed jagged outcrops on a serrated knife edged ridge towards Corrag Bhuide Buttress, with Lord Berkeley's Seat in the way. The Seat dares, or perhaps entices, one to stand on it. One thing I can say for sure: this is no place for feint hearts, nor is it a place for clumsy stumblers. Falling is not an option. There is one thankful positive: the gritty sandstone provides a bit of grip and a feeling of security. Perhaps one negative for us (according to guidebooks, none of which I read prior to our round, so I was blissfully unaware) is that it is best tackled in a clockwise direction. We were traversing the anti-clockwise route. Lord Berkley's Seat was soon towering above us and craving our attention. The story goes that Lord Berkley sat out at the prow of the outcrop with his legs dangling down each side. Apocryphal tale, who knows? Whatever, it was now our turn to scare the breeches of ourselves. With his anxious dad hanging onto him, Stuart walked out and stood, calmly, on the prow. He eased back with the comment: 'Well, I did it. It's your turn.' And so it came to pass that it was indeed my turn. I shuffled forward till my toes were about two feet from the edge, no further.

I am not one easily 'gripped'. However, this place does induce an interesting feeling. The seat projects out and over-hangs the adjoining cliffs and terraces. I have launched myself from an Olympic-sized, ten-metre board into Portobello swimming pool. In this case the water, in the shape of Loch Toll an Lochain, lay not one, but about fifty, ten-metre boards below. The sheer exposure had an effect on my equilibrium. I found it impossible to simply turn round and leave my perch, so I carefully shuffled backwards a few half steps before I was able to turn and leave. Phew.

We continued over the precipitous ridge. It was exhilarating, it was fun, and before we knew it we were on the Corrag Bhuidhe Buttress. It was tricky, and at one point I tried to find a different route by back climbing down on the lochan side. It was fierce and there was no way through that way, other than a one thousand-foot jump. Stuart sat on a ledge above me and waited patiently. I climbed back up, and we continued on our difficult traverse. Then we were over, Cadha Gobhlach now barring our way.

Time was moving on and we decided to bail out. But how do we do that? Going back was not enticing. However, there was a narrow and seriously steep gulley on our left, leading about 1,000 feet or more down to the lochan. No choice – no time to dither, it will have to do. The descent was steep and thigh-popping, and it required care. It was pretty full of snow – yes, in July; something I had not reckoned on. So we took it in sections. Stuart waited whilst I descended to a suitably narrow part where I could get well fixed and shout on Stuart to follow. I waited in the 'fielding' position until he got to me. It took us three such hops to get past the steepest sections, then it was a straightforward descent until we cleared the gulley and the steepness eased. On exiting our steep decent route, my first action was to hurry over to Loch Toll an Lochain and divest myself of every stitch of clothing, to the incredulous question in my ears: 'Dad, what are you doing?' I did not hear his other remarks, as I was deep in the freezing water of the lochan. A few minutes splashing about was enough, and I was out before my heart stopped with the shock.

A quick dry with my sweaty vest and then off home. We headed down Coir a' Ghiubhsachain by gently angled terrain with a few areas of easy walking slabs. Finding a meadow pipit's nest was a wonderful interlude. The house-holder was trying its best to frighten us off or lure us away with loud and incessant twittering. We quickly moved away to allow it to reunite with its perfectly symmetrical nest. After nearly three miles – just before a lovely waterfall section – we happened upon a short track that led to the A832 road, a short distance north of Corrie Hallie. All that was left of a wonderful day on a spectacular prehistoric raised river bed was a couple of miles or so along the road to the hotel.

An Teallach is a wonderful mountain, certainly one of the fiercest and perhaps the most impressive in Britain. The full traverse is a magnificent scramble that will live in my memory forever. It was a privilege to have undertaken that adventure with my ten year old son, who was not in the least fazed by any of the grade-three scrambling and whatever else An Teallach had to offer. Apart, that is, from my swimming episode in the lochan, when he was most definitely 'fazed'. The unnamed gulley we used as our descent route looks like the same one used by Muriel Gray in her television pro-gramme about climbing Munros, *The First Fifty*. I have since Christened it, *Neish's Folly*.

Stuart has gone on to climb many a rock and ice route, and entered the realms of Mountain Rescue. With Mick Tighe guiding, Stuart and a couple of the Ochils Mountain

Neish's Folly on the day we used it as descent route

Rescue Team put up the first direct winter ascent of Five Finger Gulley on Ben Nevis a few years ago. It features in a Cicerone Guide Book entitled *Winter Climbs: Ben Nevis and Glen Coe.*

Four or five years after our An Teallach adventure, he and I traversed the length of 'The File Mountain': Beinn Eighe, a Torridon classic. It was a foul day; wet did not describe it. Extremely wet, accompanied by a blustery gale. In August! Stuart had picked this landscape for part of his Higher geography exam, perhaps the equivalent of A Level? We leave our transport and follow the Allt a' Choire Dhuibh Mhor. It traverses round the west end of our mountain for the day. After a while following that, we swing east and round to the back. Well, relative to the adjacent public road, that is. The magnificent Liathach was hiding its mass in low clag immediately to the west of our route. Funny how grey cloud and mist, clinging and swirling about a peak or a mountain, has the illusion of making it appear larger than life. Well, it looked foreboding on this day, like a surly giant looming over us and daring us to head west.

We stick to our plan and go round Sail Mhor. The view north is over a boggy wilderness with dozens of lochans. Stuart is photographing rocks with glacier gouges (striations, he tells me), the wasteland... in fact, anything he might use in his exam. Hanging valleys seem important. We press on, and the ground rises past some waterfalls then opens out to allow us to stand at the entrance of one of the most magnificent views in the country. We gaze across the loch into Coire Mhic Fhearchair, to the towering triple buttress. As we progress into the coire from the open end, we are being enclosed on three sides by the five hundred metre walls that are Sail Mhor to our right, Coinneach Mhor, with the triple buttress in front of us. Biggest of them all, Ruadh-Stac Mor is to our left. We are open-mouthed. Today it has a roof of grey cloud, which adds to the feeling of walking into a cathedral; the triple buttress being the organ. The whole effect is stunning.

As we walk, I am thinking; how do we get up there? Referring to Ruadh-Stac Mor. I see a party ahead, and they seem to be following a path into the back left corner of the cathedral. We ignore that and strike out directly up the west flank – a direct, if steep, route straight to the summit, getting there in front of the party we saw earlier. This summit, the high point of the mountain, is on a northern outlying ridge, so we head south to connect with the main Beinn Eighe ridge. Before striking out east along it, however, we detour west to take in the ascent of Coinneach Mhor then Sail Mhor. Then we turn around and head east along the shattered, undulating, banana-shaped main ridge of Beinn Eighe, going over Spidean Coire nan Clach which was later, in 1997, elevated to Munro status by those who know about these things and obviously have a better inch rule than Munro. Then the steep section up Sgur Ban. The wind was gusting fiercely by now and screaming at us as we moved along the ridge, particularly through that latter section. At a couple of the narrow sections, we resorted to crawling, or lying flat and holding on until it eased. It did not let up, and our passage over the Bodaich Dubhs – with sensational drops to our left – was executed with extreme care.

As I write about that day on Beinn Eighe and, in particular, my recollection of how fierce the wind was, I am reminded about a solo trip years later over Conival and Ben More Assynt. If I thought the wind was fierce on Beinn Eighe, I had not experienced the Assynt equivalent. The ridge between these Assynt mountains is a narrow shoulder; not knife-edged, but steep sided, over shattered, unstable rock, requiring care and accurate foot placement. Even on a calm day. It was anything but calm the day I headed over it. On some sections the gusts were so fierce I had to lie down and hold onto a rock. Other times I stood with my back to the blast, leaning over onto my single walking pole. It was spectacular in so many ways; not least the grey clouds, like speeding wraiths, spinning up the steep east flank to curl over the ridge and spin down the other flank, as though watching my every move and intent on intimidation. At all times accompanied by deafening and disorienting screeching. As I neared my goal for the day, the wraiths got more and more furious at my audacity and threw all they could at me. I was the only human on the ridge at that time, so the wraiths could vent their spleen directly at me.

The last few yards of my journey to the exposed summit of Ben More Assynt were executed in a crawl, occasionally jamming my walking pole between broken rocks to keep me on the ridge, to the accompaniment of the screaming wind section of nature's extensive orchestra. I will forever remember being serenaded by the Assynt wind section. I did not linger long and, after a few minutes – sitting at the summit with my back jammed against one rock and a foot jammed against another – I exited stage left and was soon, gingerly, retracing my steps along the ridge. Then a remarkable thing happened. The wraiths acknowledged their failure to scare me from their hill and, as though on some unseen, unheard command, off they swirled to perform their ghostly deeds in some other venue. Within an instant all was calm, the clouds moved over, the sun broke through, and I was gazing over the wild expanses of Sutherland and to Caithness, over Loch Shin to Ben Klibreck and snuggled below it, so bright in the sunshine, a small white spot in that wilderness: The Crask Inn. The Inn was built in 1815, and four years later Thomas Telford upgraded the single track road that supplied it with travellers and still does. I had stayed in the Inn before, and would enjoy its friendly welcome again.

My wraith-free trek back over Conival and down Gleann Dubh to my transport at Inchnadamph was bathed in a wonderful evening glow. Is this one of the rewards of braving it out? Well, if that was not, what followed certainly was. To repeat, it is not always about the mountain. Before I reached my car, fate intervened in the way of the occupier of a cottage in the glen; a perfect stranger. He had just finished fitting a brass ship's porthole in his front door and was admiring his handiwork when I 'hove to'. We got on the chat and he asked if I needed a refreshment, which I could not refuse. On entering the remote cottage, I met his wife, sitting by the window knitting, her work illuminated by the dying embers of the evening sun. So peaceful, idyllic. The refreshment involved the opening of a bottle of 'uisge beatha', and the rest is history. Other than the mistake I made. I had been due to meet a companion at Inchnadamph and, as we sat in deep conversation, all notion of time headed off – just like the wraiths of earlier in the day. The lady of the house brought me back to reality by the simple phrase: 'Are you supposed to be meeting someone?' Bloody hell, about an hour ago. 'Well,' she said, 'could that be him?' as she pointed out to the track. It was indeed Alex. He too was soon 'hove to' and got ensconced by the fire, partaking of the amber nectar. I cannot describe how pleasant such unexpected encounters with seriously decent people can be. They restore my faith in human nature.

Back on Beinn Eighe however, the rain and clag had not relented one bit, making the serious section of our traverse a tad uncomfortable. Bent over, trying not to stumble, followed by a bit of crawling – but making steady (well, not always steady) progress. It was a relief when we finally slithered through the Sgurr nan Fhir Duibhe and Creag Dhubh section of the ridge and away from the main blast of the wind. Then it was plain sailing, and in easing weather we descended by the strikingly uniform, straight and steep west ridge, leading us directly to Allt a' Chuinn and into Kinlochewe. That is the architect straight ridge – like the corner of a roof – that features in photographs of the mountain, taken from the Kinlochewe aspect. Stuart got shedloads of material, and sometime later passed his exams. I had been out of the hills for a while with a damaged right hip, and that nine-hour day surely tested it. The lay off had not increased my fitness and, while my leg was not much better, I figured it just needed forced on a bit. So I finished the day a bit done-in. But what a place, what a mountain, and what a day. The wild weather and the company only added to the whole experience.

Chapter 4

DO you have a favourite Scottish mountain? A friend of mine once used statistical research software, Priority Search, to establish Scotland's forty favourite mountains. He did it for a bit of fun, so don't take it too seriously. You may agree with the result, perhaps you don't. So for a moment let us detour to that list. I have no doubt you will have a favourite that does not appear. Is there a set criteria for what is a good mountain? Priority Search, however, is a serious application that has been successfully used in the marketing world and by local authorities, to establish the ranked preferences of services by service users. In this case it was about 'favourite mountains', nothing else. A few experienced mountaineers, eight or nine, who had climbed all the Munros and many other Scottish mountains, were asked – as a group – to list their favourite Scottish mountains. Clustering their choices resulted in forty mountains featuring in the next stage. That list was then passed amongst a lot more mountaineers and each was asked to indicate their preferences. The results were then entered into a brainy computer, and it spewed out the ranked order of Scotland's favourite mountains, as indicated by this survey. The observant amongst you will note that only those mountains selected by the initial respondents could be considered. The top five, in ranked order, came out as follows: Liathach, Sgurr nan Gillian, An Teallach, Innaccessible Pinnacle, and Beinn Alligin.

So, what would your ranked top five be, and would it contain different mountains? An Teallach ranked third. I would have ranked it at the top. However, if pressed, I would pick a wee hill – one that did not feature in that Priority Search exercise, and in fact one that many would not even consider. So what is it? Dumyat in the Ochils, or – as Rennie McOwan christened it – 'The Teaching Hill'. Ranking favourite mountains is subjective, and will undoubtedly be influenced by one's experience on a particular hill, on a particular day. A singer/songwriter friend of mine will pick Stac Pollaidh, every time. It has special memories. It is the mountain he climbed, when a young man, to grieve his dad, so many years ago. In the early 1960s, never having been in Scotland before, he headed by train and bus, from London to Ullapool. After that he relied on the kindness of locals and passing motorists until there it was, Stac Pollaidh. He was not looking for that mountain; in fact he had never heard of it before that day. Kismet led him there. He immortalised that moment

Stac Pollaidh

with a poem dedicated to the mountain and, more importantly, his dad's memory:

Stac Polly

wester ross
a still april evening

in perfectly visibility
i observe four compass points

no littered streets or lamp posts here
no graffiti tattooed walls
no chimney pots or tower blocks

the only blocks that towered here
were sandstone
home to hawk and eagle
carved by the chisel of nature
in acres of sky

bereavement
had drawn me like a magnet
five hundred miles from home
just long enough to stand in leave taking
and place on the cairn
a stone

Cliff Wedgbury

I will return to the Ullapool and Little Loch Broom area, which, in reality, I did often. The Dundonnell Hotel, right below An Teallach, was, in these days, owned by Selby and Flora Florence. I was privileged to call them friends. My acquaintance started through another friend, a police colleague, who was married to Selby and Flora's daughter. Not only did I bring in many a 'new year' and summer interlude at the Hotel; I also, on occasion, used it as my 'top end' bothy when in the area, winter and summer. It is not the first time I have left the hotel late on a winter's night, heading home to the Stirling area in a blizzard. Sometimes just getting as far as Inverness was a challenge, never mind the A9 south over Drummochter. Travelling Highland roads in wild winter weather never put me off; it was just part of the experience. I have slept in the car more than once. In fact, as I gained more experience and learned the ropes I changed my style of transport to an estate car, as that gave me enough room to lie down and sleep in the car if required – and I have used that option.

During the 1980s and 1990s I got into a routine of taking part of my annual leave in mid-May each year. There was a reasonable chance of catching good weather at that time. The following group of experiences are about hill days just about that time. My May Meanders. What you will read over the next few pages is merely a flavour of these meanders.

I previously mentioned seeing the Fisherfield area from An Teallach. The Fisherfield circuit – or, as commonly known, the Fisherfield Six – comprises (yes, you guessed it) six mountains. When I first did them, the six were all rated as Munros. In recent years, Beinn a'Chlaidheimh has been remeasured and found to be below Munro height, and therefore relegated to a Corbett. I reckon if Munro regarded it as a Munro, that will do for me. Anyway, the effect of post glacial

– or isostatic – rebound (to give it the proper terminology), where, after an ice age, the land that was pressed down by the ice bounces back and rises, may well result in our mountains growing a bit taller, so perhaps it will re qualify. There are six big hills in there and they pose a serious challenge, in any weather.

The area is properly known as the Fisherfield Forest, sometimes the Great Wilderness. Completing them all in a single day is a serious challenge and not to be taken lightly. I still had five of them to experience, having picked out the solitary Ruadh Stac Mor in a wild, cold, blizzard-strewn winter day in 1991. We were late travellers that trip, and the hotel (yes, my 'top end' bothy) was in darkness when we arrived from the south, so a sleep in the car followed. We blagged some breakfast in the morning before a snowy tramp into Shenevall, where we billeted that night.

An early rise the next morning found us looking up at a glowering, leaden sky. It was wet and sleety as we crossed the freezing river, followed by a long trek up Gleann na Muice – which cuts the group in half – up steep snow slopes on our right, involving careful crampon treading onto the summit of Ruadh Stac Mor. It is positioned, towards the centre of the group and kind of adjacent to A' Mhaighdean, making them a convenient, if isolated pair, sitting furthest out and apart from the main group. We had planned to do both; however, light was limited at that time of year and our progress was slowed by the wild weather and an issue with my new, crippling plastic boots. So, with discretion being the watchword, after gaining our first summit we turned and retraced our steps – yes, including re-crossing the freezing river. So today's trip, in May 1993, would involve us tackling the outer five of the group, thus circumnavigating the 'big red peak'.

These are really remote mountains; it is a big day, requiring fitness and endurance, and must not be underestimated. Particularly in bad weather. On that trip I was accompanied by Ben, a mountain rescue colleague. Driving up from the south, followed by a two and a half hour walk into Shenevall Bothy with big bags, took up our first day. A cosy spot in the bothy, a big fire, plenty of food, drink and chat with a couple of other visitors made for a good evening. Before I get into the torture of the Fisherfield circuit, however, let me relate a tale from the previous week. I had been in the same general area the week before for a couple of days with another friend of mine, Brian. Sleeping was usually divided between tent, bothy and perhaps hostel, dependent on where our plans were to take us. On this occasion we stayed in that top class bothy I mentioned earlier, The Dundonnell Hotel. I had not warned Brian about this and simply told him we would be in a better class bothy. He had no idea, and made up meals for cooking in the bothy. We arrived at Dundonnell quite late, in the dark, and Brian was anxious about getting settled in to our chosen bothy. He was also a bit anxious to know where it was. I studiously avoided a direct answer. (The makings of a politician?) Once parked at the hotel we headed inside, where Flora met us and ushered us into the cocktail bar, which she then locked. After a dram or two, a set of keys was propelled over the bar accompanied by the words, 'Ian, you and Brian are in room seven.' Brian was a bit puzzled. 'Are we staying here?' He was correct; we were not only staying at the Dundonnell, we were getting full board. Now that is a 'top end' bothy. Brian never let me forget that, particularly as he had prepared meals for our weekend.

After breakfast we headed out, back to the main Inverness to Ullapool road, turned left at Braemore Junction, headed north and parked at Inverleal, a few miles short of Ullapool. We were heading for Seana Bhraigh, regarded as one of the remotest Munros – A' Mhaighdean in Fisherfield being one of the others. A good stalker's path leads well into the hill but starts to fade before eventually petering out, leaving a meandering trek through and over an area of annoying rises and falls. Once through the annoying bit, one's day is lifted by views into the spectacular Cagha Dearg and the remote headwaters of Glen Douchary and its resident River Douchary, running north. It is the prospect of such views, in such out-of-the-way places, that enhances one's hill experience. It is so remote, in terms of Scotland, that the percentage of the population who will gaze on such a view has to be miniscule. I, for one, was always thankful that I combined a level of fitness and experience that enabled me to get to these gems.

We stood on the lip of the impressive red slope, Cadha Dearg, and down Gleann a' Chadha Dheirg, the host glen of the River Douchary. I took my map out and traced the route of the river as it swung north east into Glen Douchary, before its sharp left turn to the west and into Loch Achall, which in its turn outfalls into the Ullapool River before splashing into the sea at Loch Broom in Ullapool. This is an example of that other dimension that so excited me about hauling myself off the beaten track and away from the 'ready reckoner'; that is, the popular transport network. But that will have to wait; we still have the last pull onto Seana Bhraigh to contend with. It is not difficult from there, and we are soon over the easy, Ochil-like rounded slopes and onto the summit. Just over four and a half hours of walking, and about eight miles from our car. Whilst having some refreshments, we wander over a few yards from the cairn to a shock. We are standing on the edge of a vertical cliff, looking down hundreds of feet to Loch

Luchd Choire, ringed by even more cliffs. Quite un-Ochil like. This is not only remote country; it is a spectacular hidden treasure, and well worth the trek. It looks like a giant, with knife in hand, has cut the back from the mountain. Our final approach, over gently rising ground, conceals and gives no clue as to what lies beyond. Scotland has many hidden treasures, some just take a bit of effort to find. Seana Bhraigh, with its surprise of vertical cliffs concealed by that easy rolling approach, has to be one. We retrace our steps and have enough energy reserves left to wander up Eididh nan Clach Geala, my two hundred and nineteenth Munro. Back to our high end bothy for a shower and dinner.

Next day we are back at Inverleal to go over three more, Beinn Dearg and Cona Mheall, then, just to prove we can, Meall nan Ceapraichean wraps up another great day. We are firing on all cylinders and going well. The surprise package that day was a six-foot high by six-foot wide dry-stane dyke that runs from the summit of Beinn Dearg northward for a few hundred yards until it stops abruptly. It is huge. Why is it there at all? Victorian landowners built a lot of march walls and fences; I assume we have just encountered one. Another good day. Back to the Dundonnell Hotel and another warm welcome and dinner. We did not stay that night and, by the time we left to drive back to Stirling, it was dark and there was a good-going early May blizzard. It was an interesting drive home. Going over Destitution Road and the Dirrie More required some caution, not just because of the treacherous road but because we were visited by scores of red deer. They were lined along the side of the road, probably down to see the lone car. We tucked in behind a lorry as we climbed out of Inverness and followed in its tracks and its welcoming red lights. By the time we reached Drumochter Pass and then

Shenevall Bothy in 1993

Perthshire, the roads were black and the rest was easy. The heavy snow would return later in the week, to enhance the Fisherfield trip. Yes, the story I interrupted to deviate to Beinn Dearg, et al.

So, where did I get to? Yes, ensconced in Shenavall bothy with Ben. As mentioned, we had spent a pleasant evening by a roaring fire and had turned in for an early night in anticipation of an early start. We bedded down in the loft area of the bothy, reached by a set of aluminium builders' ladders. We are up at five, ante meridian, on a snowy seventeenth day of May 1993. After shuffling about getting breakfast, donning clothes and trying not to waken our fellow inhabitants, it is six and we are off. First hurdle – well, water jump might be a better name – is a knee-deep, bloody freezing river, Abhainn Strath na Sealga. Having crossed it and other rivers before, we come prepared with flip-flops. They do not stop your legs or feet from freezing, but do help you get over the sharp edges and boulders quicker. Then we are over, legs and feet dried, socks and boots back on, and off we go into what turns out to be a minor (well, perhaps not so minor) epic. Straight up the steepish, rocky north ridge of Beinn a' Chlaidheimh. Fresh wet spring snow is treacherous and slippy, and slows our progress a bit. Over the top, there is only time to place a stone on the summit cairn. I have placed a stone on every summit, whatever category of hill.

Then we are off and down another steep edge, through the same slippy snow to Loch a' Bhrisidh at about 700 metres, before the pull up to Sgurr Ban. Our leg muscles have thawed out by now, and we are moving reasonably. No drama, although a few slick boulders to negotiate. Then it is Mullach Coire Mhic Fhearchair, the highest in this round at 1,019 metres. It also has the steepest approach, requiring the occasional hands-on moment. The snow has returned, we are in thick clag and the compass is out. We press on to Meall Garbh, the 851 metre top that marks the point where we swing right, to the west. We are not paying enough attention; striding out, trying to make up time. We miss the turn, not that we noticed, until we were dropping in height and there was a stream on our left. Whoa! We should be on a ridge, not in steep grass, nor anywhere near a stream.

Stop and take stock. We were not too far from the proper route. We cannot see the ridge, only steep grass and the stream disappearing into cloud. Don't panic; take your time and check our Harvey map for streams, direction of flow and slope angle. Sorted. We carefully retreat into the mist and are soon back on track. Crossing Bealach Odhar and heading over our fourth Munro, the 937 metre Beinn Tarsuinn, marks a slight upturn in our fortunes – well, for a spell, that is. The cloud has lifted, leaving a pleasant descent along the north-west ridge and exposing our gaze to expansive views in all directions. This is remote; this is where the fun is. Then we are descending from that glorious spot into a horrible trudge through the Pollan na Muice bog that seeps into Gleann na Muice on our right. Up through a short steep craggy section before the straightforward, two-and-a-half kilometre pull to the 948 metre summit of remote A' Mhaighdean. A bit of a grind for tiring legs and requiring patience and rhythm. But so worth the effort. The clag has cleared and, whilst still over-cast, we have visibility. This is a quality mountain; wonderful views in a seriously remote part of Scotland. Over to the north east is the dome that is Ruadh Stac Mor, with its seem-ingly impregnable rock 'headband'. The view west over Dubh Loch, Fionn Loch to the Minch past Poolewe is spellbinding. In fact, the views on all sides are spectacular and getting to this peak has to be one of the jewels in the crown of any Munroist.

We have completed the five and we are well out from our sleeping bags, so let us get out of here. We drop down the rocky, bouldery north-east ridge to the Fuar Loch Mor. It lies directly under the cliffs and steep scree of Ruadh Stac Mor, and I am glad we do not have to drag ourselves up there. We find a stalker's path and are soon at the next problem of the day – and not the last. There are stepping stones over the Allt Bruthach an Easian, the stream that flows south-west from Lochan Feith Mhic'-illean. Normally one simply steps over them and 'voila', one is on the track that leads back down the glen to Loch na Sealga, Shenevall and our warm sleeping bags. The week of snow and melt has completely hidden the stepping stones; the stream is a raging torrent. No way across at that point. We examine the map and have two choices. We can swing right and keep to the south side of the lochan, traversing over some foul, boggy looking terrain for a couple of kilometres before swinging left around the far end of the lochan to find the track. Or we can head to our left, downstream and away from our sleeping bags, in the hope of a crossing point. We stupidly choose the latter. Why? Perhaps tiredness and the knowledge that a perfectly good path lay so close to us, enticingly just across the burn. There must be a way over there, without us having to drag our weary bones over more bog and peat hag. It is now eight post meridian, we have been on the go for fourteen hours, and we are knackered and perhaps not thinking straight. Our first option, even though leg-bursting, was safer. We chose the less arduous, but seriously more dangerous route. What made us think it would be any less of a torrent further down? Well, it wasn't. A couple of hundred yards downstream, we came across a section that seemed not so wide and perhaps possible. That meant it was narrower, with water flowing faster and deeper through the channel. There were two huge boulders in the stream at that point. So, after a try or two, we managed to kind of lunge over – throwing ourselves over is probably a better description – and cling to the first boulder. Now we were seriously committed, and in the middle of the torrent. No going back now. In fact, I don't think it would have been possible anyway, as the bank behind us – the one we had launched ourselves from – was higher than our position. How we got onto the second boulder, with white water breaking over it, I will never know. My fear (well, one of my fears) was that if I fell into the torrent, my rucksack would drag me under. I had visions of my body being dragged from the Dubh Loch some months later. Actually, I don't think it would have mattered whether I was wearing a rucksack or not. A tumble into that white maelstrom would have posed some difficulties, whatever I might have been wearing; in fact, Speedos and a snorkel would not have helped. The second boulder was wider, and that got us a few feet from the far banking. A plan was now hatching. One of us stays put with the rucksacks while the other makes a bid for freedom. The rucksacks could then be launched over and hopefully retrieved by whichever of us had reached terra firma first. I had a bizarre thought at that point. *Why do we not sit it out here?* I mean, the water will subside. I was obviously affected by the cold, the noise and perhaps the fear. I kept that idea to myself. Things were fraught enough. Then Ben launched himself for a second time and landed on the far bank, with feet dangling. He quickly scuttled up to safety. We did get the sacks over, not without a bit of effort. I was then left to make my second launch of the day. I needed a bit of purchase and a bit of room to accommodate my long jump technique. I have to say, my launch pad was not ideal. A rounded, wet and slippy boulder with water breaking over it was not quite Olympic standard. Anyway, be that as it may, I had to do something. I shuffled back a bit then sort of teetered forward, intent on the launch. At the last instant, I hammered on the brakes and came to a kind of ungainly, leaning-forward stop. In fact, I nearly toppled into the torrent, and as one foot shot out from under me it took all my powers of recovery and balance to stay on my safe boulder. I took a couple of deep breaths, stepped back and went for it again. This time my teeter seemed a tad more purposeful and I launched forward. 'Toppled' might describe it better. I landed, nose first, on the 'safe' bank, with feet dangling in the torrent and face deep in wet heather. I clung on. Ben grabbed an arm, I got a knee into the heather – kind of precarious – then with Ben hauling and me crawling and scrabbling for purchase with my knees, at the same time grabbing handfuls of heather, I was over. It is no exaggeration to say, I was relieved.

It was only left for us to trail down the remaining eight kilometres or so to our much needed sleeping bags – yes, the ones I mentioned earlier. Getting bloody delirious. We still had our final decision of the day to make. But that could wait; although tired, we were still lucky enough to be in one of the best wilderness spots in Scotland. Time to enjoy every last minute of it. It was just about then that one of these wonderful, *National Geographic* moments happened. As we passed the remote Lochan Feith Mhic-illean, over to our right, we heard the call of what we assumed was a red-throated loon. Loud and piercing, like a prolonged terrier yelp. But besides that, it had more of a plaintive quality and in the gloaming of that evening – any evening, in such remote country – the sound is haunting and somehow forlorn. It has the quality of making the hearer feel quite isolated, which we were. However one might describe the call, it is a wonderful sound that seems to touch your soul. What you have just read is my description of the call. The *Collins Bird Guide* has a more sophisticated, perhaps more accurate description and it goes thus: 'Red Throated Loon, male; far carrying duet of loud grinding, "oo rroo uh, oo rroo uh, oo rroo uh", with the female of the species sounding off with a higher pitched, "arro, arro, arro"... Also a drawn out, wailing "eeaaooh". Some calls can resemble that of a barking fox'. The description of the Black Throated Loon is as follows; 'a wailing "aaah-oh", often at night. Or sometimes a harsh, croaking, "knarr-knarr". The song is loud, desolate but evocative, rhythmic whistle, "clooee-co-clooee-co-clooee-co-clooee", each "clooee" a strong rising whistle'. To be honest, I am confused about what we heard, being anything but an expert. But the barking bit is the clincher, coupled with the fact that the red-throated variety is a commoner species, so I am settling on that. Mind you, as we never saw the creature, who knows? Maybe it was a musical fox. You know something? It does not matter; getting into such areas, their territory, their domain, in which we are merely visitors, is a privilege, whether red or black-throated. We are lucky.

I have heard and seen the loons calling often. Some years later I got the best view I have ever had of a red-throated loon (definitely, this time). I was descending Sgurr Dhomhnuill, west of Loch Linnhe, near Strontian. It was early evening on what had been a beautiful summer's day. Whilst picking our way though a cluster of small lochans, still at an altitude of about two thousand feet, we saw two gliding down to land in one of the bigger lochans. We waited a while before crawling through deep heather, right to the edge of the lochan. The pair of red-throated loons were at the far end, little more than one hundred yards from our position. Alex and I settled into the heather and watched. The pair seemed oblivious to our presence and slowly glided nearer. They came to about twenty yards from us and one boomed out that wonderful call. It was mesmerising, and the four of us enjoyed each other's close company for the next ten minutes before the pair beat their wings, lifted out the water, cleared the far bank by a few feet and flew off into the low golden sun. They are beautiful birds and – to reiterate the expression I used earlier – we are so lucky, so privileged.

Back to our strenuous day at Fisherfield. We continued down Gleann na Muice Beag and reached the river barrier in darkness, in a clear, cold, moon-and-starlit sky. It was so quiet, so serene, it seemed wonderful. I felt we were an unnecessary intrusion into such a tranquil scene. Everything was so still, and the moonlight only enhanced the atmosphere of peace. Our final decision loomed. Cross two rivers, or stay on the path and cross where they conjoin just before entering Loch na Sealga. The conjoin option was agreed, with undue haste. Why, simple really: neither of us could be bothered taking our boots off and putting them back on again two times. So then it was boots off and tied around our necks, flip flops on, and into a freezing river again. It got deeper the further we waded and, by the time we were halfway over, the water was above our thighs and getting deeper. We were heading for the outer curve of the bend in the river. That always seems to be the deeper part. Loch na Sealga on our left looked so tranquil and glistening in the moonlight. Sometimes you have to pinch yourself. To think that a few thousand years before we passed this point, a huge grinding glacier tore Strath na Sealga out of the sandstone and left this beautiful place. Just about eleven o'clock, thigh-high in a slow-moving river and our whereabouts unknown to all, it was so peaceful, surreal. Neither of us spoke as we waded over. The only noise, the water we were disturbing. I felt so at one with nature. Like a similar moment on the Skye Ridge from another time. I was exactly at the centre of the universe, the place destiny had situated me, and at exactly the right time. I felt weightless for that instant. The moonlight was now reflecting from the wake we were creating in the still river.

We reach the far bank and look up. It is above our height, and slightly overhanging. My moment of reverie, my trance, was over. This is not going to be as easy as we may have imagined. The only technique I can muster is to reach up the banking, as far as my short frame will allow, grab as much vegetation, grass and heather as I can, then heave myself up, at the same time scrabbling about with my feet on the muddy undercut bank – still under the water – trying to find pur-chase. Then it is a matter of sort of levering one's tired frame higher, out of the river and on to the bank. It is none too ele-gant. During that frenzy of splashing action, so out of place on such a beautiful, still night, I dislodged and lost a flip-flop. My Jimmy Buffet moment. Then I go though much the same rig-marole as I had gone through a couple of hours earlier, alt-hough this time in less danger of being swept to a watery grave. After much undignified heaving and dragging I am kind of sprawled – nearly in balance, but maybe just on the ful-crum – on the steep banking, still not completely on terra fir-ma, hanging on for dear life to fresh vegetation, feet waving about in mid-air, whilst dragging myself away from the edge until my knees make contact. Do not relax just yet; keep a firm grip of the grass and crawl forward. Phew, done it. Energy reserves take a severe dunt with that rush of activity. Boots back on. Any wildlife in the vicinity must have awakened from their various states of slumber to wonder at the perfor-mance down by the river. Not one came to look. Ben escaped the river just upstream at the same time. Mind you, his tech-nique did – as far as I recall – seem more elegant. He is a lot younger.

It is probably the right time to insert a thought or two. Some, perhaps most, who read this will be thinking, 'I don't think so.' Some others will be thinking, 'I have been there, done that.' It is part of the experience; it is living, and when your mum told you not to look into the eyes of the sun, you must never forget: 'That's where the fun is'. Or, to be correct, the moon on this occasion. We got back into the bothy a few minutes later after about seventeen hours out. John Heath, the custodian, was in situ, and he had a roaring fire on and the kettle ready. We partook of tea, a bite to eat, a couple of drinks and a blether with John before collapsing into our sleeping bags and a well-earned rest.

We were up in plenty of time in the morning; a quick breakfast, clean up our bed space, thank John and exit one of the best bothies in Scotland. As one climbs steeply out of the strath, one cannot resist looking back and marvelling at the breathtaking scene that is Strath na Sealga with the loch of the hunter out to the north-west, magnificent jagged sandstone mountains along the flanks and the Bothy, way below on the valley floor, looking so small and insignificant.

I struggle to imagine that these great Scottish peaks were born in the Iapetus Ocean, some way south of the equator, 1,000 million years ago. It is also hard to imagine the great glacier that gouged out the whole strath more than twelve thousand years ago. I feel somehow exhilarated to think I am walking through such history. I belong amongst these rocks and feel strangely comforted by them and by the thought that they will survive far beyond humankind and that no matter

Strath na Sealga and Shenavall

what we think, we will not even be an afterthought. After the long walk out to the car, we pick up our bikes at Dundonnell and head off to Cannich. Not without first partaking of Flora's tea and scones at the hotel. Because, no matter the ancient past and the distant future, one must search for a perspective and a great scone is a great scone.

By the time we spend a day meandering over to Cannich, we are feeling refreshed and ready for two big days in Strathfarrar. Maps and guidebooks call it Glen Strathfarrar. Translated that equates to 'Glen Glen Farrar'. I guess when mappers were at work in this area, their grasp of Gaelic was lacking. The name holds some mystery in terms of its origins. It appears in some texts as 'Varar', a name that would appear to precede Scottish Gaelic and perhaps have Pictish connections. 'Var' meaning to wind, or perhaps to curve. The loch certainly curves. So it is the nineteenth day in May 1993, and off we go. The glen is barred by a locked gate and, at the allotted time, we are waiting for Grace to say 'open sesame'. We take the car as far as the glen will allow and, after driving over the two Loch Monar dams, we park a kilometre or so beyond the nearby power station. In 1956, before the loch was dammed, Iain Thomson, his wife and two children – near the spot we are parked – launched their furniture-filled boat and huddled for shelter as a storm tried all it could to dissuade them from travelling the full length of the curving loch, to the very remote west end where they would take up residence in an estate cottage and there live in serious isolation for four years until 1960. That story is to be read in the excellent book, by Iain Thomson, entitled *Isolation Shepherd*. In 1962, not long after the Thomson family had vacated their remote home at the west end of the loch, the horseshoe-shaped concrete dam at the east end was completed and another piece of the hydroelectric jigsaw was in place. Damming the loch extended its length by several kilometres. At the western end, the pre-dammed loch ended just about Pait Lodge, not far from the Thomsons' dwelling. After 1962 it extended about four kilo-metres or so out west, past Pait Lodge, swamping the cottage in the process. Whatever its name, Glen or Strath or Glen Glen or Glen Strath, it is a beautiful part of Scotland, and ex-tends from the Beauly to Cannich road, through a majestic strath that reaches west for thirty miles into one of the great wilderness areas left in Scotland, and nearly to Strathcarron. It is flanked by mountains to north and south, among which is the dominant and shapely 1,159 metres of Sgur na Lapaich. We take a stalker's path and, at a left fork, ascend into Coire Gnada before exiting the coire to the west and continuing up steep rocky slopes by Meall Garbh, then the shoulder of An Riabhachan, till we eventually get to the 1,129 metre summit cairn. A big cairn.

It is a mixed day with cloud blowing in then moving off. We get occasional glimpses of a vast wilderness around us as we continue along a nice ridge to the western top, 1,086 metres, then backtrack the ridge past our summit before de-scending to Creagan Toll an Lochain. Then the drag up to Sgurr na Lapaich, 1,159 metres, our second Munro. I make an elementary mistake and still have the scars to show, a quarter of a century and more later. Our route will continue east and down a steep rocky ridge for just short of a kilometre to Bealach na Cloiche Duibhe. I hazard a guess at 'The Pass of the Black Rock' (or 'Rocks')? Whatever its English transla-tion, there still was an inviting snow slope, maybe three hun-dred feet or so, just to the side of the ridge. So, no big decision really: jump onto the snow and scoot down to the Bealach. For 'scoot', insert 'glissade'. That is a way to descend a snow slope quickly in a squatting, kind of seated position, soles of boots on the slope and ice axe held under arm pit, the pointed end pushed back against the snow to act as a brake. It is normally very effective. Not this day. The snow was crap, a granular late-season crystalline structure, like sugar. That means very little control when glissading and, specifically, very little breaking efficiency. The second impediment was a fault of mine, which I will come to once I have set the scene. Ben and I were parallel on the slope, a few feet apart. We were like children, whooping at the speed and the exhilarating feeling. We were picking up speed and travelling fast. About halfway down, with our rocky terminus looming fast and gentle attempts at a controlled descent failing, I became aware of a strangled cry. It came from one of us; maybe both of us. 'We better get stopped.' Not perfect grammar, but perfectly understandable nonetheless. Stopping our careering descent required a different ice axe technique from the one we were employing. We needed to quickly roll over, lie face-down and use our ice axes in earnest. The same technique used in the aftermath of a tumble on snow or ice. We both rolled over onto our fronts with ice axes in the arrest position and dug in, then dug in even deeper. Whoa. This is not working. My left hand was now seriously sore. An important rule of winter climbing; wear gloves, especially if one is to take your ice axe from the stowed position on your rucksack and carry it. Put your gloves on, every time. So there you have it, mistake two. Gloveless in Strathfarrar. (Is that a pipe tune?) We were seriously putting every ounce of weight into our axes, with minimal effect, until we slid into Cloiche Duibhe and flatter ground, before eventually stopping like the Red Arrows in formation. Perhaps not. I stood up, my left arm hanging down, taking care not to look at my hand. Ben asked if I was alright. 'That was a bit too exciting, but I am fine. How are you?' I replied.

Ben then asked: 'Where is all the blood coming from?'

'Ah, that will be me.' I had ripped the skin and flesh from between joint one and two on my ring finger, with similar damage to the pinkie knuckle of the same hand. Both injuries were pouring blood. My hand, a combination of being frozen with exposure to the snow and the damage, was really smarting. I did not know where to put it. There was blood all over my boots and the snow. Ben patched me up with a bandage and tape and I put my winter mitts on. Too late. No sympathy required for stupidity. Move on, up and over Carn nan Gobhar at 992 metres, before descending easy-angled slopes back to the car and down the glen before the gate was closed and locked up for the night.

The following day was a real belter. Down to the gate with biscuits for Grace and the promise that we will try to be off the hill in plenty time. 'But will you let us out if not?'

'Just knock the door,' she replied.

Sorted. Off we head to a spot about a kilometre west of Braulen Lodge, where we stash the bikes, before heading back down the glen to just short of Cambussorray. Just at the spot where a stalkers track heads north into the hill. Our route that day will take us over Sgurr na Ruaidhe, 993 metres, followed by Carn nan Gobhar, 992 metres. Those reading and taking the slightest bit of interest may well be thinking, have I not read this bit before? Did he not go over that yesterday? You will be correct; I did, but it is a different mountain. For some reason, maybe in the dim and distant past, the person appointed to give mountains a name had misplaced his book entitled *Names Suitable for Mountains in Scotland*. So two mountains, on opposite sides of the same glen, have exactly the same name. Even more spooky is that they are exactly the same height, 992 metres. It is followed by Sgurr a' Choire Ghlais, 1,083 metres, and finally Sgurr Fuar-thuill at 1,049 metres, with a couple of tops in between. Just west of the last Munro is the 1,015 metre top Sgurr na Fearstaig. I failed to find that word in *Dwelly*, and the closest I did find was *Farsain*. It means 'wide' or 'large'. Anyway, it marks the northwest corner, creating a left-hand turn, leading us south along a ridge before dropping down to our left to meet the stalker's path beside the Allt Toll a' Mhuic and back to retrieve our bikes, then an easy cycle back to the car and out the glen. The high level ridge walk was glorious, easy walking in a clear, sunny day with stupendous views over to Torridon and Glen Carron and much more, mountain peaks by the dozen. Part of the fun is in trying to identify each. Having been on a mountain before does help one identify it, well sometimes it does. All seemed so close, with a totally different perspective from that experienced in the shackles of the road system. Strathfarrar is a glorious glen. My hand was pretty tender and difficult to operate for a few weeks after that, particularly as it scabbed up.

We returned almost exactly a year later to snag the Munro beyond An Riabhachan, An Socach. Why we did not do it in 1993? I have no idea. Perhaps time and a locked gate? My hand had healed, leaving a fine war story scar to tell my grandchildren about (or anybody that will listen, because they certainly did not). Stupid Grandad. So back up the glen to Loch Monar, park and hike out the same route we had followed the year before: Coire Gnada again. Our way this year is barred by steep slopes of snow and ice. Despite our best efforts, we are thwarted from that route. We are carrying ice axes, but this time – in May – carrying crampons is usually an extravagance. Got it wrong again. We skirt along the north flank of An Riabhachan and up the north-east shoulder, again through a deep snow band. There was scarcely a spot of ice this way so kicking steps, although somewhat laborious, was quite straightforward. Then we are over the summit and along the twisty, lofty and narrow ridge to An Socach, 1,069 metres. A steep final part, again through a tricky snow band, is the wee sting in the tail. Well, not much of a sting. The ridge was a pleasure, and why it is not featured in guide books I don't know. The views out to Skye and over the western islands make this a brilliant, if remote, viewpoint. I like this mountain. It is real wilderness country, bounded on the south by Loch Mullardoch and to the north by Loch Monar. The cloud ceiling was a few hundred feet above us; however, the clarity of vision that day was excellent. We descend by the north ridge, into Coire Gorm Mor, then contour east till we reach the stalker's path just after the obvious gap at Clach an Daimh. Simple walk back to the car and another great, if really cold, day.

Herds of red deer abounded as we headed out. I bump into (not literally) a Justice of the Peace from Alloa on the hills that day, Sam Bowie. Call that a small world. So there you have it: another example of a typical May week in the Scottish mountains, plus a wee extra from a year after. I will cover some of my mountain marathon type exploits later, and a couple of excursions to the European Alps – including climbing Mont Blanc. Before heading there, let me tarry for a minute to make you aware of an alternative entertainment one may experience when tramping the Scottish hills, particularly in May and June. I refer to flying displays. I am not referring to our feathered friends, although they do provide some beautiful and breathtaking moments. Have you had the privilege to watch as ravens display for their partner? I interject with two short alternative flying tales, both spectacular and breathtaking in their own way. The first involves a manoeuvre by two USA F15 Eagle jets in the West Monar Forest area of Scotland in May 1993. Ben and I were descending the northeast shoulder of a Corbett, Beinn Tharsuinn, just short of Bealach Bhearnais, on our way to ascend the west ridge of Sgurr Choinnich, before heading back to Gerry's Bunkhouse at Achnashellach. It had been a hard day, as we had gone over the same Corbett on our outward journey to the Munros of Bidein a' Choire Sheasgaich and the remote Lurg Mhor, before retracing our steps. Sheasgaich (or, as some irreverently call it, 'Cheesecake') is visually intimidating. It seems to be ringed by impregnable-looking slabs. It wasn't, and – while it demanded care – there was a way. Anyway, it was now behind us, and we were heading down the ridge I just mentioned. It also forms the west headwall of the Loch Monar valley. As we gazed to our right onto the impressive sight of the Loch (because, make no mistake, it is impressive), we were about to be even more awestruck. All that day, in a clear blue, cloudless sky, we had been entertained by a NATO exercise involving many jet fighters swinging, curving, diving and climbing, complete with curved contrails painted on the sky by each plane. Oh, and the noise. Amongst them were F15 and F16 aircraft. As we descended, the sound of jets reached our ears. We scanned the skies in vain. The sound got louder and nearer. Where were they? Then we saw them. Two F15 jets screaming towards us at loch level, way below our position. I have no idea how low they were, but each was followed by a swirling tail of water, pulled up from the surface of the loch. An amazing sight. As they closed, we were about to witness something even more amazing. They

79

were low, and for a moment seemed to be heading straight into the ridge we were on. Where are they going? Then they did something that had us speechless. They stood on their tails and screamed up the contour of the head wall from loch level. What happened next was death-defying. Just at the 'V' – where the ridges met – both jets, line astern, spun onto their backs (yes, upside down) and contoured over the low point, before diving toward Bealach Bhearnais. Just as urgently, they spun back into an upright attitude and, in the same manoeuvre, turned sharply to their right – still at a very low altitude – twisting and turning away from us down Gleann Fhiodhaig till out of sight to the east, round a curve in the valley. Spellbinding hardly does it justice – not only to the visual display but, more importantly, to the skill level of both pilots. Ben and I looked at each other. We will never see anything like that again.

Some years later – however, not in May this time, but in February 2005 (the second, to be accurate) – I witnessed another interesting flying moment. I was on Meall na Leitreach, an easy walking Corbett, adjacent to the A9 road at Drumochter Pass. It is the hill that flanks the south-east side of Loch Garry. I was with two friends, Alex and David, and we were descending back to Dalnaspidal Lodge to finish our day. It was getting dark and there was snow on the ground. Our vision of the A9 was to the north-west into the gloaming of the Drumochter Pass. Because we were on the north-facing shoulder of the mountain, we could not see the A9 to the south. We were at about the 600 metre mark when we were startled by the sound of an aircraft on our right. As we looked, a Tornado appeared in all its glory below our altitude, travelling north, following the line of the A9 trunk road. We stood and watched as it headed north into the fading light of the day, its navigation lights bright in the gloom, highlighting its position. As it got into the narrow part of the Pass, just where it curves to the right, where it opens out into Badenoch, we saw two other sets of lights, to the north and to each side of the Tornado. It was all very quick and, for an instant, we could not work out what we were seeing. A trick of the gloom. Then we saw the other two airplanes, in the Pass and heading south, in the opposite direction to the Tornado, at what looked like the same altitude. We had no time to gasp; time was suspended for an instant. Then, as quick as a flash, there they were: two RAF trainer jets, flying side by side. The Tornado had flown between the trainer jets. The Tornado disappeared round the corner in front of us and the trainer jets continued south, passed our position and out of site over Atholl, and we were left to wonder. Was that meant; was it part of a training exercise? Was it a 'near miss'? We never did find out. Whatever it was, it was 'interesting', and either showed precise flying or – perhaps – sheer luck. (By the way, the term 'near miss', is worth a thought. Should it not be 'near hit'?) So, to repeat, it is not all about getting to the top – and trust me, there will be rewards. These were just two of the many.

Chapter 5

NOT all my intrusions into the hinterland of Scotland were on foot, and quite often I employed the help of a bicycle – a hybrid, in these days. Not a road bike and not a full-blown mountain bike. Whatever it was, it served me well for years. Why a bike? Sometimes it gave a good start to some of the more remote hills – speeded up access and, if I am being perfectly honest, the trip out was where a bike came into its own. Tired feet, or just plain tired, a few kilometres sitting down and moving faster than walking pace, well, just took the edge off that track. As the years passed, certainly in my case, a cycle ride just on tarmac was good fun and I enjoyed a few of them. I certainly did not, and would not, class myself as a cyclist. But it was good, still is good, to let the wind get into your hair and speed along a bit. So if you bear with me, I will relate one or two of my cycle adventures at this juncture.

The first is a purely road-based traverse of the Outer Hebrides on a bike: Barra to the Butt of Lewis, and a wee tail on the end. I am not sure where the idea came from; just a chat once, after a hill day perhaps. I had, over the years, gazed out over the shimmering Minch, from the 'hill of the hoof' or 'the forge', or from some other lofty western perch, out beyond Skye and other gems of the Inner Hebrides to that mysterious, hazy blue archipelago that is the Outer Hebrides, filling the distant horizon and in doing so stemming the wild storms that well up in the Atlantic and race, unfettered, towards our shores from that distant mass that is North America. It was probably during these moments that the notion to travel there emerged. I am not sure.

Anyway, I held onto the idea for many years but did not act on it. Why so? I, like many others, was trapped in a cycle of work and domesticity. (Was that a pun I just uttered?) Oh, don't feel sorry for me. I found time to meander the mountains and glens, do all the big hills, a smattering of classic rock routes – both summer and winter – not to mention some fine expeditions to the Alps. That chain of bluish smudges on the distant horizon beyond Skye would get visited, maybe next year. Then one century clicked over and, through the hysterical millennium moment of aeroplanes falling from the sky, crashing computers and whatever else the fear-mongers could dream up, that oft-held notion of getting to the long island became quite important to me. *Just do it: maybe you will not be able to next year.* The last comment is probably an age thing. You know what I mean. (Well maybe not all of you, but just wait: you will.) So the urge was on me and, like a lemming over a cliff, I was off. The plan was to cycle the complete length of the island chain, from Vatersay to the Butt of Lewis. To add insult to injury and confirm my idiocy, a finishing leg from Ullapool to Inverness was thrown in. Adding to the pressure was my intention to raise funds for Macmillan Nurses. David, a climbing companion of many years standing, agreed to participate in the adventure. He had cycling experience, which turned out to be very useful. The only real 'planning' involved booking some bed and breakfast

84

stops at what seemed like achievable distances, booking the outward and return ferries, and taking account of the likely prevailing wind. We took no cognisance of the terrain and just went for it. The logic seemed to be that, well, we will have to get over it anyway; it cannot be that hard. So, it was time for the off.

Dawn breaks on a wet, cold and gloomy late May morning as we leave Stirling, bound for Oban. A friend drove us there. Then we are aboard and swinging away from the pier. The prospects do not bode well as we coorie out of the wind and rain, enjoying a serious breakfast on *The Lord of the Isles* as she ploughs her furrow along the Sound of Mull on her six-hour journey to Barra via Tiree. We get into conversation with some of Strathclyde Police Force's finest. They are bound for Tiree to take part in a mock major incident. A plane is to crash on Tiree's small airstrip and they, along with others from the fire service and Civil Emergencies Planning fraternity, are to pore over maps as the drama is played out in the form of a table-top exercise. I mused, *why travel to Tiree?* Is there not a suitable office on the mainland? What about video conferencing? But hey, nice work if you can get it.

The approach to Barra is enjoyable. The weather has changed and it is a calm, sunny afternoon. We wait our turn, which will be at the coo's tail, once all the others have left the boat. Only then are we are allowed to cycle up the ramp and onto Barra. That notion, dreamed up on some mountain top years before, is now reality and as I stand in Castlebay and look around, my first thought is *it is not misty, nor is it bluish.* I am actually on the Outer Hebrides, and I am really looking forward to the trip. We seek out our lodgings; a bed and breakfast, no distance from the jetty. The owners are really nice people. McNeil is their name. I got the impression if you let your mad dog loose, it would bite a McNeil. To do with numbers, not the personalities. Our host had spent his working life at sea, and his knowledge of ships and shipping lines was second to none. A really interesting man.

After introductions and getting settled in with a welcome cup of tea, we headed out to circumnavigate the fourteen miles of the island, including the detour to the beautiful Caribbean island of Vatersay, before dinner. No, I am not lost; not on this occasion. The beaches are straight from the Caribbean. (Perhaps that is to do Vatersay an injustice. Perhaps the beaches of the Caribbean should be measured against those on Vatersay.) The detour over the causeway to Vatersay introduces us to one of the steepest wee hills we will encounter on our trip. Once up and over we walk on the Machair and watch the sun get lower over another golden strip of sand. This beautiful and peaceful scene is where, in 1853, the *Annie Jane* – with its cargo of eager families from Liverpool, heading for a new life in Canada – foundered. That machair now overlooks the resting place of those three hundred and fifty men, women and children, commemorated every year by a carpet of yellow primroses. Barra is also a lovely island of shimmering stretches of sand and interesting, explorable inlets. We hear corncrake at two points on our circuit, the first time I have heard these birds in over thirty years.

Next morning we set out early to catch the Eriskay ferry. We have time, and so we detour from our route to watch the British Airways scheduled flight from Glasgow land on the beach. Then we are on our way, and we board the small boat that will take us on our short hop to Eriskay. It is a beautiful clear morning, albeit a bit breezy and cool. On the short journey over we see a great skua harrying a gannet for its hard-earned catch. Despite our best efforts we do not find

the resting place of the SS *Politician* and its cargo of whisky.
Neither did the exciseman, aided by all the polis on the west
coast. Not the bosses anyway. The short snab of a hill that
leads away from the jetty is a bit 'breath-catching'. Then it's
over the short causeway to South Uist, and the start of the
serious cycling.

We are soon in rhythm and eating up the miles. We
take a short unscheduled stop to see the monument to Flora
Macdonald, the lady who was imprisoned in 1746 for her part
in aiding Bonnie Prince Charlie evade capture and the inspiration of *The Skye Boat Song*. We next happened upon the island museum and our second unscheduled stop. This time to
partake of the delicious soup and sandwiches – oh, and some
home baking. My minimal pre-trip planning had uncovered
neither of these. After that my memory is of miles of lochs,
inlets, sand, causeways and easy cycling, as we steadily progress to our evening rest on Grimsay, just north of Benbecula
and some sixty miles from our start that morning. I am struck
by the birdlife, with redshank and snipe abounding. We
stayed at the home of a friend I first met many years before
whilst curling in Stirling. She had moved to Grimsay some
years before, and now ran a really welcoming Guest House
with a quality breakfast.

Saturday morning dawned a bit overcast; cool, but dry.
We head for the ferry to Harris by way of the west and north
coasts of North Uist. As we cycle through a small hamlet on
the north-west of the island – perhaps Middlequarter or Sol-
las, not sure – we happen upon two Sikh gentlemen, travelling from door to door, each carrying a suitcase of goods to sell
round the village. A sight David and I had not seen in the
Central Belt for many years. We press on and, in good time,
we are crossing the causeway onto Berneray. Just beyond the

ferry terminal we find a purveyor of fine foodstuffs and tea; a serious boon. On the short journey back to the jetty we hear what sounds like the faint sound of a dodgy starter motor. Puzzled, we look about, and high above a snipe is diving and displaying. The sound we heard is properly known as Drumming, but a starter motor refusing to fire sounded more like what I heard. Puzzle solved. The display has us transfixed for a minute or two, and then it is down to wait for the ferry. We do not have long to wait, and soon we are aboard and gazing into the Sound of Harris as the ferry follows a maze of navigation lights and buoys whilst zig zagging this way and the next as it negotiating numerous rocks and small islands in very limited visibility.

Then we are on Harris, in the ferry port of Leverburgh. It had previously been called Obbe, derived from a Viking word for bay, but was renamed Leverburgh in 1920 after the English businessman William Lever, First Viscount Leverhulme, who owned a large part of South Harris including Obbe. We are soon cycling again and decide to head up the west side; the Atlantic coast of Harris. Why, with the prevailing wind coming in from the south-west and taking account of the terrain, this will be an easier ride. The rejected alternative would have been the Golden Road. It was first constructed in the late 1890s and fully tarred sometime in the 1940s. It twists and turns through a wonderful landscape, joining the many small communities that nestle behind rocky outcrops and alongside the many sea inlets that snake in from the Minch. It was Christened 'The Golden Road', it seems, by mainland press who were adversely commenting on the cost, or so it is said. If that is what they wrote then it was wrongly named, as it was relatively cheap given that the road materials were all locally accessed, as was the labour. Our decision, however, considered none of that. It was the dozens of steep rises and falls – well, the rises – we did not fancy. So *west is best* was our chorus as we headed out of Obbe.

Soon we hear, as on every day of the journey, a cuckoo. I am lucky enough to spot this one. Then, as we pass the road leading into Northton, the vista opens out to a 'wow' moment. Miles of massive gleaming beaches. The views are stunning as we cycle along, thinking – well, I am thinking – *why have I never visited this place before?* It was sunny by now and it looked like a scene from the Adriatic, only better. Then we spy Taransay. Yes, of *Castaway* fame. From Taransay, it is said, one can see the number of the Tarbert bus – without binoculars. So our castaways were not quite as 'Robinson Crusoe' as the programme perhaps suggested.

The road angles a bit east and the bigger hills start. Nothing like what we will experience on day three, but gears are dropped and breathing is controlled. Nearing Tarbert, and getting more serious. The scene changes to miles of huge ex-

Seilebost to Losgaintir, Harris

panses of rock; a lunar landscape, no less stunning than the earlier sand. At the higher part of the road, we can see over the Minch to Skye, to the very mountains I stood on years before and imagined this place. Well, now I am here. Then it is downhill – well, mostly – all the way to Tarbert, and some high-speed freewheeling is enjoyed as we look forward to our dinner.

After getting sorted in our guest house, we head out for sustenance. On our way into the village, we see a small lamb tethered in a garden, closely watched by a crouching collie. The garden is a small triangle of grass; a really small triangle of grass, right outside the front window of a cottage. As we pass, a male appears, bedecked in baggy jeans, trainers, a grimy baseball hat and a grubby, BBC-emblazoned fleece. He tells us he is bottle-feeding the lamb, adding that he is also bottle-feeding himself, kindly inviting us inside for a 'wee dram'. While being overcome with his friendliness and gener-osity, I decline his offer and am pleased at my will-power, musing that it was not always so evident.

Sunday brings glowering skies and rain, and we are bound for the hills. A fine breakfast, and we set out. In no time at all we are at the foot of 'The Clisham' and the real climbing begins. That is when I discover my mistake, brought about by my cavalier planning regime for the trip. It is long, unrelenting and steep, particularly the first section. Breakfast is letting me know the folly of eating so heartily, and so soon before a serious climb. The hill continues and the steepness relaxes a bit. Actually, when one gets into a rhythm of spin-ning legs and breathing and the breakfast settles, it is a really nice cycling road and most of the rises are long and easy an-gled – a pleasure to cycle, eventually. After a few miles we reach the drop-off at the other end, back to sea level. It has me clinging to my brakes. Meanwhile, Dave disappears into the distance as though he has no brakes, as usual. Bloody moun-tain bikers.

Not long after getting back to sea level we are at the Lewis and Harris border, right at the end of the arm of Loch Seaforth that links it to The Minch. A sea loch with glorious views. It is a long morning as we happily make progress. It is Sunday on Lewis; the roads are quiet. As we negotiate our way through numerous villages in the Parish of Lochs, the churches are busy. Two are spilling as we pass. My memory is of stern-looking men in dark suits, wearing hats. The women were quite sober in appearance and all – the women, that is – were in their Sunday best of long frocks showing under long coats. Like the men, they were also topped by headgear. Col-ours predominantly dark. I wished we had been earlier and had been able to listen to their psalm singing. I was privileged enough to listen outside a free church in Easter Ross some years before when I worked there. The unaccompanied music was like water flowing over rocks, and seemed to grow in vol-ume as the verse went on. It was led by the presenter, who seemed to – as far as I could tell – sing the first part of each verse, solo, as if reminding the congregation what the words were. It made me a touch unsettled; it was almost eerie. Back to my Sunday in Lewis, and I remember thinking that our lycra attire was perhaps a tad out of place.

In the early afternoon we reach Leurbost, only a few miles from Stornaway. A quick change of plan sees us take the west road; we are Callanish bound, some twelve miles distant. It is a long straight road through bleak country, not made any less bleak by the rain, driving across us from the south west. My abiding memory of that day, and of all my time in Lewis, was the lovely smell of peat smoke as we passed cosy wee cottages. I wished someone would open their door and let us in for a heat and maybe a wee stroupach. On arrival at the well-appointed Callanish visitor centre, we discovered that it was shut. We were able to peer longingly through the window at home baking and apple pie; not for us on the Sabbath. The stones, however, were memorable – smaller than I had imagined, but nonetheless mystical.

Heading back along the peat-smelling wet road to Leurbost, then Stornoway, we take a short cut at Achmore and detour over a hill road, passing numerous small shacks on the high moor. I resolve to find more about them after we had completed our tour. We find our lodgings for the night, and what a choice. The Rowans: a modern house, new and spacious, containing two lovely owners who could not do enough for us. Our host drove us into the town centre later and dropped us off at a good eating place.

The final day of our Hebridean Challenge is bright and breezy, and we were soon scudding along out of Stornoway on the undulating Barvas moor road. The road swings north at the village, and we head for our final destination with a handy tail breeze. Was I getting fitter? The torturous return to Stornoway will soon disabuse me of that stupid notion. At a small shop at Borve, the lady inquired as to the purpose of our trip. When I mentioned the charity element she simply handed me a ten pound note and said: 'For your charity. God speed.' Then we are off and scudding along again in a high gear, making progress.

Ness soon enters our vision, the lighthouse on the horizon being the clue. Nearly there. We turn into a quaintly named section called Fivepenny (Coig Peighinnean Nis). My musing as to the name did not last long. David, as usual, was a bit in front and missed the welcome that awaited me. I had no sooner turned left toward the Lighthouse when the 'Fivepenny guard dog' spied me. It was a black and white border collie that had, I assume, taken exception to my spinning legs. It appeared from behind a nearby building, like a frenzied black and white harlequin, with its bark set to 'really fierce'. I nearly wet myself. I pushed on and looked back. Was it gaining? It certainly was, and it would have gained more if I had not then taken a quick look the way I was heading. I was hurtling headlong towards a deep ditch and a sudden stop was looming, as were a set of snapping gnashers. My avoiding action had me swerving about the road and, while I managed to keep on the bike, old black and white flash was bearing down on me. Whilst swaying about I nearly taint my reason all together, but – like Tam o' Shanter's guid grey mare, Meg – I gained the 'keystane o' the brig', figuratively speaking. Well, to be truthful, the timely intervention of a lady rescued me. She appeared from the same hidey-hole the dog had sprung from and reeled it in. I heard her shouting but did not look back, being too busy flailing my legs in an attempt to gain yards. Then the barking subsided and, on looking back, my adversary was meekly following the lady back into the corner it had sprung from. Meanwhile, my helpful companion – a distance beyond and apparently oblivious to the near carnage in his wake – had not even altered his pace nor even looked behind.

Then it was the uneventful last few yards to journey's end and we were there. The Butt of Lewis. Nothing between us and the Americas, apart from that serious big slap of water that is the Atlantic Ocean. We walked about for a time, took the necessary photographs and rested. Munching on the majority of our sustaining food parcel and drinking most of our water. We would regret that extravagance later. There is not a lot up at the end of the Outer Hebrides. Yes, an impressive lighthouse, but not a lot else. Except, that is, for the hypnotic ocean coupled with the feeling of space and wonder that brings. We are surrounded by beauty, both in vision and sound. The Fulmars seem to glide effortlessly, for an eternity, along the cliff faces, with nary a wing beat. The gannets soar gracefully on their gleaming white, black-tipped pointed wings then suddenly, as though on a secret signal, they lift into a short climb before instantaneously folding themselves into inverted, white dart-shaped missiles, executing their trade-mark, steep-angled dive, hitting the water at breakneck speed and disappearing below with hardly a splash. An image of raw power, grace and elegance.

Then, if that was not enough beauty for the day, our gaze is diverted by the tweeting of the rock pipits, the colour-ful machair, the pink thrift. The place is alive; who said there is not a lot here? Then there is the ocean itself, running high, with white horses dominating the seascape. It has nowhere to go and, having travelled for thousands of miles unfettered and building up a head of steam, something has to give. So it throws itself against the immovable rocks and cliffs of the land boundary. Is it frustration, anger, or part of a greater plan? Whatever, the energy released is spectacular. There is some-thing mesmeric about large waves crashing headlong onto the rocks, the cliffs and the shore. There does not need to be any-thing else. Marvel at the power of nature and appreciate your ability to witness it.

No, there is not a lot up here, that is if you have no feelings, no imagination, and no appreciation for your sur-roundings. It is simply teeming with experiences, a wonderful place. The 'Fivepenny dog' still intrigued me, however. Not so much the dog; no, the name. Why call a place Fivepenny?

No matter who I asked, there was no clear answer. *It has always been called that*, was the common response. Not that I am suggesting I asked everyone, and perhaps I just failed to ask the right people. So a bit of research brought this explanation. I hope it is reasonably near the mark. Seems it harks back to bygone times and the worth of an area of land when land tax, or scat, was being levied. Based on that convention, the names 'Penny' and 'Merk' appear in some place names. Both being synonymous with Scottish money. (There was also a bawbee, although I am not sure if that appears in place names. I am happy to be enlightened.) So 'Fivepenny' is linked to the size of an area and its corresponding worth to the assessor. I am sure it is a bit more complicated than that, but you get the picture. That made me think of other 'interesting' place names. Those based on the quaint custom of using the cardinal point of a compass, coupled to a term denoting a divisible part of a whole. Such a convention can lead to quite (well, in my opinion) mundane and perhaps utilitarian names – for example, West Quarter (near Falkirk) and North Third (near Stirling). I am sure you can think of others. I will return to place names later, in a different context.

But enough. Let us celebrate. We had done it; cycled the Outer Hebrides chain of islands and enjoyed every minute of it. It is a spectacular place, in so many ways. We leave The Butt by a short detour, down by the football pitch, giving the 'Fivepenny guard dog' a wide berth. Not far out of Ness on our return, we encounter the small hamlet that is Habost. It has a rural museum and tea room, situated in what looks like an old shop; perhaps a co-operative. We had spied it as we scooted through earlier. So a snack beckoned. Taking on calories is essential to the survival of a cyclist. The lady in attendance was very pleasant and, probably because we were the only customers, we got to chatting. I mentioned that she did not sound local.

'No', she said, 'I am from a small village in the mainland you probably will not have heard of.'

'Oh? where is that?' I asked.

'Bonnybridge,' she said. 'Have you heard of it?'

Well, as it turned out I had not only heard of it; I was brought up there. Small world. We devoured tea and cake, served in a three-tier cake stand. Quality.

Then came the cycling shock of the trip. If you were paying attention you will have remembered me mention the brisk wind that blew us up the island. Well, it was still a brisk wind – but while we had turned, it had not. So we faced a seriously hard grind into the teeth of a gale as we struggled the thirty miles back to Stornaway. If I had given the impression that cycling was hard work up till that point, I was mistaken. Fighting the gale was hard work, and any energy reserves I had retained soon disappeared; cycling on empty. We even had to cycle down the hills. After passing through Barvas, still a dozen or so miles to go, I am really on my chin strap – as I find out whilst negotiating the undulations on the road. I have now reached rock bottom, and I find myself slowing and weaving about the road. I am becoming a liability. Dave is away out of sight. I pull over and sit down on the verge for twenty minutes, during which time I devour my last bit of Mars Bar and the last of my water. Feeling slightly refreshed, I set off. No more drama, but still a bit weary, I am soon scudding down the hill into Stornoway and roll up at the bed and breakfast to find Dave getting his bike put away for him. Turns out, he is equally as cream-crackered and had only arrived no more than five minutes before me. We discover that when I pulled over in a dip in the undulations to take on the last of my sustenance, Dave had stopped a few dips in front of me. Our kind hosts, realising that we were somewhat 'done in', quickly produced much needed refreshments – tins of beer, to be accurate – and the use of their private sauna. Five star accommodation indeed. We enjoyed a relaxing evening, eating in the town again, before collapsing into an early bed as we had an early rise for the seven o'clock ferry next morning.

It was a bit cool the following day as we entered the terminal and waited patiently for our turn to board. Then we were on and, once we got the bikes stowed, we found space in the forward viewing area. It was a calm morning on a beautiful crossing over a mill pond-like Minch, with visibility unblemished. The whole of the north-west coast of Scotland was laid out in front of us. We spent time identifying mountains. It looked like the ferry used Stack Polly as a navigation aid, because for a lump of the crossing we headed directly for it. We managed breakfast on board.

We got into Ullapool on time, and hung about for a while to grab a coffee and a sandwich for the journey and to let the ferry traffic clear. The sandwich shop was busy and, as I stepped forward to be served, the lady behind the counter asked if I was cycling. A perfectly reasonable question to a male clad in cycling lycra. My answer was too quick, too flippant. I responded thus: 'No, I just like wearing lycra.' A cheap reply. Amidst the laughter, I apologised and told her what I was up to. She contributed £5 to the charity. She would have been in her rights to also contribute a slap.

The cycle to Dingwall was a treat. Oh, apart from the mile or so of steep, one in ten ascent up to Braemore junction, just at the Corrieshalloch Gorge. It is a long drag, steeper than The Clisham. If left alone, one gets into a rhythm and just beats it out. The problem is, you are not alone. This is the main route from a busy ferry port, and it is narrow. Soon the engine noise, including the noise of changing gears in a lorry right behind, is creating a bit of stress. Certainly to me, and probably to the lorry driver. I am moving at no more than seven miles an hour, tops. The lorry driver, and no doubt the stacked-up traffic behind the lorry, must be getting a bit fed up. Thankfully, there is no opportunity for any of them to pass so, while I might be annoying them, they cannot lunge into a suicidal overtake – I hope. Just as it starts to ease off there is a lay-by and, on that day, there was an ice cream van in residence. Ice cream time. Dave is already in the queue. The ice cream and the relief of getting out of the traffic for a few minutes is welcome.

Then we are off. The long rise from the ice cream treat at Braemore Junction, then up the Dirrie More to Loch Glas-carnoch, the water shed between the west and the east of Scotland in that area is easy enough. It is about six miles or so of reasonably easy-angled rise and is constant. We stop at the top, in the layby at the east end of Loch Droma. The view back west over the loch to An Teallach has to be one of the top ten roadside views in Scotland. I stopped there late one

West over Loch Droma

glorious summer evening some years ago and stood in awe –
without a camera, nor camera telephone (as they still had to
be invented). The reason for my awe? The sun, a huge yellow
ball, was sinking out of a clear golden, cloudless summer sky
into the jagged profile of An Teallach. It was breathtaking. I
said at the beginning, *National Geographic* does not get all the
best views. I repeat, this is Scotland. Please get out and experience it.

Back to my bike. The journey alongside the loch is flattish, then it is virtually downhill all the way to Garve. We
were in Dingwall, just in time to meet our host for that evening; an old friend and police colleague of mine, Hugh 'Abrach'
Mackay. He was standing on the front steps of the National
Hotel in Dingwall, in his best attire and welcoming us to join
him for dinner with Dingwall Rotary Club – 'in five minutes',
he added. So, bikes stowed, out of clinging lycra gear, a cold
water sluice down, on with jeans and a creased T-shirt and
into the dining room. We were, well, a bit underdressed. It
was a good night. Then up to Hugh's for a dram. Oh, and
another dram. Late to bed at the end of a memorable day.

So we had done it, and all we had to do now was get to
Inverness – which we did. By the way, I raised over £1,400
for Macmillan Nurses... and I got a sore arse. Dave got sore
ears, I suspect, but he is too much of a gentleman to mention
that. Back to the colourful huts, those which Dave and I had
encountered on the cycle over the hill road south of Stornoway. Our host on the night described them as 'airighs', an
ancient 'common grazings' culture of the Hebrides. In the
summer months, usually for a few weeks in July and August,
crofters would move livestock away from the 'home' croft or
pastures to the virgin, lush grass of these less-used, remote hill
pastures – principally, as I understand it, to fatten their live-

stock before the autumn markets. It had the added advantage of giving the home pastures a chance to regenerate. The airighs I saw looked like shacks; perhaps huts might describe them better. They are sometimes referred to in the Gaelic as *bothan*, meaning hut or bothy. They certainly bore no relationship – visually, that is – to the remnants, the stumps, of stone dwellings I had come across in various glens and hillsides elsewhere in Scotland, or indeed the beehive dwelling architecture I had encountered in a couple of places in Harris. The shieling culture, pretty much as just described by my Stornoway host, is the seasonal migration of livestock to summer grazings from lowland pastures to higher ground, to feed and fatten them on the rich hill grasses. It is a centuries-old, European-wide practice, and takes place typically from June right through till September in some areas. It is called 'transhumance' and was, still is, practiced in some countries. The *Oxford English Dictionary* defines 'shieling' as follows: 'Shieling {also: shealing} (pronounced: sheeling) (1) a roughly constructed hut, for pastoral use. (2) pasture for cattle. (Of unknown origin.)' The term shieling may refer to the grazing area and the dwelling. In the earlier days of this practice in Scotland, certainly on the islands in the far north and west, the dwellings tended to be oval-shaped; hence 'beehive'. On the mainland they followed the more familiar, square or rectangular shape.

The buildings Dave and I came across in Lewis, however, were more traditional huts, with a chimney in the gable end; something unknown in both earlier versions. In Scotland the tradition can be traced back some centuries. Because of an increase in the sale of 'black cattle' to the English markets during the sixteenth century, mainly to feed the soldiers and sailors of our colonial exploits, the tradition expanded. Scotland was described then, rather condescendingly in my opinion, as 'a mere grazing field to England'. It was usual, after the summer pasturing, that livestock – 'black cattle', mainly – would be driven south over the drove roads that criss-crossed the country; to the markets at the Trysts of Falkirk and Stirling, for example. Many of the routes followed by the old drovers are still well-used to this day; not by drovers any more, but by estate workers, foresters and mountaineers, the latter to gain access to remote mountain areas. Mountain bikers also have good sport following them.

While the Gaelic, *airigh* was used in the Gaelic speaking north and the islands – and still is, areas under Norse or perhaps, Viking, influence – words like *saetr* and *skali* were common. *Skeling*, or the Latinised *scalinga*, were in use in Perthshire in the 12th century. English-speaking areas in southern Scotland and north-east of England, meanwhile, used 'shiel' or 'shieling', seemingly with origins in older Scots, influenced by Old Norse. Transhumance all but died out in late medieval times over most, but not all, of Scotland. In 1862 a survey of such dwellings took place in the Outer Hebrides, mainly Lewis and Harris, by Commander F.W.L. Thomas, Royal Navy. His findings, entitled "Notice of Beehive Houses in Harris and Lewis; With Traditions of the 'Each-Uisge', or water horse, connected therewith", are to be found in the papers of Antiquaries of Scotland. It makes interesting reading. Part of his conclusion is that the ancient dwellings he surveyed were mostly Scottis (Early Scots) or Irish type, of the earliest domestic artificial dwelling, introduced to these islands after the invasion of the Northmen at the end of the eighth century. He then adds another comment. He believes some to be earlier, pre- the Norse invasion, and in fact Picts houses as found on Orkney. He makes particular reference to a discovery at Nisibost in Harris that he surmised to be a Pict's house. It is a really interesting paper, and the language used to describe the islanders he met is perhaps typical of what one might expect in these days from a person of his background.

So, why mention Transhumance in a book about meandering through Scottish mountains and glens? Simply because, as you travel through our mountain areas, you will stumble across the evidence of that practice from time to time. Many of these locations are marked on Ordnance Survey maps to this day. Occasionally place names in Scotland can give a clue to the shieling culture. Names containing 'shiel' and 'ary', or 'ari', being examples. So the next time you are planning a mountain trip, have a look on the map – there may well be shielings indicated in the area you are headed and, who knows, you might just find time to have a closer look. Many are to be found in glens throughout Perthshire and across the central belt into parts of Argyll. They can be difficult to spot, even if in the right area. More often than not, what remains will likely be a knee-high cluster of stones in the vegetation and quite easy to write off as nothing more than a rocky outcrop in the long grass. Be patient. On closer examination you will note that the cluster of stones has a regularity about them, usually in the shape of a rectangle. Often there will be patches of healthy nettles in the vicinity of these buildings. Once satisfied you have spotted one and have a better idea what you are looking for, cast your search a bit wider; there may well be others. One thing I guess that will surprise you is how small they are, and you will puzzle as to how a family lived there. I photographed one settlement in Glen Tarken, to the north of Loch Earn, shown on the map as Clach Mhor na h-Airighe Leithe – in English, 'Big rock of the grey shieling'.

Shielings: Beehive on Harris, and more conventional at Clach Mhor na h-Airighe Leithe in Glen Tarken

Back on the Outer Hebrides, on Harris, I came across a well-preserved 'beehive' dwelling, shieling, at south end of Sron Smearasmal, just south of the rocky nose of that hill. It is described as post-medieval. It is much better preserved and so much easier to spot than many I have seen on the mainland. There are many such settlements in Scotland. I cannot simply walk past these wonderful reminders of our past without stopping and having a look around, maybe even making this the refreshment break. Whilst I tarry, I can almost see the long-departed occupants still there, milking cows, making cheese, bonnyclabber, sewing, knitting, listening to the mooing of the cattle and simply smiling at the voices of their children, over the gurgling water of the burn. I can smell the peat fire and imagine the blue peat smoke curling into the evening sky and melding into the towering peaks surrounding the place. Am I just a dreamer? It is all gone. We are in a different world. (Bonnyclabber has its origins in Ireland, by the way, and is thickly-curdled sour milk). The books of Alexander Fenton, *Scottish Country Life*, and *The Shieling 1600-1840* by Albert Bil, give an account of transhumance in Scotland.

I will finish this small snatch of Scotland's pastoral past with a fascinating puzzle I came across when researching this interesting subject, and in particular the link to descriptive place names associated with it and the fankle I got into when trying to decipher one such place name. Just north of Callander there is a place called Arivurichardich, as it appears on the OS map. I pick this example not just because I find it intriguing – that bit I will come to – but because it was the scene of an unfortunate incident: landowner versus mountaineer. In short, I was approached by the landowner and threatened that if I did not leave the land, I would face the consequences – whatever that meant. It happened like this. In 1981, a friend and I were heading into the hill behind Callander to ascend Stuc a' Chroin by way of Braeleny Farm, Arivurichardich, then the long south-east shoulder, just north of Gleann a' Chroin. I knew the farmer and he assured me there was no deer stalking going on, so there would be no problem. As we approached The Shieling of the Moravian Tinker, we saw a Land Rover-type vehicle speeding our way along a track that headed in from the east. I just knew we were the issue. We got to the 'shieling' just about the same time. A well-built male alighted from the vehicle first. He was wearing the full 'estate tweeds', including plus two trousers. He had a single lens binocular hanging round his neck. (That would be a 'monocular', I suppose.) As he purposefully strode forward to meet (or was it intercept?) us, a woman got out of the vehicle. She was similarly adorned in tweeds. She was not tall, and had longish dark hair. He did the talking and opened by asking where we thought we were going. I told him. He replied, 'No, you are not'. I asked what the problem was. He simply said that this was a working estate and that I had not asked for permission to be on it. I said that I really did not need to do that, and that I had been informed there was no deer stalking that day. He seemed to bristle at my response and he said we would have to go home or face the consequences. I asked what that meant. He did not explain, but said again that I had to turn round and go home. I then asked if he could suggest an alternative route. He was not interested in any compromise, and repeated his order for us to leave his land. At that point the woman spoke, quietly. She had an 'educated' voice and said we really should leave her estate; we would frighten the sheep. I was getting exasperated by now and said that I have been trying to be reasonable and I am willing to detour and take a different route. Yet they would not compromise. I added: 'I am going to the top of that mountain, and if you don't suggest a compromise alternative route I will choose one myself.'

The male did get a bit more aggressive at that and told me, 'There is no alternative. You are leaving the estate.' At that point I said that he had limited choices. Compromise, which you reject. Then you could use violence, which will be unwise, or you could simply apply at the Sheriff Court for an Interim Interdict to prevent me going further. You have a problem with that – namely, you will need to know my name and, more importantly, you will have to have a reason. In any case, I will have climbed the mountain and will be back home before you will have even briefed your lawyer. He then said that I seemed to know a lot about the law. I decided this had gone far enough and I informed both that, despite their attitude and decidedly unfriendly approach to people who will cause no harm, I will propose a compromise. I told them I would detour west, over the reservoir, and go along the ridge to the west of Gleann a' Chroin. Then over the Corbett, Beinn Each, over Bealach nan Cabar and onto the mountain that way. Well out of their way, and a considerably longer route than I had initially intended. Neither responded, and we set out on that route. From the shoulder we could see down into the glen. They were not stalking but they were moving Garron Ponies about. Our initial route would have caused not one whit of problem to their estate activities. By the way, our compromise route was probably better fun anyway; we really enjoyed it. My friend, who had not spoken once during that little unpleasantness, said that he would have been intimidated into going home.

I will return to the place name conundrum, if I may. I note that Albert Bil spells it slightly differently: Ardivourdicherich. Bil suggests it translates from Scottish Gaelic thus: 'Shealling of the Moravian Tinker'. The obvious eye-catcher is 'Moravian'. When were there Moravians abroad in deepest Perthshire, never mind that they were workers of metal? It appears Bil got that from the Old Statistical Account, and Scott of Scotstarvit in Fife of the 1600s. That source subdivided the place name into three elements. 'Ari', a shortened version of the Gaelic, *Airigh*, meaning Shieling: element one. Element two: 'Vuri' is where the puzzle starts. There is no V in the Scottish Gaelic alphabet, so why is it here? So stick with me and I will see if I can explain it. I am no Gaelic expert – in fact, I am not even a Gaelic speaker, or expert in anything for that matter – but I will do my best. Remember, the definition and that spelling seems to have come about during or even before the seventeenth century. In that time in Scotland, while many did speak Gaelic, many did not. Couple that with another fact: a lot of the population did not read or write. Information, news, stories, place names – whatever – were often passed on by oral transfer. Perhaps the simple mistake of non-Gaelic speakers was to confuse the 'mh' sound with the 'v' sound? So for *Vuri*, insert *Mhori*. However, that cannot be correct, as the 'i' has no place next to *Mhor* in Scottish Gaelic. One assumes therefore that the 'i' was in fact not a suffix of *Mhor*, rather that it was in fact *a'*, the present participle and used to prefix the next word in the place name, *Ardich* (or *Cherich*). It is easier to explain, as I suspect it also has fallen victim of mishearing from the oral. More, I suspect, because of the Gaelic pronunciation of the word rather than the spelling.

If I have it correct: for Arivuriardich, or Ardivourdicherich, read Airigh Mhor a' Ceardachd. Translated thus: 'The Big Shieling of the Metal Forge'. To explain the Tinker element means heading into the intricacies of the Gaelic language and much study of *Dwelly*, the authoritative book on Scots Gaelic. Suffice to say, the term 'forge' connects with metalwork. A person who works with metal is *Ceard*, a Tinker, although that word is seldom used in that sense and is more usually used in composition with another descriptive word. For example, *ceard-airgid* (silversmith), *ceardachd* (business of a Tinker – forging metal).

So there you have it. Seems there were no stravaiging Moravians in Perthshire, and is that not a shame? But, hold on. Moravian, from the Latin, was used in Scotland in medieval times and Moray was actually known as Moravia. Furthermore, the Latinised version for Scotland – before it was Scotia, in the high medieval period – was Albania. It seems that was amended to Albany during the Middle English period. Is that the source of Alba? And there is more. It appears an Ayrshire preacher, John Caldwell, was involved in organising a Moravian worship in Ayr in the late 1700s. In 1903 the *Kilmarnock Standard* reprinted an earlier pamphlet that listed the Brethren Societies in Scotland, including a reference to Moravian Chapels. So perhaps we dismiss the Moravian element with too much haste. I wonder? Now the reader will understand my fankle. Perhaps it was simply Travellers from Morayshire who set up a forge and settled just north of Callander. I thank Peter McNiven for his invaluable advice and assistance in navigating me through this interesting place name conundrum. Phew! By the way, according to a Czech friend of mine, the Moravian word for a ferry is *Vuri.* I will stop while I am ahead, if I am ahead that is.

* * *

Allow me to return to my cycling theme, after that short interlude. Another trip of note was when I cycled from the Scottish Parliament in Edinburgh to Paris. That was as part of a group, thirty of us, organised to raise money for charities in Malawi. It was a great experience; however I will only mention the last part of the trip. We had cycled from the town of Compiegne, about forty miles north of Paris, into the northern suburbs – one of the numbered arrondissement areas, some eight miles from the centre of the city. We waited there to be met by the Gendarmerie.

While waiting; a word on Compiegne, or – to be more precise – the forest surrounding it. That is where, in 1918, the Armistice to end World War I was signed. The signing took place in a railway carriage in a siding. It was also where the French surrendered to Germany in 1940; same siding, same carriage. (Who said the Germans had no sense of humour?) When our police escort arrived, I was taken aback by the size of it. One white van, complete with camera crew and four police motorcyclists. I assume the Traffic Department, or their equivalent. We were given precise instructions and told to stay in a tight bunch and obey any signals we were given. We had donned Scottish cycle tops just for the occasion. Blue lights on, then we were off. It was just after midday, and we were to be escorted straight to the Place de la Concorde. Yes, the same place the Tour de France swoops through several times on the final day of the Tour. I was buzzing. What really surprised me was that we were not stopped – not even once. Traffic at every junction we passed through was halted for us, and we sallied through as though we were important. Shoppers in some of the outlying suburbs stopped and applauded. It was mind-blowing. It was now early afternoon, on a busy Saturday in Paris city centre, and we were being given Presidential Parade status. We passed through a few of the famous underpasses alongside the River Seine and, as we emerged from the last one, we were adjacent to the river and the Eiffel Tower was not too far from us. We swept to our right and into the Place de la Concorde. Then it got even more surreal. There was a big crowd of people cheering, and a band struck up. We were ushered to a stop beside a raised platform where the Assistant Commissioner of Police was standing at attention and saluting. Directly behind him was a statue of Georges Clemenceau, 'Le Tigre', Prime Minister of France during World War I. Leader of the Radical Party. A French hero; perhaps not to everyone, but name a politician who is. My mind was spinning. The organisers had not pre warned us about this. I was in a daze. The band stopped, and we were individually escorted to meet the Assistant Commissioner. He shook our hand and hung a medal round our neck. Not all of my cycling experiences finished like that. We did enjoy our night in Paris afterwards.

Chapter 6

MY penultimate cycling odyssey tale involves a mainly off-road trip into mountains, following a famous route on an old drove road. Then I will end the bike interlude with a mixed climbing and cycling day and a short mention of an inspirational figure I happened across one day, on a bike, in the middle of nowhere.

November 2008 and a group of 'auld gits' is meeting in Blair Atholl. It is about 7.30 am and the gathering is upon us. There are nine auld yins – oh, and one young git: my son Stuart. Yes, the An Teallach bairn. Stuart was asked along to help with punctures and mechanical issues. He was not fore-warned of this responsibility, but as the trip developed it became obvious. So, on a cold November morning in Blair Atholl the intrepid auld fools gathered. (Fools may be replaced by Gits; you decide.) After warm greetings and some packing and repacking of panniers we are ready for the off on the first part of our weekend cycling adventure to Ruigh-aiteachain in Glen Feshie, via the 24 miles thereby of old drove road, the Gaick Pass. The pass is one of many historic cattle drove roads that criss-crossed Scotland, referred to earlier. Some of these passes were later upgraded to road and rail passes, Drumochter being perhaps amongst the most famous. Some are now long distance footpaths. We set off in dribs and drabs; no peloton for us. Our first ten miles or so, additional to the twenty four miles of the Gaick, takes us along the old A9 road from Blair Atholl, past Bruar and Calvine to Dalnacardoch, where we will leave tarmac and head into the hills.

Just north of Calvine we encounter a large red deer stag on the side of the road. He has his head down in vegetation and was oblivious to our approach. We are within a few feet of him before he becomes aware of us and crashed off through the trees and undergrowth. He probably got a whiff of Dave. Then we are at the end of the old road section, just where it forks left to Trinafour and on to Kinloch Rannoch. We are, however, not heading for the bright lights of Trinafour. Our journey leads us north at that point, over a dual carriageway section of the new A9. Dodging fast traffic and trying not to trip over our bike or drop anything from our panniers, we cross with no incident – apart from one Auld Git, who left his cycling helmet and had to triple dodge the traffic. The deer-proof gate is closed, so lifting bikes, gear and auld bodies over an eight foot-high barrier followed.

Then we were over, and the Gaick beckoned. I understand *gaick* is Gaelic for 'cleft'. The pass is a glacial valley with very steep sides and a wide flat-bottomed floor. A bird's eye view will show that the line of the main A9 road between Dalnacardoch and Kingussie traces the shape of a bow, with the Gaick making the string of that bow. It is good that we have already got our second wind, having already cycled ten miles, because the first mile after the deer gate is a steepish uphill section. At the top of the incline we emerge from forest onto open hillside and see our track winding away to the north. It is going to be a good day. We are soon scudding along a good track. We pass a lonely uninhabited cottage,

Badnambiast, on our left. It is perched high above the river we are following at that part, the Edendon Water, which emerges from the Cama' Choire – a spectacular steep-sided choire, complete with waterfalls, cut into the eastern flank of the Drumochter hills over to our left, between the Munros of A'Bhuidheanach Bheag and Carn na Caim. We cannot see that from the track, but it is definitely worth a visit if in the Eastern Drumochter hills. After about six miles we reach Sronphadruig Lodge, the end of the routine cycling for a time.

As an aside, this is the same spot Dave and I encountered a remarkable gentleman a couple of years before when we cycled there to climb two hills. It was a very warm summer day. Just at the spot where we were to leave our bikes and head up the hills on foot, there was a tent and a good tourist bike beside it. The bike was upright, but not leaning against anything. It was being kept upright by the clever positioning of a taut piece of cord affixed to the top of the bike frame at one end and tied to a tent peg, stuck in the soil at the other end. A clever balancing act. When we returned to our bikes, lying, slovenly on their sides in the long grass, the well-looked-after bike owner is sitting at his tent boiling water for a cup of tea, of which we are asked to partake. We chatted for a while. He was seventy four years of age and was a veteran cycle tourer. He asked what date it was. When told he said, 'My goodness! That is a month since I left my house in Preston. I never miss a Cycle Touring Club AGM, and cycled from the house over to York for it. Since then I have been cycling north. What day is it?' He then talked about years of cycling in Scotland, of bothies he had stayed in and of routes he had travelled, in all weathers, including early or late snow. He always carried a thirty metre piece of thin climbing rope. Just in case he reached a place where it was too steep, or a cliff was in his way. He could lower the bike and go round the long way and retrieve it. What a spirit; we were full of admiration for him. We left him getting his supper ready as he planned an early start the next morning. He was on his own, and was heading further north for few days before turning and meandering, on his bike back to Preston. An inspirational figure.

Back to our Auld Gits torture for the day. We dismount and push and drag our bikes across half a kilometre or so of seriously mucky peat hag. Our bikes are soon covered in glaur, as are we. If you have never tried dragging bikes – laden down with bulging panniers – in and out of acres of peat hag, you are not missing anything. Honest. It would have been interesting to be about when cattle were driven through the Gaick, in particular this stretch of peat bog. After what seems an age we are on the narrow path that runs along the west side of Loch an Duin, on the east steep flank of An Dun. It is not recommended that one cycles that section, although one or two of the more daring of our group cycled part of it. Most of us had a hard enough time walking, at the same time stopping ourselves falling from the precarious path into the bloody loch. To make it more interesting, there was a fierce gale howling through the pass that day, strong enough to spray loch water on us and with enough power to blow one of our group's cycle goggles from his head, never to be found. There were also patches of hard snow on the track. Part way along the path it is crossed by a line of stones, running down the east flank of An Dun into Loch an Duin below us. Blink and you miss it, particularly when trying to keep on the path. That line of stones and boulders is the March Dyke that marks the Perth and Kinross regional border with the Highland regional border. Teetering along the track was exhilarat-

ing and – despite our moans – we were soon at a more man-
ageable part, on our bikes and freewheeling down to the north
end of the loch. There followed a tricky moment or two as we
crossed the outflow, with care, using our bikes to help us keep
our balance on not very obvious (or stable) boulders. We then
'cooried doon' in the lee of the bank, to shelter from the cold
wind and have a well-earned food stop.

After that, we were off again and back on the cart
track – or, to be modern, Land Rover track. The next few
kilometres were downhill and reasonable cycling – if a little
teeth-rattling rough in some sections. I think that part of the
Gaick sometimes gets referred to as 'Domingo's Road', after a
guy called Domingo Bezzeler – a member of a syndicate who
had the shooting rights in this area. Not particularly 'ancient
history', but a snippet of information to impress your companions if you're ever passing this way. Ahead of us lay Loch
Vrodain and our biggest challenge, the crossing of Allt
Gharbh Ghaig, which emerges from the huge plateau to the
east and can range from a fearsome, uncrossable torrent to a
wide, easy-running stream, about two feet deep. If the former,
then we are headed back to Blair Atholl. It was behaving itself today and, with only the risk of wet feet, we safely
emerged beyond it. One of our group managed to cycle right
through it. Bully for him.

Loch Vrodain, or the Gaelic, Bhrodainn, has an interesting, mystical and ancient story attached to its name. It con-
cerns a magical, jet black hunting dog called Brodainn, or – as
described in another account – a semi-supernatural dog, gifted
by a stranger to a hunter. It did not take the hunter long to
realize the dog he had been gifted was indeed as described,
magical. At that time there were stories of a white fairy deer
over west at Ben Alder. So the hunter set out to catch the

fairy deer. The deer was spotted and an epic chase ensued, as dog pursued deer over mountain and glen. Eventually both passed over the Gaick, and the deer plunged into the loch with the magical dog hard on its heels. They clashed in mid loch and, with the deer firmly in the grasp of Brodainn's jaws, both disappeared into the black water, never to be seen again. From that moment the loch would carry the dog's name for eternity: Bhrodainn. Is the dog story true? It must be. Who could make that up? Incidentally, another ancient map marks the loch as Yrodin.

Not all tales from the Gaick concern the supernatural. Over the years many avalanches have been witnessed and recorded in the steep-sided, narrow pass. On New Year's Eve 1800, Gaick Lodge, as it stood then, was overwhelmed by a huge avalanche. The search for survivors found the remains of five men and their dogs. They had been sleeping in the bothy. One of the bodies was not discovered for three days, about

two hundred yards from the ruins of the bothy. There were no survivors. Ancient folklore has it that avalanches were caused, either by the Devil or the Almighty, depending who was angry enough at the time. No avalanches for us, as we scoot through on our bikes, although it is uncommonly cold. The track past Gaick Lodge and then Loch an t-Seilich is good quality, and obvious-

The Gaick, with Loch Bhrodainn the distant loch to the north

ly used regularly by vehicles visiting the lodge. At the north end of the loch, near Poll Dubh, one encounters a Water Board station and the track changes to a tarred road.

The hard part of the Gaick is over for us, and we simply cycle the last few miles to Tromie Bridge and Drumguish where we turn right into a forest track as we head over to the Feshie. We still have five miles or so to negotiate before we get into Glen Feshie and reach Ruigh-aiteachain Bothy. None of it is too onerous – apart from one stretch, on wet grass, where a couple of us, without knobbly tyres, did a bit of slipping and sliding, but miraculously stayed upright. Then we are at our destination, after about forty miles of moderate cycling and a wee bit of pushing. Our day produced sightings of one red deer, a few mountain hares, a roe deer, what might have been an eagle and several ravens. There were a myriad of small brown jobs, but I am not quite up on them.

For those with no experience of bothy living, what follows might be of interest. There are already some people ensconced in front of a roaring fire when we pile in. Protocol suggests you try not to disturb them too much. We spread our gear in the concrete floor of the freezing fireless room next door and set to work getting our cookers going and preparing our respective meals. A bothy tends not to be well equipped with a plethora of chairs and tables, nor is it blessed with a ballroom of floor space. With our group installed and with many hungry mouths to feed and space at a premium, the 'waltzing' and 'shimmying' begins. Otherwise known as busy bothy behaviour – or, as I like to call it, the bothy shuffle. Each unit in this traditional dance routine glides across the concrete floor, carefully manoeuvring between other units, so as not to clash or knock over pots of boiling liquid. It is amusing to observe, and would be worth a study for behavioural psychologists. So, even with the dancing, we are soon fed and watered. Alcohol is calling. We make our way into the other room – the only other room, the one with the lit fire and people already clustered around it – in deep conversation. It does not take long for our larger numbers to take over, and soon we are singing, telling tall tales and laughing, even though we hear the same tales every time we gather. Oh, we also partake of the alcohol. (It is not about the alcohol; it is about reducing the weight of the pannier.) We eventually head back to the cold room, where we pull and drag our sleeping bags around us – yes, on the freezing concrete floor – and get snuggled in. We are a tired bunch, and a hush transcends on the refrigerated space we occupy. The snoring will emerge eventually. Getting out of the bothy in the pitch dark, carefully tip-toeing over recumbent snoring bundles, to answer calls of nature is for another study – and best forgotten. Remember our age profile. I have not even mentioned the bit about getting back into your sleeping bag again.

Morning dawned clear and cold. After breakfast the party split into two groups – though before the end of the day, it would further subdivide. The majority headed east, intent on returning to Blair Atholl via the Geldie and then the Tilt. That matter-of-fact comment hides a seriously long and difficult day. I will return to their fate later. Stuart had to be back that night as, unlike the retired auld yins, he had work next day and had to be there. So, being aware of the possible difficult river crossing the main group were going to face and not wanting to be stuck in Braemar with no transport, he and I headed back a different route. After wishing the rest luck, we retraced our wheel tracks back to the top of the Gaick at Tromie Bridge, then detour over to Kingussie, passing Ruthven Barracks on the way. In Kingussie we pick up the Inverness to Perth, Sustrans cycle route and are soon scudding south, Blair Atholl bound, with no drama. Well, not quite.

Stuart and I were making good progress on the cycle track. We had not long left Newtonmore and were about a mile or so south of the Ralia Cafe when we came across a woman walking south on the cycle track. I thought, *Bike-less in Ralia*, as my over-fertile imagination for some reason reminded me of the Aldous Huxley classic novel *Eyeless in Gaza*. I have no idea why. That thought soon vanished as we saw the woman was distressed and in tears. We got off our bikes to offer help and more detail emerged. She was in her stockinged feet, clutching Ugg-style boots under her left arm and a packet of fruit sweets against her ample chest. We were in a remote part of the track and there was not another person in sight. How did she get here? Where on earth is she headed? Her good luck fairies had just arrived? A retired senior police officer and a serving fire officer – who, incidentally, was in a mountain rescue team, as had been the retired police officer. We could not get her to calm down, and struggled to get any sense out of her. 'Are you hurt, and how did you get here? Can we make contact with someone for you?' were the obvious starter questions. We were making slow progress. One thing was obvious; her sweets were going nowhere, as she steadfastly kept them pressed against her chest. All was not lost, however, and after much persuasion she put her Ugg boots back on. We were now employing our high-level empathy and sympathy training, and slowly a tale began to emerge. She had been in a car being driven by her husband. They were on their way from their home near Glasgow to visit relatives near Nairn with the family Christmas presents. They had stopped in a nearby layby where she had alighted from

the car. (Scotrail jargon for 'got out of'.) Anyway, for a reason that was never explained, she somehow fell down the
steep embankment that separated the main A9 road from the
Sustrans cycle track. It was never clear how or why she took
that tumble onto the cycle track. While Stuart stayed with
her, I hurried back a couple of hundred yards and climbed the
steep embankment. Lo and behold, a layby. There was no car
in it. She had no idea where her husband had gone. We got a
rough description of the car: small and grey. She had no idea
the make or the registration number. Stuart whizzed off back
to the Ralia Cafe on his bike, in the off-chance of finding a
small and grey car and a bewildered and solo husband.
Meanwhile, I waited with the woman and tried to talk her
into giving me a sweet. I wasn't successful. I did notice, however – no matter the conversation – the sweets continued to
be clutched very tightly. I was becoming more and more puzzled. The steep banking immediately adjacent to the layby was
covered in impenetrable bushes and trees. She could not have
fallen through them. There was not a scratch on her, and her
clothing was not torn. Stuart arrived back, empty-handed.
Then, miracle of miracles, just as we were thinking of giving
up and contacting Scotland's finest, a small and grey car pulled
into the layby from the north. The missing husband, we pre-
sumed. Stuart and I managed, not without some difficulty, to
assist her up the embankment and reunite her with her husband; well, I think that is who he was. Neither seemed to delighted about the reunion, and he seemed less than talkative.
He let a dog out of the car to answer the call of nature; it ran
up to her, tail wagging, and she gave it a big hug. It seemed
pleased to see her. Evidence that a family was indeed reunited.
They all (I include the dog) got back in the car, and it did a U-
turn then sped off to the north, without as much as a by-your-

leave – and without as much as a 'thank you gentlemen, can I give you a sweet?' Then they were gone, leaving Stuart and I to wonder.

The rest of the day was uneventful and easy. As we were getting back into Blair Atholl, Stuart opined: 'You know, Dad, there are not many of your age still doing this stuff.' Did he mean trying to steal sweets from a distressed woman? I think he probably meant the weekend venture, and I think maybe he had a point. The average age of the group had to be nearing seventy years, and the route was a serious physical challenge – for any age group. Particularly the group who headed out to negotiate the Tilt. All in all, it was a great weekend; it was living, it was hard.

Oh, and how did the other party fare? On leaving the bothy at Ruigh-aiteachain, the main group headed east along the River Feshie for a few miles to where it is joined by the Eidart burn, just where the latter emerges from the Cairn-gorms. The Feshie turns south at that point, and our intrepid band continue their eastward journey over about three miles of trackless hinterland until they reach the Geldie Burn. Cycling is not always a possibility through parts of these sections. At the Geldie they encounter a Land Rover track and make good progress for another few miles. Then they are at decision time. They have reached the spot where they will cross the Geldie, and pick up the track heading south to Blair Atholl via the Tilt. Bearing in mind that if they cannot cross, then onto Braemar is the only option. The second and unscheduled split in the team is now a reality. The river is high and fording it was difficult, and would not be without some risk. Two decide on caution and head for Braemar to find beds for the night. They will work out how to reunite themselves with their cars in Blair Atholl after sleep and breakfast. Meanwhile the others plunge into the river and emerge unscathed, if a tad wet, on the far bank. Once remounted, they follow a good track as far as the ruins of Bynack Lodge, where it turns back to a walking path. Time is passing, and they need to get a move on before dark. Seems as though it was every man for himself after that point, as they all push on as best they can over more difficult ground. Then they are in the Tilt, and – after a while – a good track. They speed on to Blair Atholl, getting there well after the sun has headed off to New Zealand (or wherever it goes at night), leaving the intrepid Auld Gits in the pitch dark. Stuart and I were home by the time they got to their cars.

Postscript: after some telephone calls, one of the Blair Atholl crew drove all the way to Braemar and joined the stranded. He stayed overnight and, in the morning, drove them back to Blair Atholl. Mountain people are nice people.

I must warn the reader that my concluding cycle-related story does involve a bit of a conflict. It does not, however, contain flashing images, so it is not that much of a risk – but be warned nonetheless. It was, as planned, a mixed day of driving, cycling, mountaineering and – in my case – a solo cycle into mountains to my resting place for that day. It all started so well and, about six o'clock that morning, we headed north out of the Central Belt. After an uneventful three hours or so we were on the Kessock Bridge at Inverness and skirting the western end of the Black Isle. In spite of its name, it is neither an island nor black. It is in fact a peninsula, and it is thought the 'black' reference was due to it not retaining snow cover as long as the surrounding land, and hence it looked black against the white of the snow. An old wives' tale – who knows? It seems that an edition of the *Encyclopaedia Britannica* suggests the Black Isle was historically known as

Ardmeanach. Seemingly from the Gaelic for a 'high religious house', somewhere near Milbuie. I have to confess, I did check out some reference books but failed to find that meaning. I did, however, find one reference to it, meaning 'middle ground'. I am not sure if there is truth in that; a reader or two will enlighten me.

However one may label it, we were soon over the spine and crossing the Cromarty Firth to the 'mainland' at Ardullie, midway between Dingwall and Evanton where, with breakfast beckoning, we stopped at the relatively new visitors' centre and coffee shop and eatery, Storehouse of Foulis. The 'Storehouse' part, is an 18th century, grade 'A' listed building, adjacent to the old ferry jetty, where trade and passengers alighted for Resolis on the Black Isle, right up to the late 19th century. The building, similar to many along the coasts of Easter Ross and Sutherland, was also known as a *girnal*, or 'rent house', and they were used to store grain. It is after ten o'clock before we emerge into a cold day and continue our journey. We detour over the Struie Hill road and the views over the Dornoch Firth are as spectacular as ever.

Before leaving the Struie, let me tell you a wee story. A long time ago I travelled to the top of the Struie hill, from the Edderton side, in a Bren gun carrier. That is a square metal box running on 'tracks' like a tank or bulldozer. I believe its correct name was 'universal carrier'. An armoured military vehicle designed between the two World Wars to carry troops and equipment and, in particular, weapons. It was also used as a machine gun platform, hence the nickname 'Bren gun carrier'. Production of this vehicle, certainly in the UK, ceased in 1960. In its time it was reputedly the most-produced armoured fighting vehicle in history. Steering as far as I could see, certainly in the one in which I travelled, was achieved by pulling in two brake levers, thus sending the vehicle into a shuddering and violent turn to one side or the other. Using that method my trusty colleague and driver weaved an uncomfortable path up through the steep hillside to the very top. You might wonder why I was taking this trip. Well, it had nothing to do with warfare or transportation of weapons; it was far more mundane. Our job that day was to take a barrel of creosote to the top of the Struie Hill, then paint the wooden hut that sits atop the hill. It is no ordinary hut and is, or was, used to house the sophisticated electronics needed to run the radio mast on the hill. In fact, to this very day a radio mast still adorns the summit. When our messy task was at an end, we sat beside the newly-creosoted hut and had our lunch whilst taking in the breathtaking view over the Dornoch Firth. It was then I heard the sound of chattering voices getting ever nearer. Despite looking all over the hill, I saw not a living soul. As the voices got even louder, I was beginning to wonder about my eyesight. Then I saw the source of the chattering. A huge skien of grey lag geese to the north, winging up the Firth and lower than my lofty perch. It was a wonderful sound, and still is. I can never hear chattering geese now without recalling that wonderful day on the Struie Hill.

Back to my cycling day. Ardgay is soon behind us and we head west on the delightful single track road that leads down Strathcarron to where it changes from a tarred road to a cart track that leads all the way through the mountains to Ullapool. That is for another day. We had turned left just before that point, at The Craigs, and after a short distance we parked at Glencalvie Lodge. A quick change of gear, bikes out the car, and off we go cycling south along the cart track in Glen Calvie. A glen that played a poignant – no, a tragic part – in the Sutherland Clearances of the mid-1800s. It was a thought-provoking cycle down the glen as one could only think that it was once a community of people who were, in 1845, forced from their homes to never return. On high ground to our right we could not fail to see a large modern house, at Diebidale. It is a fine-looking building; however, there was something incongruous about its presence in a place that carried so many stories of despair. In fact, it made our cycle down the glen almost irreverent; pointless, in some way. Anyway, we got down the glen and ditched our bikes. After a quick snack, we headed off on foot to catch the stalker's track that wends up the north flank of Carn Chuinneag, our mountain destination for that day.

It is a cold day with a grey covering of high cloud. The track leads almost to the summit, so route finding and walking is a doddle. Like many Corbetts – hills between two and a half and three thousand feet high – this one sits apart from the other, bigger mountains, making for expansive and spec-tacular views. We had another snack on the summit and gazed back down to the fateful glen. Our thoughts drifting back to 1845 as we tried to imagine what it would be like to be dragged from our houses and cast to the four winds to fend for ourselves. What about the old, the infirm, the children – who cared for them? It was not long before we thought to nearer times and similar expulsions of communities, all over the world. What kind of people are we?

Where was I? Atop Carn Chuinneag. The views are stunning. The track we cycled up is seen to swing east, just where we left our bikes, and meander like the silver track of a snail for miles into Easter Ross somewhere in the direction of Alness. Ben Wyvis, to the south-west, looks within touching distance. Over to the west, one can pick out the Ben Dearg hills near Ullapool and more. Then it is time to vacate our lofty perch and get back to the bikes, followed by twenty minutes of cycling back to the car. I pack two panniers and a tent onto my bike. Dave deserts me to drive back along the road through Easter Ross, heading for the Altguish Inn on the Ullapool Road where he would meet up with some Auld Gits at the bunkhouse for a couple of days' hillwalking. I would join them late the next day, or perhaps the day after that, depending on how my solo adventure pans out.

I set off west past Alladale Lodge, then south-west down Gleann Mor to my 'campsite' for the night at Deanich Lodge, about nine miles ahead. My cycle down the glen was uneventful and very pleasant. The track, obviously well-used, provided a good off-road cycle route. In the early part, at the Alladale Lodge end, one cannot help but notice the work going on to erect miles upon miles of seriously high and strong fencing. It tracks straight up steep hillsides and can be seen in some bits arching along ridges on the skyline. Just like some of the great walls built across mountains in Victorian times. I also read a couple of notices that inform me a 'zoo' licence has been applied for. I am reminded that the landowner has an idea, a plan, to return some 'extinct' wild animals to these parts. Wolves and lynx, if my memory serves. Not sure about the tent if that goes ahead. Personally, I was not certain then, and I am still not certain, if said animals will ever set foot on the hillsides behind the high fences. What I am certain about is, neither will human backpackers or even day walkers, and one wonders about the real purpose of the fences. They certainly nullify the 'right to roam' legislation.

Whatever, it is a lovely evening and I am spinning my wheels down a nice, open, picturesque glen – apart from the monstrous fences at the start – and enjoying every minute of the freedom. There is something liberating about being alone in mountains, whether on foot or on a bike. After a while, maybe slightly over halfway down the glen, I come upon a lovely wee fisher's shelter built into the bank of Abhainn a' Ghlinne Mhoir; the resident river of this glen. Trouble has been taken to build the banking up round three sides of the wooden shelter and put turfs over the roof. It is unobtrusive, and melds into the landscape. It is unlocked, so I use it as my brew up and dinner stop. The shelter hangs right over the river, and that side is completely glazed. What a wonderful spot. I reluctantly leave it to head down to Deanish. Given the circumstances of later, I should have stayed put.

As I continue down the glen the sun is lowering, and the evening views in the glen are stunning. I have to gingerly circumnavigate a herd of Highland cattle, complete with calves. They were not interested in this lone cyclist in their midst, but I keep my speed up just in case. I next encounter half a dozen Highland Garron ponies. They seem to be taking

Deanish Lodge in distance over Abhainn a' Ghlinne Mhoir

more interest in me than the cattle did, and two trot over towards the path. I am no horse whisperer, so I am a wee bit wary. It seems, however, they are more interested in finding a soft place to rest and calmly sit down on the grassy edge of the path, completely ignoring me as I cycle a few feet from them. I did, however, listen intently for the next few minutes, just in case the sound of hoof-beats could be heard. It actually is an interesting sensation. I am neither a cow herder nor a horse handler – or should that be whisperer? – so meeting them in the middle of nowhere, with nowhere to hide and certainly not being in a position to outrun them if they turned frisky, does play on one's mind a bit.

Anyway, with these silly mind games receding I eventually close in on Deanish Lodge, just a short distance on the other side of the river, around a buttress to my left. So, over the handy bridge, round the corner and cosy in my tent in no time. Or so I thought. The area I planned to pitch my tent was bristling with about a dozen identical large tents. Obviously an organised group. I saw a Land Rover-type vehicle and a minibus, parked near the lodge. Undaunted, I cycled on and found a less-than-satisfactory spot about four hundred metres beyond them. I then set about getting my tent erected. It was about eight thirty by then, and I was looking forward to my supper and my cosy sleeping bag. Then I saw the lone ranger, or was it the 'born leader' striding with purposeful gait through the tented village, heading directly for my solo tent. He was not carrying a friendly mug of steaming hot cocoa for me. I smelled a rat. He opened by asking if I intended camping, adding that the access laws made it legal. I found that an interesting, but less than welcoming, comment. He went on to tell me he was in charge of an educational party of young people and that he was responsible for their safety, and that I had just arrived from nowhere. I asked him what his point was and informed him I had not arrived out of nowhere – that I knew exactly from whence I came. His next retort was astonishing, and I am sure many readers may well have been a tad annoyed if directed at them. 'As I am responsible for the safety of the young people and I don't know anything about you, and with the issue of paedophiles, I have to be careful.' Yes, that is what he said. I did respond, and he was soon on his way – leaving me alone to get my tent up and my supper cooked. An interesting encounter, leaving me to won-der, *what is this stupid bloody world coming to, and how did he get to be in charge of anything?*

It was my intention to climb a couple of hills the next day. However, my slumbers were interrupted about five in the morning by the faint pitter-patter of raindrops on the tent. A lovely noise. A peek outside to a vision of glowering grey cloud cover, hiding all the hills. I breakfasted inside the tent, and listened as the pitter-patter got stronger. By eight it was a full-scale downpour, and it did not look like moving on any time soon. Decision made. Abandon the stupid hill idea and get down the glen. Packing a tent and loading gear into panni-ers with the rain bouncing off everything is not a recipe for keeping dry. In fact, it is not even possible.

Bike and I are as one in our misery as we splash down the ten miles of Strath Vaiche, heading for Black Bridge, on the main Ullapool road. Visibility is limited in the clag and downpour. Soon I am on a long downhill section, and all I can think is 'I'll have to cycle back up here some day'. On I splash for about five miles and halfway along Loch Vaiche. At Lubachlaggan I pull off the track and eat the second sitting of my breakfast. The rain has eased by now, so I decide to tackle Beinn a' Chaisteil from that point. It is a steep grind up by the south west ridge. By the time the ground eases a bit, the rain is back with a vengeance and the wind is howling. I cannot see much and, as I have left my map safely stowed in my waterproof bike pannier, which is still attached to my bike, I am mapless. I bail out. The hill of the castle will have to wait on the pleasure of my company some other day.

The track out onto the main Ullapool road, another five miles of it, is uneventful, although enjoyable enough, as the rain eventually stops and the clouds open to allow a glimpse of blue sky. A few Highland cattle adorn this end of my journey, calves and all. They were too busy eating to take any notice of me, so I sneaked past with nothing to report. I am soon onto tarmac and the last mile or so on the Ullapool road to the Altguish is easy. I hang my wet gear in the drying room, have a shower and head for the bar. The Auld Gits will eventually find me. Soon, I was not caring if they found me or not. There are a lot more cycling, off-road experiences I could tell, but these few are a sample of what can be a grand variation, a counterbalance, to the main hill experiences – and all the more enjoyable for that.

Chapter 7

BIKE safely stowed in garage, boots back on, and off to Skye to get my feet onto the range of iron and magne-sium – ferromagnesium – mountains that dominate Sligachan and Glen Brittle. The eroded remains of the magma chamber of a huge volcano that erupted sixty million years ago. The range is better known as the Black Cuillin; An Cuilthionn or An Cuiltheann in Gaelic. It is believed by some that the name comes from the Norse word 'Kjollen', meaning 'keel-shaped', referring to the shape of the ridge.

The Norse visitors to these shores some centuries back arrived in boats, and would simply name it as they saw it – or in the case of Trollaval, on the adjacent island of Rum, as they heard it. Trollaval, 'Mountain of the Trolls', seems to have been named because of the strange, eerie cooing noises that emanated from the mountain at certain times, giving rise to the belief that trolls lived there. Trolls are a mythical creature from Nordic folklore, said to live well away from humankind – often deep in forests or in remote mountains. The moun-tains off Rum certainly qualify. The Norse invaders were mis-taken. The noise was made by Manx shearwaters, not trolls. These amazing birds nest on cliffs and in burrows high on re-mote mountains. The adult birds range over vast areas of the

The Cuillin Ridge, with Bla Bheinn in foreground

sea, fishing for the small fish they survive on. When they arrive back at their nesting burrows, as on Rum, they call out to their young. Having heard their calls, I can attest to the fact that they sound eerie and ghostlike. Having never heard a troll, mind you, I cannot compare.

A large part of the Black Cuillin – the rock that scrapes the skin from your fingertips – is Gabbro, a granular igneous rock that forms when molten magma is trapped beneath the earth's surface. It forms, as I understand, like a massive bubble that cools and forms below the surface until, after several million years of weathering, the covering surface wears away to expose the Gabbro rock that we walk upon today. One last geological note of interest: it is not the oldest part of the island. The oldest rocks found on Skye are Lewisian Gneisses. They appear in the south-east, around the coast of the Sleat peninsula. They formed as granite igneous rocks in the Precambrian era, some two thousand, eight hundred million years ago.

If I said that A' Mhaighdean in the Fisherfields was a jewel of mountains, I meant it. The Black Cuillins, on the other hand, has to be the jewelled necklace of Britain's mountains. Where to start? Why not with the anxiety-inducing Inaccessible Pinnacle – or, as Munro referred to it, 'The Inaccessible Peak'. Or, as many refer to it, The Inn Pin. Whatever moniker you might apply, it remains the bottleneck; the dreaded, exposed rock climb; the crux for anyone intent on doing the round of the Munros. It is regarded, in many ways, with foreboding – or perhaps the Victorians and those of Munro's time may have used the old fashioned, quaint term 'disquietude'. I like that.

Listening to the 'lucky' ones who have safely ticked it off is no help. Nor is looking at photographs and listening to tall tales. Yes, it is exposed – and yes, it is perhaps best left alone in a gale. And yes, it is advised to take a rope to get off; trust me, jumping is not an option. If you thought the Black Cuillin was a narrow, acrophobia-inducing ridge, the narrow and exposed section that is the east ridge of the Inaccessible Pinnacle adds to that impression. At one part you can straddle the crest with one leg hanging over Loch Coruisk and the other over to the Minch. The views are stupendous and the exposure is spectacular; yes, you do need to look. Hundreds of nervous non-climbers manage it every year. It is classed as a rock climb, rated 'moderate', so not too difficult.

If the actual 'rib', for that is what it is (well, a Basalt Dyke to be correct), was laid out in the local park, you would go up it with little anxiety. Basalt is very similar in construction to Gabbro; however, it is finer grained, so less abrasive and in fact quite smooth. When wet, it is treacherously slippy. It forms in large cills – or, in the case of the Innaccessible Pinnicle, a vertical dyke. It also was formed in the magma chamber of an active volcano. Under the tremendous pressure of that process, it gets forced into fractures, cracks and fissures in pre-existing rock bodies and, in that way, can and does protrude through and above the surface. It is not the actual hands-on bit that brings the difficulty; it is one's imagination.

Best to leave that in your rucksack. My first trip up its long side, the east ridge – a few years ago now – was on a gloriously sunny July day.

Tom and I set out early from the memorial hut and wander up the Coire Lagan path. It is a nice approach. Not far up the track is Eas Mor waterfall, at the back of a lovely wee gorge area on Allt Coire na Banachdich. Take your camera. As you ascend further up the track, the views

The Inaccessible Peak

back over to Eigg and other islands are worth the effort so far. After a while you scramble over the slabby rim of Coire Lagan and come across the lovely lochan, a perfect spot for a snack. For those of you with no wish to scale the peaks, please believe me; the effort required to get to this spot will be well-rewarded. It is spectacular; no, *really* spectacular. High on one side is the Cioch. I think it has a very 'proboscis' look about it. It is properly known as Cioch Buttress on Sron Na Ciche. Did you ever see the film *Highlander*? If so, do you remember the sword-fighting scene with Sean Connery way out on that airy, fearsome overhanging ledge? That is the proboscis you are now looking up at. You are surrounded on three sides by fierce beetling black cliffs and jagged ridges. On the fourth side you are on a viewing platform, with scenes you could not believe. It is also a sun trap.

Tom and I cannot wait about for long; much to do. We decide not to take the book route, which will lead us to the back left-hand side of Coire Lagan and up a steep scree scramble. We simply strike out directly up the south flank of Sgurr Dearg to our left. It was a spur of the moment decision. Why? A steep gulley to start, then a mixture of slabby ground and large blocks; altogether steep and interesting. We eventually get onto the Sgurr Dearg ridge and head right. Soon we are below the short, west face of the Pinnacle. A couple of climbers are rappelling from the top. After another snack break we pick our way down the south side of the 'fin' to reach the obvious broken part; our access point. Tom sets out in front, and we are soon on the ridge proper. It is steep, narrow and exposed. It is not, however, technically difficult, and we are soon making progress.

Then I become aware that Tom has stopped. At first I assume he is taking in the view, so I relax and have a look about. It is amazing. Magnificent. A couple of minutes pass, and I begin to wonder what Tom is doing. I ask, and he tells me he is gripped and cannot move. I try to encourage him to make the next move, but to no avail. After a couple of minutes I decide I had better do something. I have no intention of going back, and there is no point in taking the rope out of my rucksack; I would have to get beyond him to do something with it. I am going to have to get past him anyway. Decision taken. At the narrowest, most awkward part of the whole ridge, I tell Tom I am going to climb over him. I urge him to stay absolutely still: 'Do not move'. Then I simply clamber over him. Interesting. Once in front, I tell him not to look anywhere other than my boots and just watch exactly where I step, then follow.

That works, and soon we are atop the Inaccessible Pinnacle. After a few minutes soaking up the sun and the view, it is out with the rope; I get it looped round the handy belay.

Funny how we should just trust a pre-placed belay. Anyway, we did, and with Tom exiting first we descend the eighty foot west face. So there it is. It was not as hard as I had feared, but really exhilarating. Time for a quick snack, then off we go again as we have another rendezvous – this time with Sgurr Mhic Coinnich, named after a Skye crofter called John Mac-Kenzie who, born in 1856, was reputedly Britain's first professional mountain guide.

We head off down by An Stac and look over to the buttress we have to ascend. From a distance it looks fearsome. How are we getting up there? As we near, the route becomes obvious, and we soon scramble up the north-west corner onto the summit ridge. It is shattered and airy. Makes the Aonach Eagach look like a stroll. While not technically difficult, it is nonetheless quite an undertaking for anyone with no rock climbing experience, and not the place for those unsure of airy stances. There is a lot of exposure and, because it is mostly basalt, it is treacherously slippy in wet weather. Despite that, or perhaps because of that, it is great sport. Wonderful. At the small airy summit we sit about, not doing much, just taking in the view. This summit has to be one of my favourite places in all the earth. I will return, and I did return on my own – one balmy day in May a few years later.

Heading along the shattered ridge that day, I found a sun trap corner, with views over to Rum and the glistening Minch. It is not only a seriously precarious place; that day – to me, anyway – it was a seriously precious place. I don't think I have the skill, the language, the vocabulary, to adequately describe my feelings just then. I, for a few moments, was in the perfect place. Destiny arranged that I be in exactly this place at this time. I felt complete; there was no other place in the universe I could, or should have been. I was in perfect harmony with myself, the mountains and the universe. A magic moment of perfect contentment, one of the calmest moments in my life; it was though I was hardly breathing. Similar to the midnight dip in the river in Fisherfield near Loch na Sealga. Different location, different circumstances; same universe, same contentment.

Returning to Tom and our Inn Pin day. We left by the book route, down scree slopes into Coire Lagan, then down the track and back to the car. A refreshment in the Carbost Inn put the lid on a brilliant day, and in one of the best mountaineering areas anywhere. One small impediment that might give you a smile. At that time I lived in Clackmannanshire and was a police officer. The Carbost Inn shares the village of that name with The Talisker Distillery. By sheer coincidence there was work being carried out to one of the copper stills in the distillery, and a company from Alloa was doing the work. As we happily munched our dinner, a group of the copper workers were enjoying some refreshment at the bar. One of the workmen, a male with a prominent moustache, spied me and took an instant dislike to me. Seems my police activity had crossed paths with his personal life back home, and he now saw the chance for revenge. The first I was aware of him was the shout in my direction, asking me to step outside – where he intended to settle whatever score he imagined needed to be settled. I ignored him. However, that seemed to enrage him all the more. Tom thought we should leave, but I disagreed and we stayed put. I think I was enjoying my meal more than Tom seemed to be. I continued to ignore the challenges, although I was beginning to feel a tad sensitive; a bit embarrassed, perhaps. I laid down my knife and fork and my napkin – carefully, John Wayne-style – then slowly, with purpose, kind of sashayed over and suggested he was upsetting customers, so perhaps we should continue outside. I never found out if he would actually have ventured outside, as his workmates spoke to him and they all left. I went back to my table, finished my meal, and – upon leaving – all was quiet.

There is so much more to talk about in relation to Skye and the Black Cuillin. However, I will move on with these few comments. Over many visits I traversed the majority of the ridge, ascended all the Munro Tops – some more than once – and scraped the skin from my fingers often, by spending hours climbing and scrambling with hands on the Gabro, the rock with a surface the consistency of the roughest grade of sandpaper imaginable. The west ridge of Sgurr nan Gillian, the awkward step on Am Bhastier and Bla Bheinn rate more than this brief mention, because they are real climber's ridges and must not be missed. The first two of these tower over The Sligachan Hotel and campsite, and they dare you to meddle with them. All in all this is one of the supreme mountain spots in the whole of our islands.

Let me change my mind and back track on myself. I cannot miss the opportunity to mention my initial failure at the bad step on Am Bhastier. I was on a family holiday with Tom and his clan. We had begged some space to get our feet on the hill, and Am Bhastier was our goal. It was not a nice day; wet and windy. We were at the bad step and I was in lead position, sitting astride the ridge looking down at the route. Yes, it is not wide. I was also looking at the vertical drop immediately on my right and the very steep rocky ground to my left. I sat there for a few minutes, getting soaked and buffeted by the wind. Decision made: not today. So bail out it was. I could not settle that night and thought: Bloody coward; it can't be that difficult. *It is a Munro, and hundreds get over it. In fact it hardly rates a mention, so it really cannot be that difficult.* Begging bowl out, and a second day on the hill is sanctioned by the committee. So – same weather, same time –I am again astride the saddle of basalt that marks the bad step. The ground is just as steep on either side as it was yesterday; no change there, either. So, here we go. I turn and face the way I had come, then gingerly lower myself down the step, holding on for dear life until my feet find a small platform to take my weight. I bend my knees and lower my upper body a bit, at the same time letting go with my right hand and feeling about the rock at around waist height for something to grab. Then there it is: a hold as big as a jug-handle, and easily grabbed – which is what I did. I cautiously lowered one foot from the ledge to the bigger ledge underneath. I repeat with my other foot and look down. Terra Firma, and sorted. I move my hand lower, and use the other to retain my balance as I turn round. Bad step conquered. It is only nine feet or so; not a lot. The exposure gives it an edge. It is an easy slope to the summit from that point. It is nothing on the way back, and in fact made me wonder what I had been playing at the day before. I have been over it twice since then, and cannot believe balking at it the first time. I heard since that some dare devils just jump over it. Hmm!

Just to add a bit more to my own experiences in this area at a different time, Brian and I arrived at the Sligachan campsite late one Friday. We found a space, pitched the tent with undue haste and retired to the bar. That is where we met another of the amazing characters that one happens across when regularly stravaiging this wonderful country of ours. This one was Sam Gilbraith. He was with his wife Nicola, and we spent a delightful two hours in their company. He had been a neurosurgeon and was then a Labour Party Member of Parliament. He was a keen mountaineer, and had climbed all the Munros as well as climbing in the Himalayas. He was a very humble man, and a gentleman. We were lucky to have had the fortune to have been able to spend time in his and Nicola's company. It is not just the mountains that are awe-some.

It is time for a change – not only from my boots to a boat, but from Scotland to New Zealand. There will be a bit of boots involved here also. It was only meant to be a simple 'hello', just a phone call to my son, Stuart. Then, before I can say 'joey' – or, to be accurate, 'kiwi' – I am committed to tak-ing three short hops (well, not so short, really) halfway across the world. I had never before seriously contemplated going to New Zealand. I once read a book, *There but the Godwits* by James McNeish. A haunting impression of a windswept, lone-ly spit of sand somewhere in New Zealand. Some scattered dwellings, a forlorn character or two, a telephone box, and of course, godwits. Will it be like that?

The start of my journey was quite inconspicuous. Brit-ish Midland from Edinburgh, transfer to a Singapore Airlines '747 Megatop' at Heathrow, then up and away. Soon I peer down through broken cloud over Germany, then the Baltic Sea, over Latvia, with clear views to its west coast. The more geographically astute amongst you will know it hasn't got an east coast. We wing over Russia; it is coyly hiding under a blanket of cloud. Just to the north of the Caspian Sea we bank to the south-east. Another boring film, and then we are over the 'Eastern Approaches': Tashkent and Samarkand. Magical names that conjure up visions of the mysterious east: the Silk Road; flowing robes; skilled horsemen; caravans of burdened camels; bargains struck. What commodities are now trafficked, what deals now struck on that road, as we speed overhead in our high tech beast of burden? A turn takes us over the western corner of Afghanistan, a deviation sends us south-east across the top of India, then – after an age of gazing down over a continent in darkness – we depart somewhere over the coast near Calcutta (now Kolkata). The latter part of that leg was accompanied by huge electrical storms over the Tibetan plateau. Pyrotechnic displays, like a huge artillery bombardment. While all else sleep, I stare in awe. Then to the last part of that hop; over the Bay of Bengal, the Andaman Sea, down the Malaysian peninsula into Singapore, arriving about an hour and forty minutes late.

I scurry about and am rushed onto the New Zealand aeroplane that has been held up awaiting my arrival – well, not just *my* arrival. Before I have time to blink, I am off on the final hop. I leave Singapore with a vision of a huge anchorage, full of ships of all sizes. Where are they all from? The rest of my trip seems to pass relatively quickly as I doze most of the way to Auckland. As I leave the plane to meet my son and my daughter-in-law for the first time since July, a steward tells me that Scotland has won the 'Five Nations' rugby. He seems genuinely pleased. He then tells me that he has a ticket for the 'Old Firm' game the next week, and I know why he is pleased. I also realise what a small world it is, and the extent of the spread of the Scottish influence. My luggage has a more leisurely journey and arrives a day later.

I have just arrived in New Zealand – Rotorua, to be exact. It is about 2.00 a.m. and my first impression is of drifting smoke and the smell of rotten eggs. I have been travelling for more than thirty hours and just want to sleep. My slumbers are rudely interrupted by my son at about nine in the morning, who tells me to get up or the jet lag will only get worse. He has a busy day planned; no dozing about for me. A quick breakfast, and then we are off into the Red Woods for a wake-up, jet lag-reducing walk in borrowed footwear. My stuff is still 'jet-bound' somewhere. It is beautiful; we are dwarfed by huge ferns and giant fir trees. I am having trouble actually believing where I am. It is a clear sunny morning; a bit cold, but hey – who cares, I am on the other side of the world; somebody pinch me.

The three hours seems like three minutes. I get my first glimpse of fantails. Lovely, flitting fairies. Then back to the house for lunch. A note on the table changes that plan. 'White Water Excitement' are running a free promotional trip down the Kaituna River, and there are two spaces available. I soon find out why. Our guide, Nick Gutry, fits us up with wetsuits and goes over the safety drill, and after a short portage we are on the river in our inflatable raft. More instruction follows as we bob through exciting and 'dangerous' white water. Did I have a surprise waiting? For the uninitiated, it might be of interest at this stage to explain that travelling in an inflatable raft requires one to sit, precariously balanced, on the side of the raft, leaning out over the water whilst propelling it forward with a paddle. Keeping out the river and 'on board' requires jamming a foot (your own, preferably) under one of the inflated cross-tubes that fit across the width of the raft to keep it rigid. An uncomfortable position. We are descending a grade five river, and will go over a series of waterfalls. One of these will be the Okere Falls, some thirty feet of vertical drop and apparently the highest commercially rafted fall in the world.

As we pleasantly drift, we receive important 'in-flight' safety instructions. Apparently, and most crucially, we have to paddle really hard as we near the top of the falls. This will keep us in control. We don't want, under any circumstances, to get out of control and go into the waterfall sideways or backwards. I nod sagely. *No, we certainly cannot afford to go in backwards.* In fact, I am not sure I even want to go in 'frontwards'. Seems there is a fifty-fifty chance of remaining upright, with even shorter odds of us all remaining in the craft. Now he tells me! We certainly will not stay dry.

The river now enters a meandering narrow gorge, dank and gloomy. The sheer vertical walls are covered in vegetation; mostly ferns of one sort or another. I also see fantails flitting about. To complete the picture, a thin mist hangs in the air. A hundred feet or so above us is a narrow strip of blue. *That must be the sky*, I muse. Then I hear the falls. A faint, non-threatening sound at first, getting louder by instalments. I was so busy with the paddling, balance and keeping the craft headed forward, I failed at first to notice the change in the surrounding sound. Then we are moving markedly faster – maybe 'hurtling' describes it best. The earlier, non-threatening sound has been replaced by the percussion section, giving it laldy. Our ears are assailed by a deafening crescendo that echoes along the steep-sided gorge and assaults our very being. The non-threatening has been replaced by threatening. I am paddling like my life depended on it. Perhaps it does? I look up for an instant and catch a fleeting glimpse of our guide sitting calmly on the stern, urging us to paddle quicker and steering our craft to the best position to tackle the narrow entry. For an instant I have a ridiculous thought: *More steam, MacPhail!* No going back now; no last minute escape for the faint hearted.

My memory is limited, fragmented, into a few short snapshots at that point. I recall being hurtled forward at breakneck speed, at the same time urgently paddling towards the abyss – all accompanied by the incessant, increasingly deafening roar as the torrent accelerates uncontrollably over the cliff. I remember thinking: *What am I paddling for? We're going over anyway.* Nick's cool commands permeate the roar. 'GET DOWN! HOLD ON!' I did. My stomach seems intent on leaving my body through my mouth. I am deafened by roaring water and screams. All seems chaos. We crash onto the next level, thirty feet below, and I am aware of being struck about my shoulder by a flailing paddle then beaten up by thousands of gallons of water. Our rubber craft is helplessly trapped by the awesome hydro-power and thrown about like a cork in a toilet bowl. I stubbornly cling on. Then we are released, and I am aware of cheering. I, then a fifty-two year old child who should know better, am also cheering – with relief, I suspect. We rest a few minutes, gather our wits, gaze back at the falls, and then we were off to traverse the remainder of the river.

There were plenty other white water experiences and Nick asks if any of us fancy having a shot at 'riding the bucking bronco'. (Well, I think that's what he said. With all the noise and the accent, I might have misheard). *Yes,* was the answer, although I don't think any of us had the faintest idea what he meant. We would. We had negotiated a lesser fall, maybe about ten feet or a bit more. Having gone a short distance downstream, we turned and paddled back upstream to the very falls we have just come over. So now it was the bucking bronco. An idiot is persuaded to sit astride the front of the inflatable, facing forward – feet dangling in the river, hands gripping the rope that is around the prow. The remaining crew then paddle the dinghy, as hard as they can, back into the base of the waterfall. As the inflatable enters the falling water, at speed, the bow is forced into the torrent. I remember thinking, *we will never get through there.* How astute of me. The front of our craft is directly under the cataract, and the 'rider' is violently pounded senseless by its brute force. As the craft loses forward momentum, the paddling stops. The sheer raw power of the waterfall dips the front of the craft down alarmingly and at speed.

Then comes the good bit. Having lost forward momentum and been forced down by the force of water bombarding the prow, hydro powers again take over and – in an instant – the inflatable is thrown violently backwards out of the torrent. On being so quickly released the front of the craft is alarmingly pitched high into the air, somersaulting the prow rider some feet backward into the boat. Keeping a grip on the rope is not possible. As I untangle myself from painters, paddles and the other 'passengers', I understand why this piece of tomfoolery is so named and I wonder: *why me?* (A 'painter', by the way, is a sea-salt's name for a rope. Showing off a bit there.) Soon we are at the end of our river trip – for that day, anyway. The Kaituna offers a relatively short outing, just over an hour... but what an hour. It is not regarded as one of the classics; however, certainly for the uninitiated, it is an exciting and memorable – if not to say mind blowing – experience. Probably not for the non-adventure seeker, but a must for anyone looking for an early wake up call to New Zealand, and definitely an antidote for jet lag.

Negotiating Okere Falls

145

As we trudge up from the river porting our inflatable, I see my first New Zealand Kingfisher.

Chapter 8

L ET me keep you out of the country for a wee while as I
head for Europe and the Alps for a short interlude. I
had always harboured the notion of climbing Mont
Blanc. Well, since I get into mountaineering, that is. Quite
interesting to note that many of the people I climbed with
harboured no such notion. They regarded it as a tourist
mountain and not a 'real' climbing challenge. But as I said,
climbing Mont Blanc – to me, anyway – was something I really wanted.

Before that, however, I looked for the opportunity to
spend time in the European Alps and get acclimatised to
them. Perhaps comfortable in them might be a better term.
That chance came along with an invite to go out with a few
guys and walk the Haute Route. Incidentally, and for any
pedant reading this (that will be me, then), 'Haute' with the
'e' suffix is female, whereas innocence of the 'e' denotes mascu-
line. It is pronounced 'oat', and literally means 'high'. It links
Chamonix with Zermatt – some stretch it to finish at Saas
Fee, under the Monta Rosa. The route goes through the centre of the Alps, over high Alpine passes and glaciers. When
first charted by the English Alpine Club one hundred or so
years ago, it was named the 'High Level Route'. Depending

on what season one choses, it can be a ski touring route, an alpine climbing route or a walking route. Over the years the route has gained several variations to the original, in terms of route and severity. No matter which of these one chooses, the venturer – I guarantee – will experience one of the better mountain experiences of their life. In our case we chose, for reasons that suited our needs and time constraints, a variation from the classic route. We would travel in early September, and would largely follow a high, glacier route – and if given the chance, we would ascend a mountain or two. That would mean carrying crampons, ropes, harnesses and ice axes. With some variations to the route, our trip would be about ninety miles – partly because we started higher up the valley from Chamonix, at Argentiere.

The early planning was kind of fluid, and two of our original guides eventually sort of moved out of the frame for various reasons. We eventually got sorted and our actual guide, Iain Peter, could not have been bettered. He was everything we needed, in so many ways – including the ability to take no nonsense, to stay calm, to fit in to the team and most importantly, to exude confidence and display a keen, if dry, sense of humour. He was, and still is, a really nice bloke and a seriously experienced guide and mountain person. That is why ten of us found ourselves gathered in Le Dahu Hotel in Argentiere, in early September 1987. A Dahu is a mystery creature of the Alps, described as a mountain goat-like creature with legs of different length on each side, enabling it to stay upright and keep its balance on steep mountain sides. A haggis-like feature, I have to assume. On a more serious note, our guide has already started the task of sussing out our characters and competences. For that part of his planning, he was joined by his very good friend, fellow Alpine Guide and top-end climber Roger Payne. Our 'induction' started with a Raclette eating competition. Iain and Roger beat us hands down. So much for the fun; now for the hard stuff, and it would be getting so as we were put through our paces on the big glacier above Chamonix, the Mer De Glace. To get from Chamonix, we took the rack and pinion railway that ascended to the Montenvers Station on the edge of the glacier. The rack and pinion design of railway is used on steep gradient tracks, typically about 7 to 10%, the latter being the maximum for friction-based track railways. The design involves having a cog wheel that meshes with the track. The cog wheel is normally between the running rails. We were not there to be tested on our engineering knowledge though, and soon we are drinking coffee at Montenvers and gazing out over the glacier.

The Mer de Glace snakes and curves out of the Mont Blanc massif to terminate above Chamonix. At Montenvers it is half a kilometre wide. It is ribbed for its whole length by regular transverse ripples that give it the look of a massive serpent. I found it an awesome sight and, just like my New Zealand experience, I had to pinch myself. I am easily overawed. My reverie is soon snuffed out as we are mustered and headed onto the back of the massive serpent. The hard work is about to start, and there will be no resting place for the next two or three hours as we don our crampons and get put through a series of competence-based routines designed to assess our strengths and weaknesses as well as teaching us some new techniques. Walking gingerly along the top edge of the aforementioned ripples, crampon-footed and unroped, we look nervously at near-vertical ice dropping away from us on either side; pleading with our balance mechanism to work for just a wee bit longer was a nerve-racking experience. But we get the hang of it, and soon we were prancing along atop ripples without a downward glance. Following that there was belay work, rope work, putting in ice screws, and then it was practising with full leg and shoulder harness acclimatisation and a few other things. I leave the worst till the end. From the top edge of said ice ripples, we had to walk straight down to the bottom of the ripple while wearing crampons. No easy 'get-out clause' for us. Nobody to arrest our painful fall down a dozen or more feet of solid ice onto more solid ice. Falling will be like crashing down into the inside of a huge 'V' shape, with no cushioning. So it's better to get this right. Then the sadistic twist in the tail. We had to do it facing out, and – just so we would know it was serious – we were doing it freefall, with no rope. This had serious leg-breaking potential. Oh, the ice was as near-as-dammit vertical; certainly in the 60% category. Seriously steep. The ice axe was our only external support. I described in an earlier chapter the technique of descending with an ice axe, called glissading. Well, this had some similarities, but not a lot. You do not glissade on near vertical ice when wearing crampons.

Then it was my turn. Face out, knees bent, kind of squatting, feet together, crampons firmly planted in the steep ice. Then a careful walk down to the bottom. *Stop whining and get on with it*, was the watch-word of the day. Knees and thighs about to burst. My sensible brain is telling me to ignore the pain, because falling will be worse. We had to go through that exercise a couple of times – maybe three, not sure. Whatever the case, it did not get easier. I can honestly say, of all the various techniques I experienced over the years on mountains – in the Alps, in Mountain Rescue – I found that to be the hardest and the most painful to endure. We were toiling under the gaze of the Dru; that famous, fearsome tooth-like pillar of black rock on the far bank of the glacier from our location.

It looked so near; a short jog over. Iain explained that it would take at least two hours to get there. Scale, in terms of visual perception of distances, is not the same as back home.

We heaved our sweaty bodies back to Montenveres and relaxed over a coffee and a bit of cake before piling onto the rack and pinion railway and then down to the 'English Bar' in Chamonix. Back to the Dahu later for dinner and another Raclette challenge. Next day was more acclimatisation under the gaze of our guides. This time we actually climbed something – the Petite Aiguille Verte, just outside Argentiere. Not the biggest peak in the area, but seriously good sport and involving the climbing mixture required by our guides. Steep alpine snow topped by a fragmented and precipitous ridge, with just a deep enough snow to keep it interesting. If the ascent is exciting, wait till you try to get back down. Its position between Mont Blanc and Aiguille du Argentiere – with its 4,000 metre-high relative, the Aiguille Verte, towering beyond – gives a spectacular vista. Then back to the Dahu for a hat trick of Raclette and preparations for our departure on foot to Zermatt. We carefully fold and stow our dancing togs into kitbags. Roger will drive round to Zermatt with them. We are left with climbing gear and as little clothing as we will safely get away with. I think our packs were about thirty pounds, maybe a bit more.

Morning dawned to a brisk, cooling breeze and broken cloud cover, and we were off on what – certainly for me – was a special journey. Europe, the Alps and that whole thing was so far from my early life, and beyond my horizons. I had read books by and about the exploits of climbing superstars: Haston, Boardman, Messner, Brown, Whymper and more. Now I was setting foot in their domain; pretty much on the lower rungs, admittedly, but still near their shadows if not actually in them.

The first day was not unlike a typical mountain day back home. Apart, that is for the altitude – oh, and the short chairlift journey and the glacier we walked beside. We were on a well-worn track that runs alongside the Glacier du Tour, to the Albert Premier Hut; our first night's resting place. My abiding memory of that day was the acres of shattered ice. So unlike the uniform condition of the Mer De Glace. It was similar to a vehicle scrap yard, with thousands of tons of shattered ice piled high as far as the eye could see. It was dirty grey with broken parts exposing gleaming white ice, laced in some parts with a kind of blue, aquamarine kind of colour. It was obviously a living thing, as it cracked, creaked and groaned – along with the occasional crashing sound as some large piece of it broke off. In short, it was fascinating.

The hut was busy, probably because it is only a relatively short trek from Le Tour in the main Chamonix valley – on a walking track, not on ice or snow. The hut is staffed at that time of year so we ate and lazed about, taking in the views over the glacier to the impressive Aiguille du Chardonnet. Breakfast was early the next morning: French bread, jam and tea. Then we were off. We donned crampons and roped up early, and headed up the steeply-inclined head section of the glacier and over the shoulder of Aiguille du Tour, eventually dropping down towards the Trient Glacier. A snack break amongst steep rocks allowed us a view of our route for that day.

After descending from our perch we were onto the glacier and continued on it all that day. A new experience for me, and I enjoyed every step of it. There were no dramas; nobody, unlike in the days to come, broke through the surface of the snow into a crevasse, so we made good progress. We were divided into two separate groups. There is a technique to walking whilst roped together; not rocket science, but requiring concentration. The issue for our single guide was our numbers. Normally a single guide will take a group of maybe up to five or six, but ten was above the 'safe' limit. Hence the assessment work before setting out. Three or four of our group had Alpine experience, both walking and climbing. They were proficient on ropes and traversing glaciers. So it was easy; we divided accordingly, the less experienced in Iain's charge. The others, on their rope, followed at a discreet distance – but always within Iain's control. The Trient Hut would have been the obvious destination; however, our guide and the guardian of the hut were at loggerheads at that time, so we swung right and descended the gentle sloping arm of the glacier towards the town of Champex Lac and the Cabane d'Orny in the hills above the town.

It was a longer walk – maybe a couple of hours, but no hardship – as we strolled along on crisp pristine, white snow, with black, jagged mountains at every compass point, all held together by a ceiling of azure. I think we were still in France, so perhaps ceiling of *ciel bleu* might be more correct. Who cares? I was in dreamland, and loving every new step. Cabane d'Orny was top quality. The light pine interior gave a clean, fresh and relaxed feel to it. We selected our bunk spaces and chilled about for the rest of the day, taking on plenty of liquid and a small beer or two before the early evening meal. Then to our bed of heavy and hairy blankets. We were too tired to care.

An early rise, and – after the ubiquitous breakfast of bread and jam, washed over by coffee or tea – we were off. The first part found us teetering along the glacier moraine;

the ridge of debris, crushed rock and stone, formed by the glacier and lined along its side. Then we were onto a normal track and making good progress to the small hamlet of Le Breya, high above Champex Lac. I was pondering the knee-grinding decent when Iain ushered us over to the ski lift. Not a grumble or a protestation about ethics from any of us as we quickly alighted the teleferic and were soon transported below to a leisurely afternoon of tea or coffee, or perhaps wine and cream cakes by the lake. *We need some of this back home*, I thought. There followed a minibus trip by a zig-zag of a road to Verbier, where we grabbed a light lunch – in my case, pizza and red wine. Oh, and more coffee and cake. Then we were herded to the high end of the town to catch the first stage of the teleferic onto the foothills of Mont Fort, where we alighted and trekked for a while to our digs for that night, Cabane Mont Fort. On our way up we had passed through a lot of cloud. By the time we were ensconced at the cabane the cloud had drifted away, leaving us perfect views down on Verbier and over the valley in the direction of our previous night's shelter. Two things I will never forget about that night: the wonderful, deeply melodic and calming sound of clanging cow bells drifting up from the pastures below, and the meal. We dined on a large bowl of wine-infused cheese fondue, supported by a whole variety of breads and dips, with the occasional beer – to balance the meal, you have to understand. The chat got more raucous as the night passed, and soon degenerated into a joke-fest. A memorable evening of friendship and fun.

Morning arrived far too early and, as we headed out and ascended towards the Col de Louvie – situated between the mountains of Mont Fort and Rosablanche, at about nine and a half thousand feet – I don't think mine was the only head fit to burst. We did encounter steeper ice and some tricky sections that day as we headed for the Cabane de Plafleuri – or, as it seems to be known today, the Plafleuri Hut. It is situated in an isolated spot at about eight thousand, six hundred feet – midway between Verbier and Arolla, on the edge of an old quarry. The surroundings are pretty barren. Not the prettiest corner of this lovely region. The quarry was worked years before to provide rock for the lower dam on the Lac des Dix, the Barrage de la Grande Dixence. The hut was accommodation for the workmen and, during our brief stay, that is exactly what it looked and felt like. Since our passage through, a new hut complex has been built adjacent to the old hut and, from images I have seen, it looks a nice billet. As we descended to the hut we saw a herd of Ibex – well, a wee group of maybe five or six. Does that qualify as a herd? They are known locally as Bouquetin, and I understand they are sexually dimorphic. I didn't like to ask. They seemed to care less about our own presence, and hardly moved aside as we passed at a distance of no more than thirty feet from them. It was self-catering that night, but cosy enough.

Next day, we headed out the quarry and continued east before dropping down into the valley containing Lac des Dix at the northern end. It was another clear, sunny day – if a bit cool – as we walked the length of the lake, snatching views over to the needle point that is Aiguille de la Tsa and beyond to the spectacular Dente Blanch, near where we would sleep a couple of days later. The route we followed today was reasonably easy, with a couple of steepish sections that required care. As we rounded the last corner of the day, our resting place for that night – Cabane des Dix – could be seen perched high on our right, overlooking the lower reaches of the Glacier de Breney. Another comfortable hut, with an afternoon of

Pigne d'Arolla from Cabane de Bertol

washing and sunbathing, before an early and comfortable night. An early rise was called for as we were heading off to ascend a nearby peak, the twelve and a half thousand feet that is the Pigne d'Arolla.

Three of our party stayed in bed as the rest of us headed out over the reasonably level grey ice of the glacier. While it was level and easy to cross, it creaked, groaned and cracked rather disconcertingly. We were soon over and onto the steep ground. Soon it was us who were creaking and groaning. It was not particularly technical; it was, however, steep and long. Like a grade two or three Scottish climb, if a lot longer.

Then we were there: on the summit. The views were spectacular. A group of Germans arrived soon after and they produced a bottle of bubbly, which they happily shared with our party. Well, certainly with Iain and myself. It was then I heard a comment I would hear again on top of a big mountain in the Alps. Iain looked around at the group and said: 'Come on, guys – get your photographs and let's get out of here before the bastard kills us.' Then we were on the way down.

One memorable moment comes back to me. When a good half way down, we sat at a convenient spot for a refreshment, overlooked by Mont Blanc de Cheilon. It was not only a bit bigger; it looked a much tougher prospect. We were not going there, however. Not far below our refreshment break spot, there was another party. Then we heard it: the yodelling. They were all singing and yodelling at the top of their voices. It echoed around the Alpine peaks. We applauded them, and they bowed. A brilliant moment, and a memory not to be forgotten.

Once back on the glacier, we dallied to allow our colleagues – who had foregone the pleasures of the Pigne d'Arolla for a leisurely breakfast – to catch up. After tripping through (and in some cases over) a boulder-strewn moraine, we were confronted by a vertical wall of rock, sporting vertical metal ladders. We had arrived at the Col de Riedmatten. We queued and climbed, and were soon at the top and gazing into a different world. An Alpine valley with a clear path winding down through sun-kissed green pastures to the lovely Alpine hamlet of Arolla, some four miles or thereby below us. No ice, no creaking glacier, not a drop of snow and pleasantly warm. I enjoyed the stroll. We soon became aware of companions, lots of them, skittering about on the grassy pasture from the shelter of one boulder to the shelter of another boulder. We were collectively enthralled not just at the flashes of brown, darting creatures, but also by their calls – seemingly alternating from a kind of cheep to a more regular short, high-pitched whistle. One of the learned members of our group informed us that the collective noun for marmots is a 'madness'. Hmm! With our usual zany sense of humour we soon renamed them 'Bovrils'. We also heard the distinctive chirping sound of crickets. At first they were not as easy to spot, until that is, we sat on the grass to take on board sustenance. They were all around us, and in some cases all over us: a crackle of crickets. I sat for ages with one on my sock and another on the arm of my shirt. I had not realised how big they were. The chirping sound emitted by them was so sharp and clear, probably because of their closeness to us. To be accurate – information again gleaned from one of our group, who displayed an authority on creatures I have only seen bettered by Doctor Doolittle – the correct term for the sound a cricket makes is 'stridulation', or so he sagely informed us. It is not – as is commonly believed, he added – made by rubbing its legs together, but rather, it comes from rubbing the upper and lower parts of its wings together. One has ridges, and the other has a surface like a scraper. So there you have it; the cricket explained. Do you know something? I could not have cared less. I was just enthralled by them. They are beautiful and fun creatures, and – to repeat something I said earlier in the book – try and find time to get out and listen to nature. Its music is so much better than that produced by humans.

Our sun-kissed day continued, and we reached Arolla in fine fettle. We got sorted into our billet for that night: a self-catering community centre. A quick detour to the local shop to get provisions, then to the small village square and a refreshment whilst soaking up more sun. An uneventful night between cooking and washing up followed, before sleep and another early rise. One of our group had damaged knee ligaments a couple of days back, so he bailed out to get public transport round to Zermatt where we would catch up with him in three days.

Day seven arrived with a clear blue sky and a good forecast. We were thankful of that, as we were heading for our highest hut of the crossing – Cabane de Bertol – at just under eleven thousand feet. A stroll out of Arolla along the valley floor soon terminated as we swung left up a steep track leading to an unnamed smaller glacier that skirted the southern flank of Aigille de la Tsa and terminated just under the Bertol Hut, which sat high astride the southern ridge of the aforesaid mountain like an eagle's eyrie. It was a hard and steep day, including two minor crevasse crossings. The cabin itself became more impressive the nearer we got to it. Not only that – its position high on the ridge above us made getting into it look a tad daunting. Once we cleared the glacier, we were faced by steep, exposed rocks that required some airy scrambling, aided at one section by a steel chain handrail. If that was not enough, a vertical rock face – complete with two lengths of metal ladders affixed to the rock – was the next hurdle. Just to add to the whole experience, the rock face was not smooth, so the ladders were offset with the bottom of the upper ladder splayed out beyond the top of the lower ladder. That meant, having reached the top rung of the lower ladder, one had to reach over and get a firm handhold on the upper ladder – as many rungs up as your stretch would allow. Second rung up, in my short-legged case. Getting a firm grip was essential before the next move. That involved standing as high up the lower ladder as one could whilst maintain-

Metal Ladders

ing balance, stretching out one leg to get a foot firmly placed on the lower rung of the upper ladder, before the death defying heave across the gap. All the time with your arse hanging out a couple of hundred feet above the quaintly-named Haute Glacier d'Arolla. Plain sailing after that as we traversed the last short section and reached our shelter. If that sounded a bit interesting, wait till we exited next morning.

I will say now that Cabane de Bertol was my favourite resting place on the trip. It was in a sensational position with views back over Pigne d'Arolla and an uninterrupted view of the Dent Blanche, and so much more. The food was also first class and – when I managed, with some coaching, to utter (or perhaps stutter) a German phrase to the German-speaking guardian – I was his lifelong friend and a free bottle of wine soon found its way to our table. We spent the late afternoon, as we had done before on this trip, basking in sunshine and snapping photographs of all that surrounded us. I again use the word memorable, because it certainly was worth the effort. Sometime after our evening meal, as we were chilling and blethering about this and that, I was approached by an older couple – not older than I am today, but older than I was then. They had been in the hut when we arrived, so I had no idea of their route. Anyway, they asked where we were heading in the morning and, when I told them, the male asked if they could travel with us. Seems they were a bit nervous and the weather for next morning was to be cloudy with limited visibility. I spoke to Iain, our guide, who refused to take responsibility for them. I was a bit taken aback. However, he explained it was about his Alpine Guide insurance and – as he had no idea of who they were or their capabilities – he was hog-tied. He then took me aside and said: 'Look, Ian; tell them no, I cannot take responsibility for them, but tell them there is nothing we can do if they follow us.' So that is exactly what I did.

Another early start, breakfast finished and out onto the descent route from the hut. The whole place was ice covered, including the two metal ladders – every rung. Getting down was a trial of care and confidence over trepidation. If I thought moving between the splayed-out ladders had been tricky on the ascent, I had not experienced the descent on the ice-covered metal rungs. Maintaining balance going down is trickier. It was a white knuckle ride for some of us, particularly short-legged *ich* (I think that might be German for me?). In fact, one or two did not risk the free climb down the ladders and opted for a belayed descent using a rope. Who could blame them?

Despite the ice, we all gathered safely on the Haute Glacier d'Arolla, got roped up into our two groups and toddled off. It was cloud-covered, so not only did Iain use his compass, he also resorted to his mountain altimeter to pinpoint our height and position. What he also did on occasion was slow down and check behind, to make sure the older couple were able to follow us. He was constantly looking back. We did take a minor detour not long after leaving the cabane, so we could climb the Tete Blanche. It is just a bit over twelve thousand feet in height and sits astride the Swiss-Italian border. We took the opportunity to step into Italy. Then we were off on our long descent and detoured back over the Col d'Herens, then down another glacier to the Schonbielhutte. It was a tricky decent, and one or two of us broke through the crust into hidden, snow-covered crevasses. Our rope management had improved during the crossing, so there were no real dramas, although there was the occasional curse as one crashed through and, for that instant, wondered when the rope would go taught and arrest the plunge into oblivion – which it always did. The old couple stuck doggedly to our heels, a respectful distance from us, and all was well.

As we descended to the end of the glacier and through the moraine, we passed through a section of steep – almost vertical – cliffs. As I gazed over, I saw movement; little goat-like creatures moving with ease about on the face of the cliffs. 'What are they?' I asked. Chamois was the answer. Our resident animal expert explained that the Chamois is widespread in Europe's mountains. They are small, hoofed animals and described as goat-like antelopes. Their young, it seems, can be referred to as kids – or, according to some, calves. I could not argue either way; I had never seen one before, and my knowledge was pretty limited. Mind you, as I watched them my heart was in my mouth. How do they do that? It looks like they had spikes for hooves. I could not believe how they moved about so effortlessly and sure-footed on such steep ground. Amazing creatures – and again, a privilege to behold. My memory flew back to my youth and the popular cleaning cloth so prevalent in these far-off days. Chamois leather, made from the hide of these delicate creatures. We pronounced it 'shami' leather and, for the life of me, in these early days of my childhood I did not connect it to the beautiful creatures I was watching that day, prancing effortlessly on precipitous cliffs. We grow up and learn.

Then we were in our last hut of the trip: the Schonbielhutte. It was busy; probably because – like the Albert Premier Hut at the beginning – it is a walk, roughly seven miles from Zermatt, with no requirement for ice axes, crampons or any of that stuff. I, for one, looked forward to the leisurely walk down into the bright lights the next day. The hut is situated right under the Dent d'Herens and the

Matterhorn, both four thousand metre peaks and classics. The views to both are sensational, just stunning. We spent hours sitting out on the veranda with beer in hand, simply staring up to them. Bairns in a toy shop. The old couple got in safely, thanked us several times, and then spent the rest of the after-noon forcing drink on us. We resisted, but they were insistent. We spent the evening playing silly table games and chatting. Another good night.

Not such an early start the next morning, then out into another beautiful day. It was a shorts day, and an easy ramble. The first four miles was accompanied by the Zmutt Glacier on our right. It was difficult to linger our gaze onto the glacier as the Matterhorn, standing proudly beyond it in all its splen-dour, took precedence. I could hardly drag my eyes from it. We were eating up the leisurely stroll and enjoying every mi-nute of it, and making good progress to Zermatt... until, that is, we happened across the small hamlet of Zmutt and the smell of fresh coffee. No requirement for a guide to advise us on that decision. In fact, where was he? We dived down off the track into the group of squat, dark wooden Alpine-style buildings, clustered together, almost overlapping and elbowing in to get the cosiest spot. Winter blizzards on their mind. Drawn to the coffee smell, our trusty guide was already en-sconced. Cream cakes of the highest quality were not resisted. A fitting end to a great week. Then into the millionaire set-tlement that is Zermatt and the end of our high-level crossing. We were billeted in the Hotel Banholf and would spend two nights there. Roger had already arrived with our kitbags. Washed, showered, changed and ready to go was the order of the day. We did relax and enjoyed every minute, even when we were disgorged from a pub called the North Face. I still protest our innocence. We took exception at not being called

Scottish by a group of central Europeans who insisted that the island we were from gave us no right to that name as we had been conquered a couple of hundred years ago. Something like that, anyway. The detail and logic of the debate got lost in the level of intellect being displayed by participants and, of course, the volume. Well, I thought that. Seems the owner of the pub disagreed, and both teams in the debating society had to continue outside the premises and not come back. We were fed up debating and headed for the Brown Cow Pub and its sister establishment, the Broken Bar Disco, and a belter of a night was enjoyed. I have a vague recollection of someone telling me, 'You have been in the mountains too long!' To this day I have no idea what she meant.

A good night's sleep followed and, after breakfast, some headed up onto the Briethorn – a four thousand metre peak. Most of us continued to enjoy simply meandering in the town. Next day we headed down to Visp and spent the night there. Whilst eating out, one of our group – to the amusement of the waitress – managed to string together three languages in as many words when he asked if she had three spoons. '*Pardon; drei* spoons, *s'il vous plait, danke.*' Then it was a train along the Rhone valley, through Martigny, almost completing the circle from whence we came. Then up to Montreux, through Lausanne, alongside Lac Leman and back to the airport in Geneva. And so ended a wonderful trip. Certainly, for me. In particular it gave me so much confidence in my ability to exist and explore the Scottish mountains. I had never felt so fit. All round it was a very positive experience, and I would not hesitate in recommending it to others.

I harboured a plan to head back out the following year and climb Mont Blanc. So I needed two things: to keep hill fit, and to find someone to travel with. I spent a lot of time in winter conditions and got up some ice and snow routes. When not doing these things I regularly – at least once a week – headed into the Ochils carrying a heavy sack. Straight up the front of Dumyat from Blairlogie car park and back into the village, timing each trip and trying to improve. Heading onto Ben Cleuch, by Alva and Silver Glen or by Tillicoultry and over the Law. Same arrangement: carry a heavy sack and time myself. I was on one or more of these routes every week. In addition, I kept up my normal hill calendar, climbing 51 separate Munros as well as some rock climbs, completing my second Ultimate Challenge, my mountain rescue activities and more.

Chapter 9

THE winter climb and the summer rock climb I relate now are not the hardest climbs in the book. In fact, they are pretty low end compared to what a top level mountaineer will be tackling. Remember what I said at the beginning: I am no top level mountaineer. I am no more than a fit, enthusiastic trier.

Savage Slit in Coire an Lochain in the Cairngorms is rated 'severe'. Mind you, there are several ratings above that, so – certainly in terms of technical climbing – it is not that difficult. Way back then, the numbers participating were a bit less than today, so we had no queue to contend with and wandered into the coire, got set up and went for it. Looking up at it from the coire floor, it is quite intimidating. The first part involves a scramble up steep blocks to the foot of the actual 'rock climb' section. That is a vertical crack set in a ninety degree angled corner, and with an awkward chockstone towards the top. The final section is a steep scramble, certainly no more than moderate in climbing terms, although pretty exposed and not the place to lose one's footing. The first and last sections we did unroped. The crack is quite wide in parts and involves some jambing, involving different parts of your body from fist to forearm and to actually having your whole

The author views Savage Slit

body in the crack, jambing your back against one wall, whilst your feet are braced on the other wall. It is a strenuous wrestle, hard work and great fun. A climb not to be missed.

During the winter of that year I was in the Lost Valley, Coire Gabhail in Glencoe. There was a lot of snow about as we tackled the adjacent climbs of Peregrine Gulley before descending Ingrid's Folly. They are rated Grade 3 and Grade 2 respectively. They were full of snow. The walk into Coire Gabhail is easy enough, although I did wonder how Clan MacDonald managed to drive cattle into the valley – where, so the story goes, they hid them. Had they stolen them, or were they protecting them from rustlers? Who knows? The steep-sided valley is a glacial creation, and is actually quite spectacular. It is a long, narrow, flat-bottomed – a secret Shangri-La, enclosed on three sides by massive rock walls. It can be a sun trap and serenely wind-free. It is a special place, and I have been lucky enough to have walked through it often.

One winter weekend, having nearly been wiped out by an avalanche on our way up Bidean nan Beath on the Saturday, followed by too long in the Glachaig that night, we once more headed into the Lost Valley. We were intent on a winter route somewhere, although I cannot remember the where. It was a Baltic cold, cloudless Sunday. Coire Gabhail was a windless, sun soaked paradise that morning, so we sprawled about on some boulders to enjoy a few moments of warmth and woke up a couple of hours later. Oops. So we adapted to the conditions and the moment, had a lazy and memorable lunch, then bailed out to find another pit-stop on the way home. I think Glen Orchy Hotel was the lucky place. Today, however, we were on a mission. Getting up from the Coire floor to get into Peregrine Gulley was actually harder than the actual proper part of the winter climb, which was a blast – particularly going through the overhanging arch. Getting down Ingrid's Folly was a bit harder, even if it has a lower grade. It is narrow and steep, and we encountered two awkward chock stones. The first completely blocked our descent, meaning we had to rappel over to get below it. Finding a belay point was the problem. We broke the ice from the rocky sidewall of the gulley and luckily found a flake of rock, about three inches long and sitting at a jaunty 30% angle from the sidewall. 'Perfect', somebody said. I was less impressed, particularly at what was to follow. It was not possible to tie anything to the flake, so a clever alternative was called for. A knot was tied in a climbing sling and the sling was eased between the flake and the main wall, with the knot behind the flake. Testing its strength and suitability was carried by simply tugging on it a few times. Then the heaviest looking person in the party was chosen to nervously rappel over the chock-stone. Once I was safely in the gulley below the obstruction, I secured a safety rope and the others followed.

The second obstruction was a bigger rock in the gulley. It, however, had a handy hole going right through it. All but one of the party were able to drop through it. I was the 'all but one' factor. I am a bit chunky – residue of my rugby-playing days, I suppose – and although I got into said hole, I got stuck at hip level. Solution? Two of my colleagues climbed back up under the stone, grabbed a dangling leg each and heaved. Unceremoniously and without dignity, I scraped through and joined them on the last escape ramps of Ingrid's Folly. I have no idea who Ingrid was or is. A helpful comment I received whilst stuck by the hips went as follows: 'Don't worry; we will just leave you without food, and in a couple of days you will fall through.' So my year continued, and I kept my fitness at a reasonable level.

Then it was a hot day in late August 1988 and I am standing by the shore of Lac Leman, Geneva, gazing past its spectacular water foun-tain. Then, in the distance, there she was: a massive, gleaming white pyramid, shimmering in the sun and seemingly suspended above the earth. Thus did the 4,809 metres of snow and ice that is Mont Blanc fill my horizon and reignite my burning de-sire to stand on its summit.

Wedged

Why? Who knows, really. The challenge, perhaps, because it is the biggest at our end of accessible Europe? Maybe it was because I was driven to prove something to myself, perhaps to more than myself. Was it simply because it will be hard? Or, perhaps, I will take you back to Mallory: 'Because it's there'. My aspirations were born among scarcely-realised influences. They developed as I extended my boundaries and experiences. No different from anyone else in that regard. Perhaps understanding dilutes the desire. Mont Blanc is a big, dangerous mountain and a fair challenge, whatever one's motivation. It has a complicated topography and, because of that – coupled with its position in the Graian Alps and its height – it can and does attract its own weather. In the oneiric-steeped Alpine hamlets, all can be calm, while the summit peak can be gripped in a maelstrom of wind, spindrift and ice. Mont Blanc can be serene and beautiful, or it can be an awesome, deadly killer – whatever its mood, it demands respect.

Before that I had to get to Chamonix. The bus from Geneva was our preferred option. A couple of hours later we are in the square in Chamonix, necks bent back and staring up at the White Mountain trying to imagine how we will get up there. It looked daunting. I introduce Tom to the English Bar, then we hop on a train for the short journey up the valley to Argentiere. We are staying at Le Dahu; yes, again. I am a creature of habit. There we meet up with Alex, who will be joining us on the mountain. Later that evening we are joined at dinner by Ken, thus completing our quartet. After dinner, Roger Payne and Dr David Jones arrive. They will guide us up the mountain. The intention is to ascend by The Grand Mulets Route, the route taken by Jacques Balmat and Dr Michael Paccard when they made the first ascent, just over two hundred years before, on 8th August 1786. They explain it is the classic route; an excellent, but very long route, not so popular these days. Day one will take us over the Bossons Glacier to reach the Grands Mulets hut, where we will stay that night. Day two will be a long day, with 1,780 metres of height to be gained, at altitude, perhaps explaining why it is not such a popular route. That route also exposes the climber to serac falls between the Junction and the Petit Plateau, requiring one to press on and get through that danger spot as quickly as possible – and definitely before the sun gets high. Ice fall activity increases as the day warms up. So be through early. Once past the Petit Plateau and that danger, one ascends into Les Grandes Montees, the Grand Plateau, before pulling up steep ground to join the more popular route on the shoulder between the Col du Dome and the Vallot shelter. So that is the route explained to us; now we have to do it.

Before that, however, we have to acclimatise and be assessed by Roger and Dave. The next morning arrives – innocent of sun, overcast, but thankfully dry. I find myself back on the 'Petit Aguille Verte'. I am now becoming a regular and can tick it off twice. Just as steep and enjoyable as I remembered from the year before. Our second 'training' day dawned to a foreboding sky. The glowering cloud was now at street level and it had brought its trusty companion, rain. Dauntless, we headed out and I was soon back on the rack and pinion railway to Montenvers, followed by a repeat session of serious knee-breaking work on the Mer de Glas. Then it was a bee line to get out of the rain, onto the train and off the mountain.

Back in the English Bar, Roger faced us with a dilemma. It was simple, really. The weather forecast indicated we were about to get a short, three or four day break in the unsettled weather before it would close in on us again. While we were undoubtedly fit – it was not that he was worried about

– he was concerned as to how we would handle the altitude without the proper acclimatisation. He said we would suffer, and he could not guarantee we would all get to the summit. His alternative was to stay relatively low and have fun on other peaks, ridges and challenges. So what to do? All went quiet until I broke the silence by saying that I trusted Roger and his advice, 'but you know, Roger, it is what I came for and I am not sure if I would get another chance, so I vote we give it a go'. That was it; decision made, we agreed to give it a go and we did. What would you have done? Oh, there was one condition: Roger reserved the right to take us from the mountain if we were not handling the altitude and were endangering ourselves. After some lunch we spent the rest of the afternoon in front of tumble dryers. I headed to bed, excited and full of expectations. Sleep was fitful and a full-on electrical storm, complete with heavenly pyrotechnic display and rolling percussion, flashed and crashed up and down the steep-sided valley, hardly filling me with confidence.

In the morning I peek out to a clear, if windy morning. Mont Blanc's head is coyly hiding beneath a billowing raiment of white silk. Rucksack repacked for the umpteenth time, then down to Chamonix. We head for the Aguille du Midi cable car and encounter a long, winding tourist queue. Roger strides past the queue displaying his Alpine guide pass, assuring us that climbers heading onto the mountain take priority, which we were and did. After a short, speedy ascent, we alight at the half way station, Plan de l'Aigille. As we sort ourselves out, we watch the remaining passengers swing and sway, ever upward, to their summit for the day. My goodness; no going back now. We get sorted and then we were off.

We descend through a steep rocky section before heading gradually back over the intervening rising ground, still below the cable car route. Before I know it we are crossing our first small area of glacier. Quite a tame stretch of ice, giving no clue as to the shock we are about to experience as we leave it. A simple ascent across broken ground is followed by a scramble up through steep rock. We then gingerly pick our way along a narrow ledge under a towering buttress and, as we round a corner, our gaze is exposed to the first real obstacle of our journey: the Bossons Glacier. It looked huge; it looked frightening; it looked impossible... or should that be impassible? Probably both. We stare for a few minutes, trying to take it all in. Time to move. We don our crampons, cross a short, icy stretch before tentatively stepping out onto the glacier for real. We rope up into two teams of three and push on. The glacier at that point is a spectacular potpourri of twisted, shattered ice and towering ice stacks, interlaced by bluey-greenish gashes in the white ice. Every few minutes we hear the sound of some serac or other huge ice monument crashing onto the glacier or down a crevasse; not the most reassuring sound, however spectacular. Roped and crampon-footed, we carefully turn and twist over narrow ice bridges or knife-edged ridges, perched above or beside another pitch black, greenish flanked, seemingly bottomless crevasse, like some wide-mouthed creatures awaiting a stumble. We encounter a well-equipped party retreating from this precarious place, warning of a 'super dangereux' way ahead. Roger lets us know that when it gets this dangerous, the military come out and install aluminium ladders across the difficult areas. He thought that moment was a day or two away. We press on.

Our passage is interrupted momentarily and we watch helplessly, for what seems an eternity, as an avalanche – way above us, to our left – booms out a warning and careers head-long towards us, only to crash behind a distant fold and never reappear. We continue through this seemingly never-ending maze of crevasses, ice bridges and other steep-angled crossing points. I remember musing that if it is this difficult going up, what will it be like coming back down? I would find out. More about that later. The final barrier is breached, not without some difficulty, and another heart-stopping uphill leap across another chasm amongst a frenzied flurry of kicking crampons and flailing ice axes. My right hand falls foul of a misplaced crampon. Ouch.

Then we are through onto steep but easier snow. It is now possible to see our haven for that night, Refuge des Grand Mulets; a silver-coloured rectangular box, perched precariously on a rocky outcrop, high above us to our left. We cover the steep ground quickly, and are soon scrambling up through the rocks and into our refuge at 3,051 metres.

The time is 1.00 pm. Boots discarded, we settle in and take on board sustenance, in the form of bread, cheese and

Author negotiates narrow ice bridge on Bossons Glacier

175

Looking down on Grand Mulets refuge

chocolate, washed down by copious quantities of warm tea. An afternoon of lazing about on sun-drenched rocks follows. What a special, if precarious, place – smack-bang in the middle of a moving glacier, with no easy way in or out. I felt almost cut off from normal, well-balanced people. The afternoon was constantly interrupted by crashing ice falls. At 6.30pm we are summoned to partake of the communal meal, prepared by the Guardian of the Refuge. Choice is limited to 'take it' or 'don't eat'. There followed a hot, greasy stew of questionable origin. (Well, not so questionable really: does anybody remember 'Shergar'?) Whatever it was, it was delicious and welcome. The day concludes in spectacular fashion, with the sun set-tling down over the jagged silhouettes of a thousand peaks. Its dying embers wash the sky from a washed blue, to crimson, through countless hues to a golden finale. I crawl onto my allotted space on the 'open plan' communal shelf and curl-up into my individual hairy blanket. I fall asleep, tired and ex-pectant.

A cheery Nepalese assistant guardian arouses the sleeping dormitory early. I am not too sure, but I seem to remember it was about two o'clock in the morning. A cold breakfast of lukewarm tea, hard bread and jam follows. We fumble about with frozen fingers in the glow of head torches, sorting out our gear for the day. A quick descent through steep, ice-covered rocks, a brief stop to don crampons and get roped into our two teams, and then we head out onto the glacier and away. The inky black sky is encrusted with shimmering diamonds, a full moon beaming its silver smile on us. So bright that it's reflected light on the vast White Mountain, allowing us to conserve our head torch batteries.

We crunch our way over the ever-steepening glacier, avoiding dark gaping mouths where we can and crossing them when we must. As we close in on the Petit Plateau, with Roger and Dave hustling us on, our meandering ascent takes us into the high-risk area and I am aware, in the light the moon affords us, of being close to high, beetling ice-covered buttresses on our right. A fresh covering of snow requires trail-breaking and a steady rhythm. It is not long before the predicted altitude sickness overtakes the party and we go very quiet as we try to walk through it – quiet, that is, apart from the noisy retching and groaning. Then we are in the area of the Petit Plateau and through that danger area. Roger mercifully calls a halt. We rest a bit and take on sustenance. I have been headachy, nauseous and dizzy for the past hour. I was so rough that my innards did not know which end I needed to void. It is a horrible feeling. Roger assured us that eating and drinking was the only antidote, so I did. It was still a bit dark, that deep darkness that beckons the dawn. I look behind and down over the glacier to the distant twinkling lights of Chamonix, so far below. My thoughts turned to cosy beds and warm duvets. Then there was a shout from somewhere below our position. Roger immediately untied from the rope and told us to stay where we were before heading back down the steep section we had just climbed, out of our sight. I also untied and followed. I suspected Alex was in trouble. I have climbed with Alex for years and know him well; he is one tough cookie. But when I spoke to him briefly, further down, I knew he was suffering. When I got to them, Roger and Dave were discussing what to do. Decision was that Dave would return to the Grands Mulets with Alex and they would wait there for us on our return. I, trying to be helpful, suggested that I would descend to the Grand Mulets with Alex and Dave in the event that Alex got worse. Roger growled at me to keep out of it and get back up to where I had left Tom. I could feel the tension and slunk away, like a scolded child. I realised a couple of things at that moment; the situation was potentially serious, and that high on the precipitous slopes of Mont Blanc was not the place for an amateur like me to stick my nose in. Unfortunately Alex had become one of the statistics Roger had warned about whilst we discussed our acclimatisation issue back in Chamonix two days earlier.

Soon after, Roger and Ken joined us and we got sorted out on the rope. My malaise had receded by then, and with the dawn and the changing of the sky from inky blackness through shades of grey then tinged by a pink glow to blue, I was feeling ready for the next phase of my journey, through the Grand Plateau. It was steep and lung-bursting, but the sun was out; I was feeling fine. Eventually we emerged onto the shoulder to join the more popular route between the Col du Dome and the Vallot refuge at 4,807 metres. The summit was tantalisingly close; not much higher than Dumyat from where we were. Perhaps it's possible after all? It was now Tom who was really suffering. He lay down at the Vallot shelter and asked if he could just wait there until we got back from the summit. Roger was having none of it. We all go up or we all go down; he was leaving nobody on their own. Sort it out. So it was sorted, and Tom was put directly in front of me on the rope. It will become clearer why as we progress. Ken seemed totally unaffected by the altitude and quietly plodded on. The Vallot refuge is not staffed; it is simply a building near the top, on a rocky outcrop at the start of the Bosses Ridge. It can be used as a shelter if required. The rocky outcrop can be seen from Chamonix. I think the term 'refuge' is not the preferred name, and I have heard it called a shelter and a bivy hut. It has a dozen bed spaces and is officially understood to be an emergency option for climbers. One cannot reserve a space. It contains a small observatory, with radio capability. It was constructed in the late nineteenth century by Joseph Vallot, a meteorologist and botanist, and used by him to carry out experiments.

Author sits by Vallot Refuge, Tom and Roger standing

After a break we set out to ascend the Bosses, the ridge that would lead us to the summit. It had settled into a cold and clear windy day, certainly at our altitude, while far below the valleys had filled with white cotton wool. My spirits are high as I traverse the narrowing icy ridges leading to the summit. Then there it is: the summit of Mont Blanc, a few hundred feet up a narrow two foot wide strip of ice, with mind-blowing drops down either flank into Italy on one side and France the other.

We then get a stark reminder of how dangerous this place can be. Above our position, a duo of climbers gets into trouble. One seemed to stumble and lose his footing on the narrow ridge. He slides down steep ice on the Chamonix side, out of control and gathering speed. Disaster looms. We look on in helpless disbelief. His quick-witted umbilical partner affects an ice axe arrest in the classic manner, by throwing his full body weight into his axe; his now-hurtling companion is heading for some seriously steep ground and probable death. The thin lifeline snakes out to its full extent, goes taut, and the descending German is yanked to an unceremonious halt. His saviour continues to lie over the quickly constructed, life-saving belay and waits until his partner regains control. We look on, powerless to assist. As we gape, the saved gets to his feet, shrugs his shoulders and applauds his saviour. A reasonable response. We reach them and offer help. All appears in order, so we push on. Was that a reminder by the mountain to take it seriously?

The last few hundred feet at the apex of the ridge passes reasonably calmly, other than Tom collapsing to his knees on two occasions, retching and moaning that he cannot go on. I realise why I have been put on the rope directly behind my friend. Who else would have been able to – in the spirit of companionship built up over many hours of climbing peaks back home – gently but firmly kick his arse with crampon-clad foot and 'encourage' him to continue. Then we rise over the final ridge and onto the summit of Western Europe. A military jet rises from our left, up the French flank, in a vertical climb, spinning over our heads in a victory roll before plunging down the Italian side. Am I so important, I mused, or was it just a coincidence? Tom has little memory of being there; he was really quite ill. I stand on the summit amidst a mixture of emotions – elation probably uppermost – as, through tear-filled eyes I try to make out some of the other great mountains that are thrusting out of the Alps massif. The Matterhorn, Dent Blanch, Monta Rosa and more... wow! What a long way for a wee boy from Bonnybridge, with not a mountain to dream on.

Then it was time to get out of there before it changed its mind. This thought was supported by our guide, Roger Payne, who echoed the words of Iain Peter from a year before. The accursed mountain had briefly let down its guard and allowed me the privilege of standing on its summit; many have not been so lucky. It can be a lonely, frightening and unforgiving place, but maybe that's where the fun is. Descending the ridge back to the Vallot, whilst not technically difficult, still demanded care. It is simply one's imagination that gets in the way – well, my imagination. The falls on either side, particularly the Italian side on my left, are mind-blowing.

We are soon back beside the Vallot and heading down the route we had ascended earlier. Because the sun had been up for a few hours, the danger of ice falls as we got beyond the Petit Plateau had increased, so we pressed on through that section as quickly as we could. Other than that and Tom still feeling wretched, we got down to the Grands Mulets with no drama. Thankfully Alex had partially recovered and was in better spirits. After food and lots of tea, Tom had the colour back in his cheeks. We spent another pleasant evening in this isolated eyrie, topping up with liquid and calorie-inducing snacks, watching the sky go through its evening chameleon routine. What a wondrous place, and how lucky I am to be there.

Our wake-up call the next morning was at a more reasonable 7 a.m. Getting down through the Bossons Glacier the next morning was a nightmare of twisting and backtracking to find ways over numerous crevasses, some of which we jumped. Two in particular I will recall. The first thought-provoking barrier came in the form of a double crevasse that ran directly across our path. As we approached, it looked like a single wide crevasse and obviously a problem. However, as we got to the edge and looked down into it, we saw it was in fact split into two parallel crevasses – the nearest about four foot wide, and the further away about eight or nine feet wide. In the centre was a three feet wide 'ice bridge'. Unfortunately it was transverse and lay across our path, running parallel to the double crevasses. It was no bridge. We were on the high side, on steep, sloping ice. The distance from our position over both crevasses looked to be about fifteen feet. There was also a vertical drop of maybe seven or eight feet. Absolutely no chance of clearing that with one leap. (Where is Bob Beamon when you need him?) So what to do? From our spot to the dividing strip was about four feet, with a drop of about three feet. Trouble was, the dividing strip was no more than three feet wide, with the second crevasse gaping just beyond. Normally jumping over a four feet wide crevasse would not be a problem, as we could land and – if required – pitch or stumble forward to safety. Not today, however. Our landing area today was kind of limited. After staring down into the blackness for a few minutes, Roger came up with a simple enough solution. Launch ourselves over and onto the three foot wide platform, making sure we did not stumble, lose our footing or pitch forward. Roger set up a belay. He then simply backed up our side a bit, quickened his pace down to the edge and leapt across the gaping jaws of the first bottomless abyss, landing on the narrow middle section with nary a stumble. Once over that hurdle, he moved to the side and set up a second belay. Then it was our turn and – one by one, like nervous lemmings – we jumped. All was fine, apart from me causing damage to my back due to wearing metal crampons and landing a bit stiff-legged onto solid ice; it really hurt and took my breath away for a while. No matter, we were safe... well, relatively safe. Once gathered on our transverse sliver of ice between the gaping crevasses, we wend our way to one side and eventually find a more conventional ice bridge to get us over. And so it went on.

The second crossing, worthy of citation, involved another crevasse – only a singleton this time, but too wide to jump over. There was a very narrow ice bridge we could use to walk over to the other side. Trouble was, the ice bridge was no more than a foot wide and about eight feet below our position on the high side. Roger again showed us how. The technique was simple – requiring accuracy, confidence and a bit of daring. One sat on the steep, sloping high side and slid down – hopefully in control – into the waiting jaws of the crevasse and, with careful aim, planted your leading foot onto the narrow 'life saving' sliver of ice bridge before pitching forward and hammering your ice axe into the ice on the safe side. Not a place for faint hearts or a bad aim. Not sure what would have been the worse fate: missing the bridge completely, or landing astride it. Ouch! We got over this obstacle and continued on that vein, twisting, turning and backtracking until we got over the Bossons, then back over to the Plan de l'Aigille for our cable car return to Chamonix. Then it was on to the English Bar and tall tales.

* * *

Postscript: Roger Payne, who so professionally guided our party to the summit of Mont Blanc, died on this mountain in July of 2012. He was caught in an avalanche on the slopes of Mont Maudit in the Mont Blanc massif, not far from the summit.

I first met Roger Payne in 1987 in Le Dahu hotel in the village of Argentiere, a small alpine village between Chamonix and the Swiss border. I was with a group of climbers, and it was the eve of our departure on what was to be a memorable high-altitude crossing of the Alps. Roger dined and took refreshment with us. He turned our simple meal into a Raclette eating competition. He was there to assist our guide, Iain Peter, and transport our spare gear round to Zermatt, where we would be reunited with both Roger and our clothing in ten days or so, after our high level crossing. They were both Alpine guides and obviously very good friends. We spent two days together in Zermatt.

I next met Roger in the late August of 1988, again in Argentiere and again in Le Dahu. We dined again, but did not eat all the cheese on this occasion. On that trip Roger was to guide our small group up Mont Blanc. We spent just over a week together on that occasion. My memory of Roger, apart from a strikingly handsome young man, was of a person of humility, humour with an obvious love of life. He was a complete professional and a mountain person to the core, although the 'mini gamp' slung across his rucksack made him look like an interestingly-clad city gent heading for the underground. Roger led us up the mountain by the central route over the Bossons Glacier, in the steps of Balmat and Paccard; the first to ascend the mountain some two centuries before. I was a plodding amateur, a client of Roger's, not a real mountaineer – I would never call myself that. Client, mountaineer, plodding amateur... it did not matter to Roger one little bit. He had such an enthusiasm for life and an understanding of people that his whole being simply radiated friendship and encouragement and, whilst hardly knowing him, he gave me so much confidence – and, in no small way, changed my life. He made me feel I could be a mountaineer. He made me feel I was perhaps not as worthless as I often felt.

Roger Payne was inspirational, indestructible; his love of mountains, and of life, brimmed over. He was the real deal. He gave so much in a world where many cannot give for taking. I will never forget you, Roger; you will never understand what you did for me. The sadness I felt in July of 2012 has not diminished.

Chapter 10

IN the midst of all my Munro bashing and Alpine excursions, I found time to get to get furth of Scotland to Wales, England and Ireland – yes, to climb their highest peaks and some more. I really enjoyed these days and wonderful places. However, I will restrict my narrative about these visits to a few short tales and a discovery about sheep.

One horrid wet and claggy morning, Tom and I ascended Skiddaw and – on reaching the summit – were mobbed by sheep, looking for a titbit from our provisions. That is when I discovered that Lake District sheep have a liking for chocolate. We climbed Helvellyn and Skiddaw on the same day. Scaffell Pike, a few days later. I found them to be very enjoyable excursions, as were some other hills I managed to ascend in England. The Lake District is a special place; not quite the wilderness of large tracts of Scotland, just a different place and no less enjoyable. Snowdon was also enjoyable. We picked the Watkin Path approach, for no other reason than the hostel we were bunking in was near the start of that route. The development to a walker's route was created from the original old quarry path to the summit by Sir Edward Watkin. It is the first 'official' footpath in Great Britain, and was opened in 1892 by the then-Prime Minister, William

Gladstone. Hence the feature Gladstone Rock, complete with suitable plaque commemorating the opening of the route. According to one narrative, it has the distinction of being the hardest of the six classic routes to the summit of Snowdon. Having done only this one, I am not in a position to judge.

We start just off the A498 road, between Llyn Gwynant and Llyn Dinas, and follow a well-marked track as far as Gladstone Rock. The wide track is left after a while and the going gets steeper and rockier, though not too taxing. It eventually does get even steeper, with a lot of broken rocks and scree, requiring some care. But it is still not too exposed through that section – until, that is, one gets to Bylch y Saethau, when it does transform into a ridge and requires care. The views and drops to your right are spectacular, with the ridges of Crib Goch and Garnedd Ugain, the Pyg Track and Miners Track, as well as the lakes of Llyn Llydaw and Glaslyn all featuring. It is a nice corner of Wales and, as far as I could tell, not as well-trodden as the others. On our way back up to Scotland the next day, Alex and I stop at Plas y' Brenin National Mountain Centre and pop in to see Iain Peter, who was the Principal at that time. Then it was back home.

My trip to climb Carrauntoohil – at 3,404 feet, the highest peak in Ireland – was straightforward enough, and hardly rates a mention. Don't get me wrong; Kerry is a beautiful corner of Ireland, and MacGillycuddy's Reeks are stunning mountains. Tom (of Mont Blanc fame) and I took the straightforward route onto Carrauntoohil via Hag's Glen, passing between Lough Gouragh and Loch Calee, before ascending the Devil's Ladder. Then into the mist and rain up the last shoulder to the top. We reverse the route on our descent. Nothing much of any controversy there. Our start, however, might raise a chuckle. We parked up at farm yard called Cronin's Yard. When checking out the map earlier I had noted there was a Hostel on the road up to Cronin's Yard. I also noted that it would cost one punt to park at the farm. I am not sure where my confusion came from. While Tom was putting his boots on, I strode over to the 'Hostel' to pay for parking. I knocked on the door, opened it and confidently walked in, punt in hand, looking for the reception desk. In front of me was an older gentleman, complete with waistcoat and a bunnet pushed to the back of his head, tucking into what I took to be his breakfast. He looked up, but stayed silent. A lady's voice to my left and slightly behind me said, in a lovely Irish lilt, 'Can I help you?' I looked over my left shoulder and there she was, complete with apron and hands in a sink of dishes. Being quick on the uptake, a thought flashed through my mind; it had no difficulty, because at that moment there was nothing else in there to prevent it. 'Oops – this is not the hostel.' I quickly retrieved the situation by apologising profusely for bursting into the kitchen of their home unannounced. I meekly proffered my punt, in the hope the gesture would reduce the tension.

The older lady, drying her hands on her apron, smiled and said, 'You are not from around here?'

'No,' I replied, 'I live in Scotland. I am so sorry,' I repeated.

She then told me her daughter had studied at the University of Dundee. Her next remark evidences all I need to say about decent folks, wherever they are from. She asked if I had eaten and would I like some breakfast. I explained that I was not alone. So that is how Tom and I got breakfast and tea at Cronin's Yard and parking, all for the princely sum of one punt.

Another experience I think might be worth exploring with you turned out to be very eventful – for me, anyway. I was persuaded by Alex Macmillan to accompany him on the 1985 cross-Scotland backpacking event, The Ultimate Challenge. The rules were really simple; walk unaided across Scotland, west to east, in fourteen days or less. In the early days there were six signing-on points in the west. (Well, I think it was six.) No matter which of the starting points on the west one chose, all routes terminated at the final east coast checkpoint, The Park Hotel in Montrose. It was not a race. The concept was the brain child of Hamish Brown in the 1970s and, on selling the whole idea to Roger Smith, the then-editor of *The Great Outdoors* magazine, the challenge became a reality. It was initially sponsored by Ultimate Equipment Limited, and the first was held in 1980. It was, for obvious reasons, called the Ultimate Challenge. Ultimate eventually withdrew their sponsorship and, in 1992, it morphed in name to The Great Outdoors Challenge – or as it became better known, the TGO Challenge. By the time you read this, it will be near (or perhaps even will have celebrated) its fortieth birthday. It is a remarkable event in many ways, not least the camaraderie amongst the participants. My view is that the Challenge is one of the best-organised events of this nature. It is almost a living thing, with a heart. Not only is it non-competitive and friendly, but participants go out of their way to support others, advise on routes, places to avoid, good camping spots and good eating spots – whatever. They do not, in my experience, hide things from fellow challengers. Alex had done it before and assured me that, with my hill experience, 'you will find it a doddle'. I can still hear him saying that. Remember that phrase, because I will never forget it.

We travel up to our starting point at Dornie, on the Thursday 9th May 1985. After a nice train journey up from Stirling to Inverness, we enjoyed the delights of the Inverness to Kyle of Lochalsh onward leg. A breathtaking railway journey. At Kyle we used our influence as serving police officers and blagged a run in a police car to Dornie, where we had bed and breakfast booked. By the way, the officer was going our way on an enquiry, so he said. Then it was D-Day: Friday May 10th 1985. As we left our bed and breakfast, it was dull and overcast. We headed down to the water for the non-negotiable photograph of a foot in the sea, with the added bonus of Eilean Donan Castle in the background.

We retraced our steps to sign in at the Loch Duich Hotel. Then we were off in what proved to be, certainly for me, an eventful and painful crossing of eleven days; a passage involving being assaulted by a snipe, breaking into a youth hostel, stabbing myself in the foot, getting a penicillin injection, having hallucinations and nearly being physically removed from the hill. Remember the fateful words of my companion: 'You will find it a doddle'. Oh, and I got dehydrated on the Five Sisters Ridge. Apart from all that, it was a doddle.

It started well enough and our route up the old road from Dornie, by way of the viewpoint at the top, was a pleasure. It was overcast, but the cloud level was about four thousand feet so it was like a grey ceiling with plenty of visibility beneath it. Views west along Loch Alsh, south down Loch Duich then west and south-west over to the wee hamlet of Letterfearn, followed by the Glen Elg peninsula and beyond to the tops of the Knoydart Munros, were all a joy to behold. It did not take long for the first problem: getting accustomed to the forty-odd pounds of backpack containing, food, clothing, extra socks, tent, cooker, gas canister, sleeping bag, bedroll and whatever else I had put in – just in case. This was in the days before minimalistic backpacking. Or perhaps I was not that switched on. The first pain emerged as an ache across my shoulders. Adjusting the straps did not offer much respite. Mind you, I was a bit inexperienced, having never worn a brassiere before.

We pressed on for a few miles and, once through Inverinate and over the causeway at the head of Loch Duich, it was time to fuel up. Soup and sandwiches at the wee café-cum-restaurant, just under the north end of the Five Sisters ridge, did the trick. Then we headed up the 'wall' that we had spied earlier. It looked steep from a distance, but that often is an illusion that reduces as one nears the object. Mind you, with enormous rucksacks it was a bit of a toil. The 'wall', as earlier described – the west end of the five sister ridge – is split by the Allt a' Chruinn, and whilst the left bank, as we looked up, was steep-sided, there was a footpath of sorts up through the craggy section. The sides eased back a bit after that, making

Resting in Coire na Criche, looking down Loch Duich

walking less perilous. However, the direct ascent into and through Coire na Criche was a steep grind. We had a much-needed pit stop at the head of the coire, with lovely views back up Loch Duich.

After that we went directly over Beinn Bhuide, Sgurr nan Saighead and Sgurr Fhuaran – the first Munro from that approach – and pitched the tent at about 3,000 feet, just before the second Munro, Sgurr nan Carnach. A perfect spot. Some food and drink, then tucked into sleeping bags. We were done in, and soon were snoozing. An early rise to a crystal clear sky and a fresh morning, evidenced by ice on the outside of the tent. We breakfasted to stupendous views of a myriad of difficult-to-identify mountains to the west and out to the Hebridean Islands. The plan then was to complete the Five Sisters ridge and go over the Three Brothers at the east end before dropping down to The Clunie Inn, where we would camp and eat. It did not work out exactly like that. Breakfast over, tent packed and on our way, we were feeling good as we hurdled the tops of the ridge. We had not long gone over the last Munro, Sgurr nan Spainteach – named after the 1719 battle that took place on its flank, when a Jacobite force of the Old Pretender, James Stuart, supported by a contingent of Spanish Marines, fought and lost to the Government forces of George 1 – when things went a bit awry. As we approached Saileg, the first of Three Brothers, I started to feel really ill and weak. We had been waterless for a couple of hours and the sun was up. While Alex was doing fine, I was obviously suffering the effects. We negotiated the first two siblings, Saileg and Sgurr a'Beilach Dheirg, but my goose was cooked by then and I really was dehydrated. The only option was to bail out to lower ground and find water. Just after that latter-mentioned peak, there is a natural and easy escape from the ridge on the south side down into Coire Tholl Bhruacha, oc-cupied by the stream that bears the same name. Water, fresh and flowing. I threw myself onto the grass while Alex opened out the camping stove and that miracle healer, hot sweet tea and more hot sweet tea. Recovery is quick, and we are soon on our way and descending to the A87 road and the Cluanie Inn. Decision time: sample the delicacies of the Inn or pitch the tent, in what order? What would you do? You are far too sensible to be reading this book. We chose the former, and did not regret it. Bearded George, the manager in these far-off days, was good craic and a fine night was enjoyed.

We pitched the tent a few hundred yards behind the Inn, just past the bridge over the west outlet from Loch Clu-anie. As we were getting sorted by torchlight, we became aware of a snipe milling about not too far away. The high-pitched *chip-chip* kind of call suggested to us there were young in the vicinity. As if we were snipe experts. I could not see them. One reference describes their call when excited as a sharp *jick*. I am not sure about that. Anyway, into sleeping bags and two tired travellers headed for dreamland, leaving the probable snipe to settle into whatever a snipe does after dark. Our journey to that wonderful place, dreamland, was rudely interrupted as the high pitched *chip-chip* suddenly in-creased in volume. It also sounded as though it was careering in our direction. It certainly was, and an instant later the mys-terious and fast-closing noise turned into an object that hit the side of tent at velocity and smacked me square in the left ear. The *chip-chip* immediately changed to a crescendo of high pitched squealing, which reduced in amplification as the of-fender fled the scene. It then settled down to a regular *chip-chip*. Poor wee thing got an awful start. I can only assume the wee bird got a fright as well. Then, just as I was settling back onto the train to dreamland, I shared a thought with Alex: 'You know, I've never been sniped before. How about you?' He answered with a snuffly kind of snore. But it was not to be the last – not the snoring; the sniping, I mean.

I break off at this point to tell you about being sniped a second time, some two years later. A winter day in Glen Lyon in December 1987, although this time the offender was not a snipe, but a sniper – well, a deer stalker to be fair. Dave and I were ascending a ridge when a deep whirring noise 'ripped' over our heads, really close, immediately followed by the 'crack' from a high-powered rifle being discharged in our direction from a parallel ridge. A high velocity rifle being fired sounds very different if you are at the business end, as opposed to the safe end. While the discharge is a loud crack, quite distinctive, the actual bullet passing sounds like ripping cloth, although I thought it sounded like a quick flying baritone bee. Decision time; go over and remonstrate with a flailing ice axe, or not? We decided on the latter and continued our day, spending a few hours navigating through snow and clag, going over Craeg Mhor and Carn Mairg before leaving the hills down steep ground and coming out of the cloud near Carnbane Castle. The castle is thought to have been built about 1564 by someone called Red Duncan Campbell. His wife, it is suggested, named the castle after catching sight of her naked husband walking near it. Rumour has it that he had given his clothes to a poor, raggedly-clothed beggar. She said he looked like a white goose. Mind you, *carn ban* in Gaelic translates easier to 'white cairn' or a pile of white stones. So perhaps the goose reference is in error, in terms of the translation. But, then again, maybe he just looked like a white goose, or perhaps he was exposing more of his white flesh than would be decent to relate? Hostile clans, representing Lochaber it seems, burned the castle down some years later using fire arrows. Back to 1987 and Glen Lyon was still not a hospitable place to visit, though at least there had been a progression from fire arrows. As we descended we saw a Volvo Estate car going slowly up and down the road, as if looking for something. How right we were; the occupants were looking for us. No sooner were we on the road than said vehicle pulled up beside us. A tall, lanky male got out and rounded on us, demanding to know if we had been on the hill earlier. I asked if he was part of the only stalking party on the hill that day. He agreed that he was. I apologised if we had got near his stalk, and explained I had telephoned earlier in the week and had been told the other two hills in the group were being stalked, hence our decision to be in the area we were in. He was very angry and said we should not have been on any of his hills during stalking season. I retorted that, even if – because of a misunderstanding – we had interfered with stalking, which was something we would never do on purpose, then I apologise. Nevertheless, we have done nothing illegal. On the other hand, no matter the circumstances, you should not have discharged a loaded firearm at us, even if the intention was to miss and scare us off 'your' hill. I said I would report him to the police. At that point the driver of the car, who I assumed was the person who fired the shot, shouted at him to get back in the car. He did, and they sped off. To my eternal regret – perhaps because I felt a bit guilty myself about getting in the way of a perfectly legal activity – I did not report him. David and I knew exactly who he was; a well-known character in the Glen. I understand his family are still resident. So there it is; you never know what the Scottish hills have in store for you. Sniped, twice in two years.

Back to dreamland in our tent near Loch Clunie. No big decision in the morning. Tent packed before a leisurely breakfast at the Inn, then off on day three. A point of interest. I did two of these crossings and, in both, I found days two and three the worst. Legs dragging like lead weights, and bag weighing more than day one. However, all that eased as the days passed and fitness increased. I will not regale you with every step of our journey, nor with the detail of every day. I thought the first two days would set the scene and give the reader some idea of what the crossing was all about.

The Clunie Inn is on the track of an old military road that runs roughly parallel and to the north of the main A87 road. We walked the track of that old military road all the way to Fort Augustus, camping on the heights just before the town. Day four started with a leisurely breakfast in the town, after which we headed for the Corrieyairack Pass – Mam Choire Ghearraig in Gaelic. It is about twenty five miles from Loch Ness over to Laggan in the upper reaches of the Spey Valley. At its highest it is about 2,500 feet altitude. It was designed by General Wade as a military road, part of a network created across Scotland to allow the military easy access to us unruly Scots. Their aim: subjugation. There was an old military-style Jeep lying abandoned beside the track. I am no archaeologist, but even I didn't think it had been discarded by General Wade. Mind you, I believed Richard Dimbleby when, on a *Panorama* programme in 1957, he said spaghetti grew on trees. I did not think money grew on trees, but was not sure about spaghetti. What do I know?

We pitched the tent at Melgarve, a few miles from Laggan. Day five was road walking, and I was footsore. We stopped at Kingussie and enjoyed a tent-free night in the luxury of the Youth Hostel, although we nearly did not. Having signed in, snagged our bed space, stowed our bags and showered, we headed for the bright lights of the bustling metropolis that is Kingussie. An establishment called the Wooden Spoon had the pleasure of our company that evening. My feet – the metatarsal area, just behind the toes, under the pads – were really sore. Taking the weight off and sitting about provided temporary relief from the pain and convinced me I should continue.

The restaurant had a liquor licence; perfect. We were joined by two fellow Challengers, both medical men – General Practitioners from Easter Ross; Alness, if I remember correctly. We had a fine evening: good food, a wee libation and good chat, and some laughs. We came to our senses when the proprietrix (or should that be proprietress) said she was putting us out, as the Wooden Spoon was closing for the evening. (By the way, if it is not proprietrix, that is shame; sounds like a

Corrieyairack Chariot

good word, and far more exotic than proprietress.) All good so far, until I looked at the time. Argh! It is after midnight, and not a pumpkin in sight. The Youth Hostel closes and locks up at eleven. A short time later, four grown adults – two serving police officers and two serving General Practitioners – found themselves standing in the dark outside a slumbering Youth Hostel, with the prospect of a very uncomfortable night separated from sleeping bags. Not a light on, and locked up. 'What next?' was the question. Choices again. This trip has too many decision-making moments for my comfort. Knock loudly on the front door, or something else? We are not happy about awakening the sleeping giant.

So, almost as on a secret signal, the traffic officer and the two medical practitioners kind of found themselves behind me, and the consensus seemed to say *Ian, you must have more experience of breaking into houses than we have*. And as though pre-ordained, I found myself in the lead role as the dastardly house breaker. With my charges following, I head round the back of the building. Kingussie Youth Hostel was an old building, and finding a way in was relatively easy. I take out my trusty penknife – the same one that will feature later on this trip in a different guise – and move up to the kitchen window. It is an old wooden sash-and-case job. The rest is easy, and soon I push up the bottom section of the window wide enough for us to climb in. Quiet, muted giggling followed, and there was talk of prison. We move like experienced miscreants and get into our respective bunks without disturbing a sleeping soul. Sad to say, the Youth Hostel at Kingussie closed its doors in 1995 – not just at eleven o'clock, post meridian, but for good.

Day six is longish and pretty uneventful. We visit the shop in Kingussie, top up our supplies, and head out past

Ruthven Barracks and Tromie Bridge following forest tracks and paths till we reach Glen Feshie. Incidentally, exactly the same route cycled by the Auld Gits, many years later. My feet are again pretty sore, so I break a branch from a tree and fashion it into a walking stick, mainly by wrapping lots of surgical tape round one end to make a skelf free handle. We get rain that day; the first since day one. A refreshment break at Ruigh-aiteachain bothy finds it full to the gunwales with Challengers, many of them having completed the crossing more than once. Some were gaining reputations as stalwarts, and many had met before. The atmosphere was friendly and buzzing. I remember Chris Mumford, who went by the bye-name of Strider; a real character. There was a little lady called Janet. She might have been small in stature, but not in spirit. I think this might have been her first Challenge. She was in her late sixties and doing it solo. She seemed to be travelling awfully light, at least compared to the load I was carrying. It turned out she had carefully picked a route that passed near several guest houses and farms. Her planning was exceptional, even to the point of placing essential provisions in these guest houses the week before the actual event. Hence the light day sack; a resourceful lady. It was also said Janet could get a 'piece' at anybody's door. That is a quaint Scottish saying which meant that she would never go hungry, as her charm would ensure she got fed. Janet did several solo Challenges after that. She sadly met her final Challenge a few years ago at 89 years of age. She just meandered on at her own pace; nothing seemed to trouble her. A lovely lady, and inspirational. The rainbow girls were about then also. Their claim to fame – well, one of them – was that they all wore identical rainbow-coloured striped jerseys, knitted by their own fair hands. The Challenge is like that; so many real characters and decent people. Many lifelong friendships emerged during the event, and probably still do. Long may it continue. I was a mere fledgling.

We could not stay here all day (much though we would have liked to – it was shaping up for a good night). We set off east into the rain along Glen Feshie for a few miles to meet the Eidart River, just where it flows south out of the Cairngorms. At that point the Eidart is crossed by a metal-framed bridge built some years before by Royal Engineers. It is about nineteen miles out from Kingussie at that point, so we set up camp. My real problems have probably already started by then; however, they do not make themselves known to me until the early hours of the morning. I am awakened by a severe pain in my right foot; my heel, to be precise. No matter how I move, turn, or rub it, the pain is not for shifting. It is throbbing and unrelenting. I am in serious trouble, and I know it. Day seven dawns and I am in agony; my heel has swelled up to such a size, I cannot force it into my boot.

First things first. Get breakfast out the way, then work out what to do. I will explain something at this juncture; a successful crossing is rewarded by a certificate and a badge. However, if one includes a dozen separate Munros in the crossing, the certificate has 'High Level' written on it; otherwise it is a low level crossing. The former is particularly prized. We were both on track for the high level, until my malaise. I was out of the high level challenge, and the chance of being in any challenge was slipping away fast. After breakfast and after stowing our gear, we were ready for the off. Except I wasn't. Decision time – yes, more damn decisions. Alex still had a chance of the high level, and to stay in contention had to go over Carn an Fhidhleir and An Sgarsoc – two big mountains a bit to the south of our position. I agree he needs to get over them and off he toddles, telling me to do the best I can and he will catch up later in the day. Then he is gone and I am sitting alone, in a really remote part of Scotland, nineteen miles from Kingussie and eighteen miles from Braemar. What to do? I am quite pragmatic about these things, and quite logical. There is only one choice: reduce the swelling so I can get my boot on, or cut my boot open. I reject option two. So how do I tackle option one? The trusty pen knife that affected our entry to the Youth Hostel is my surgical tool of choice. I hirple over to the Eidart and sit down by the water. I then, carefully and with the precision of an experienced surgeon, wield the pen knife with a certain amount of aplomb and dexterity, and saw my foot open. I am careful not to cut under my foot on the pad of my heel; I will have to walk on it later, so a stab wound on the pad will be a bit of a bummer. I carefully saw and stab at the fleshy part immediately below the heel bone and above the pad, at the back of my foot. Awkward to reach. I struggle to get purchase. Some of that because of the awkward angle, but most of it because I am a bit apprehensive at operating on myself. I am getting nowhere. So I pluck up courage and really go for it. If I said I was inflicting pain, I would be absolutely correct. Eventually I am in, and blood is flowing. I keep going until I see the first sign of yellow pus; no going back now. So, after some time sawing and squeezing until I see no more pus, I think – not without some relief – that will do. I am not sure I could have put up with much more pain. I then give my foot a wash in the river, dry it, apply some plasters to the gash and get my sock on. Now for stage two: get my boot on. Miracle of miracles, I get my injured foot stuffed into it and I am good to go. That whole procedure took a while; the best part of half an hour, maybe longer. I load up, take two pain killers and set off on the long miles to Braemar. I am in real pain – a different pain, more of a sharp pain – but I am walking. I had to try and ignore the pain; get into a zone, sing, tell myself stories, anything but concentrate on pain. I did that for mile after mile; just kept walking, reluctant to stop, sucking on sweets and the occasional pain-killing tablet. Every time I stopped to ease the pain of walking, I had another look at my map. Wishful thinking on my part, willing Braemar to get closer. I really was not enjoying this.

Then I had my second miracle of the day. I could hear music. Have I taken too many painkillers? I am approaching a ruined building, just a mile or two short of where the River Dee appears at White Bridge. The music is coming from there. For some reason I cannot recall, I think the ruin is called the Red House or similar. It is just before the spot where the Auld Gits, from another adventure I relate in this book, turn south on their bikes for Glen Tilt and Blair Atholl. I have no bike today. I find two real characters have taken up temporary residence in the ruin. They are fellow travellers; however, their application for the west to east Challenge crossing had been rejected, so they were protesting by going east to west at the same time as the actual Challenge. They called it the 'opposite protest' Challenge. I wish I could remember their names. They were both London taxi drivers and had completed the challenge the year before. I have never seen backpackers with so much gear. They had a radio, hence the music and pots and pans, and were busy boiling potatoes and preparing some kind of stew. They had stuff spread all over the place. I was mesmerised; how did they carry all that stuff? Not a taxi in sight. Food was nearly ready, and they asked if I wanted to join them. Join them I did. I spent more than an hour in the ruin. What great craic they were.

We left together and they walked along to White Bridge with me, before heading off on their 'opposite protest' challenge. More pills, and on the road again. White Bridge to Linn of Dee, where I would be back on tarmac and actual roads, seemed an awful long way and I was toiling. Shortly after reaching the tarmac, a couple of day trippers in a car – on seeing my hirpled gait – offered me a lift. When I explained why I could not take up their kind offer and mentioned the charity I was collecting for, they gave me five pounds. Then I was on my own again. Alex caught up with me at the thirty miles an hour signs on the outskirts of Braemar. He was surprised I had made it so far. I was in too much of a dream state to notice. All I had to do now was find medical assistance. That was in the form of the wonderful District Nurse. When I found her she was in the middle of a game of bowls, on the artificial grass outdoor rink. I waited until it looked like she had won her game before approaching her. Omens were good, then she examined my feet. 'My goodness! You really need to see the doctor,' she said. That is why day eight started and nearly finished with me heading the queue at the Doctor's surgery. The nurse ushered me in and there was the Braemar General Practitioner, resplendent in tweed jacket, plus two trousers, to the knee, green socks and heavy duty brogue shoes. Now, if I were to meet characters on this Challenge, which I did, this was the one who topped the bill. He examined my foot – well, both feet as it turned out – and informed me, amid much tutting, that my right foot was in a bad way. I am not sure my 'self-help' surgery impressed him. This will need penicillin, he informed me – and with that he headed out of sight into a large walk-in cupboard. For the next few minutes all I could hear were the sound of boxes and perhaps furniture being moved, much grunting and the sound of glass rattling against glass until he appeared, triumphant, with two glass medicine phials clutched in one hand and an old 'large' glass syringe in the other, along with the response, 'found the blighters!' He had indeed. Having affixed a large needle to the syringe, he inserted it into the rubber seal on top of the glass phial, drew out the required amount of liquid – checking the levels carefully – then inserted it into my arm. If I said I felt no pain, I would be lying. Next he cleaned both my heels, applied some kind of cream, then bandaged both; my left foot seemingly had an open blister that he was not happy about. He gave me some painkillers and advised: 'Your journey is over, young man. You need to keep off your feet for a few days.' I thanked him and the Nurse, then headed up to the Youth Hostel to give Alex the bad news.

We packed, and I decided to accompany Alex a couple of miles south on the Perth road to Auchallater Farm, where I could wait for the Perth bus. It is also the spot where Jock's Road starts. Our chosen Challenge route: down Glen Callater, past the loch to the end of the glen before the steepish ascent onto the east Cairngorm plateau at a Knaps of Fafernie. The road is a former cattle drovers' route, and gained the name Jock's Road after a local shepherd, Jock Winter – who, in 1888, after the landowner tried to stop access, took him all the

Bandaged

way to the House of Lords in protest and won the action. So as a result, access continued.

My story, however, did not stop at Auchallater Farm and against medical advice – and because, compared to the previous day, I felt 'good to go' – I went. We pitched tent between Knaps of Fafernie and Fafernie after a short walking day of about fourteen miles. I needed to stop anyway. After some supper I was soon fast asleep. Day nine started at five in the morning with a navigation lesson for Alex. The cloud was thick, and Alex was leaving me in the tent to head out and go over four more Munros before coming back for me. He had a wee problem. With the thick clag and visibility severely restricted, he was a bit unsure of navigating the route alone. What followed next could have come out of an episode of *Blackadder Does Navigation*, if there had ever been such an episode. I ripped a page from a notebook and wrote down an easy-to-follow, bullet-point guide to navigation, supported by a short lecture. I take the bearing to his first Munro, write it down, remind him the basic rules and wish him well. He headed out into the unknown with compass in one hand and scrap of paper and map in the other. No sooner had the tent flap closed than I was curled up and back in dreamland. I was wrestled out of my dream state by the sound of my name being called. He had been out for about five hours. Not that I knew; I had slept the whole time. It was now after 11 am, and it was Alex looking for a clue to find the tent. He had navigated round his mountains – Tom Buidhe, Cairn of Claise, Carn an Tuirc and Tolmount, not necessarily in that order – and now he could not find the tiny green tent in the vast plateau of greens and browns. He soon homed in on my sleepy voice.

We sorted something to eat and, after Alex rested for a while, we were ready for the off – the second stage of day nine. The cloud had opened up a little, and visibility was not such a trial. We trudged over Fafernie, Cairn Bannoch – Alex's fifth Munro of the day – then another two tops before going over Broad Cairn, Alex's sixth of the day and his twelfth Munro of the crossing, thus completing his high level challenge. I had done six. We were then on good stalking paths and heading for Spittal of Glen Muick and right into the Monarch's deer stalking country. Having been here a couple of times before, we knew there was a cluster of wooden buildings beside the path, not far east of Broad Cairn. They were used to stable the stalkers' Gearran ponies, so the plan was for Alex to 'horse' on and get a brew sorted. I was still limping and not going too well. The clag had closed in again and it was wet. I was happily bumbling along in a dream when overtaken by two born leaders. I thought they may be military by their identical gear and their cultured addresses to me. They asked if I was alright – which I obviously was not – and also enquired as to my destination. My reply, 'Montrose', seemed to throw them. 'I don't think you will be going to Montrose', said one. 'You just stay here and we will get help'. My response seemed to dissuade them of that notion and reluctantly they headed of on their own journey, leaving me to mine. I never saw them again, but Alex did. On my arrival at the stables Alex asked me if two guys had spoken to me. I nodded. It seems they had given Alex a piece of their mind for leaving a person – that would be me – in such a state on the hill. It was then we discovered our bad planning in Braemar. My visit to the Doctor had removed any thought we might have had to stock up with sustenance. We were low on food, but had plenty of tea. We shared a small tin of mandarin oranges and drunk a lot of sweet tea before heading out. It seemed a long walk from there to Spittal of Glenmuick in the gloom and the rain. There is a minor road from Ballater to the Spittal, so I suppose that gave me a second opportunity to bail out – which I rejected.

We drank some water and had a few minutes' break before we headed onto the hill again looking for our digs for that night: the bothy called Shielin of Mark. The first part involved followed a burn for about a mile and a half, up a well-defined gulley, easy so far. Then it opened to a trackless peat hag, not so easy. Careful navigation required. Visibility was now really reduced in the rain and the gloaming. There was an obvious junction of two burns, showing on the map as a 'Y'. Because there were no obvious land marks or objects to take bearings from, I was reduced to real map-reading. I took a direct bearing from the 'Y' junction on the map to the shielin. I had then to walk on a perfectly straight line till I found it. That meant spotting anything on the line I could use – mostly tufts of heather or indentations or boulders on the side of a peat bank; in fact, any object that was on the bearing line. None were far out from me, ten to twenty metres at most. I could not afford to lose sight of whichever one I picked. I spent the next mile gazing at such trivial signs, deep in concentration and walking in a straight line, up numerous steep peat banks and down others. Through wet pools, ankle-deep peat, and on and on. I was starting to lose the will to live and thinking I had got things terribly wrong when, out of the gloom, there appeared a chimney. The shielin was over a rise in the ground in a dip. I could only see the chimney. Found it. Alex, meanwhile, wandered about somewhere out to my right, zigzagging about trying to keep on good ground. We were exhausted. The inside was a simple single room with a fireplace and a narrow wooden slatted bed, or cot. The pillow end was raised in a curve, but still wood-slatted. We hung our wet gear up as best we could, and while one got the tea made, the other found some kindling and wood and got the fire going. We soon found our mistake. The chimney was blocked, and soon the single-roomed shielin was like a Lawrie's of Mallaig kipper smokehouse. We had to douse the fire and then vacate the building for a while, leaving the door open. Eventually we got to bed – even though everything, including us, smelled of smoke. Our paper money was soaking, and we even hung it out to dry. I got the cot, although that was a trial as it was narrow and had no restraining sides, and the prospect of rolling out onto a concrete floor kept me awake for at least a millisecond. You have worked it out; Alex slept on the cold concrete.

I was awakened by someone knocking at the door. It did not wake Alex, so I got up and opened it. There was a man at the door; a shepherd, I jaloused. He was wearing the ubiquitous tweed trousers and those turned-up shepherd boots, complete with hobnails and a leather cover over the laces. I think they are also referred to as half-sprung boots. He had a shepherd's crook walking stick and two collie dogs. He did not have a jacket or a shirt, and wore a Rab C. Nesbitt-like heavy string vest. He asked if everything was fine with us and enquired as to our destination. I told him Montrose, and said that finding the shielin in the rain through a peat hag, with darkness falling, had been a bit tricky. He nodded, then laughed and said the weather was good today and it was a pity I had not strayed from my direct bearing the night before. If I had, I would have stumbled into someone's back garden. 'Look,' he said. I glanced out past him into a glorious sunny day; not a cloud in the sky. There was a peat hag stretching dead straight, billiard table flat, for what seemed like miles to the horizon. It was what I saw when I looked to either side that had me gasping. The peat hag was only a hundred yards wide. It was lined each side with houses and back gardens, as far as the eye could see. Washing out drying, people mowing grass, doing other garden tasks and settling into barbecues in the sun. I was amazed. The next thing I remember was waking up and seriously expecting to see the sun and the same scene. I opened the shielin door to rain and glowering cloud. Does penicillin do that to you? That was my hallucination?

So there you have it; an interesting cross-Scotland walk. We are not quite finished yet. All that remained was to get to Edzell on day ten, some twenty five miles away, and then the last eleven miles to Montrose – day eleven. We were walking on empty; apart from some tea and a stray biscuit found deep in Alex's rucksack, we were foodless. We pressed on regardless and, miracle of miracles, an oasis of sustenance appeared. No, nothing to do with penicillin this time. When we emerged out of Glen Lee and joined the public road, just where Glen Mark heads into the hills on our left and where Glen Esk begins on our right, there was a cottage with an honesty table in the garden offering home-made tablet and other sweet things. There was one request: put money for goods purchased in the box provided. We deposited two wet, smoky pound notes into the box and selected a macaroon bar and some tablet. We munched and walked and, after a while, came to Tarfside and the Retreat Country Life Museum. It was open for a few hours on a Sunday, and it had a tearoom. We could not have timed it better. This was Sunday, and it was open. We dragged our smoky beings into the busy tea-room and sat down. We ordered scrambled eggs on toast and a huge pot of tea. Each table was covered by a white table cloth with one of these old-fashioned triple decker cake stands thereon. From another era. Ours had sandwiches on the bottom layer, home baking, malt loaf and fruit loaf kind of stuff in the middle layer, and actual cakes – 'fondant fancies', no less – to top it off. When the lady came back out to ask if we wanted more tea, she stared at the empty cake stand and all she could say was: 'My, we were hungry!' We thanked her and paid our way before setting out again. (Probably to the relief of the Sunday trippers. We really did stink of smoke.)

Not far along, we crossed the River Esk to continue our way to Edzell on tracks and paths, away from the busy glen road on the other side of the river. Then it was the final day – day eleven and, coincidently, eleven miles left before hitting the high spots of Montrose. I cried at one point as I walked, not just because of my sore feet, but on thinking of my mum and dad who had both died more than ten years before, my mum being taken by a horrible cancer and about a year later my dad. I don't think he really ever recovered from his war years and being a prisoner for so long. The starvation and the beatings. Mum was the reason I was collecting for Macmillan Nurses. Then we were on the beach, and I dispatched my rude walking stick to Neptune – or whatever other Gods of the oceans frequented the North Sea just off Montrose. We signed off at the Park Hotel, got my treasured Ultimate badge and certificate, had more food, and got the train

Montrose, and cheerio faithful stick

home. An eventful trip. Alex found it a doddle. I will have to redefine that word.

* * *

In 1988, I ventured out on another Ultimate Challenge – this time in a trio, with Alex again and on this occasion Tom. The trio that would attempt Mont Blanc later that year. A different crossing route this time, starting at the Kintail Lodge Hotel, over The Saddle and the South Clunie Ridge, then over to the hills of Glen Affric, crossing Loch Ness on a ferry, then the Monadhliath Range to Aviemore, before heading over to Ballater by glens to the north of the Cairngorms, then over Mount Keen to Edzell and a stroll into Montrose. The crossing took twelve days, and we ascended seventeen Munros in achieving a High Level crossing. While my foot malaise did not get better and never has, I plodded on and took pain relief. One of the highlights of that whole crossing came at Carndavon Lodge. Having walked from the bothy at Faindouran Lodge, down the length of Glen Avon into Glen Builg and south past Loch Builg, we swung east into the steep-sided glen that hosts the River Gairn.

Towards the end of that glen, about three miles short of the B976 public road, we happen across said Carndavon Lodge – a bothy at that time. It was full to bursting, and the noisy chattering and laughter was like a magnet. We squeezed into the busy living area, with a welcome fire filling the hearth. Oh, by the way – the chimney was not blocked. A whole family from Peterhead was acting as mine host. Mum, Dad, two daughters and the boyfriend of one of the latter. A roll on bacon or roll on sausage was the offer – oh, and tea. I settled down to hot tea and a roll on sausage: luxury. The sausages were from the best butcher in Peterhead, apparently. This was not your normal bothy group; in fact, they were not even hill walkers. It seems they just loved to head out on a weekend and find a suitably accessible bothy, Carndavon being their favourite. Their car was parked no more than three miles away, so bringing in stacks of provisions was easy. I wished they had a helicopter, because they would bring life to any bothy.

Suitably fed and watered, our trio brave headed off to find Ballater Youth Hostel – still a bit away. The second seemed an easier crossing. I participated in two cross-Scotland Ultimate Challenges, and despite my feet issues – something that has bedevilled my mountaineering years – I loved both trips. To wake every morning, look east and think: 'I will have to walk beyond the horizon'. What a feeling of freedom. The planning and working out of routes while poring over maps is such a buzz; this way, that way, how to cross this river, is there a bridge? Will there be snow in the northern corries, should we carry an ice axe, and on and on? By the time D-Day approaches, you are desperate to get going. Then the people you meet, the friendships, built on a combination of shared adversity and shared respect. The feeling one gets when heading down remote glens, carrying your house and your food; self-sufficient.

I am living the dream of a parallel universe that awakened in me when I looked over the impressive steep-sided Ceanlochan Glen and beyond from Glas Maol, all these years before. Nothing but you and the mountain or the glen or the river; it does not matter. It is challenging you to listen, to understand – and as you do, and as you become as one, you start to understand yourself. Then I think to the people of The Clearances who travelled down remote glens and I think: *It was easy for me. I had a warm house to go back to. I was just doing this for fun.* These poor people had nothing; they were not doing it for fun, and I feel unsure and actually a bit angry at a world that allowed that and still has not learned. Our mountains can be sobering places.

In 1895, the Tomdoun Inn – a drovers' refreshment stop at that time – was transformed into the Tomdoun Hotel, a refreshment stop for fisher folk. It ceased being a traveller's rest in the early 21st century. It is situated a few miles west of Invergarry, near the east end of a loch that opens a window into Knoydart. The Tomdoun has some great memories for me, having used it several times in my travels. I take this opportunity to slot in this tale of things glorious and mysterious, centred in that area. It is the end of May 1995, and Brian and I have just spent a couple of nights in A' Chuil bothy in Glen Dessarry, gateway to wonderful Knoydart. The weather had been a tad inclement; however, that did not stop us raking about the unseen Knoydart Mountains. Finding the weak spot in Sgurr na Ciche's defences from the high point of the Glen Dessary path in a West Highland downpour – with seriously strong winds, squelchy paths and virtually zero visibility – was a bit of a trial. We carefully worked our way up and round the west nose of Garbh Choich Mhor until we reached a sloping, yet flatter area of ground at about six hundred and fifty metres. It was obvious on our map, so we used that as our datum to take a bearing from which to locate the ramp up through Sgurr na Ciche's southern defences. We could not even see the mountain. Three times we approached on a bearing into a blind cliff, glowering at us from behind a dark grey curtain of cloud. Twice we retreated to try again. Each time with the same negative result. Brian did ask if I knew what a compass was, and then asked: 'Are we even in bloody

Knoydart?' After our third failure we changed tactics and stayed beside the vertical wall and picked our way to the west. Lo and behold, round a small outcrop – no more than fifty metres from our failure – there it was: the gap in its defences. Like wet rats up a drainpipe, we scramble up the narrow chimney of shattered pink rocks, overhung by sheer dripping outcrops. A wet place. Our way was barred briefly by a snow band, high in the chimney, then up more shitty steep ground onto the summit.

We did not tarry, and were soon heading east along the ridge where we bumped into two canoeists – well, that's what they said. *It is wet*, I am thinking, *but not that wet.* They are having a break from paddling for the day. After a slippery and skittery descent, we scramble up Garbh Chioch Mhor then the rest of the ridge without incident. By the time we navigated and squelched our way back to A'Chuil, we were wet, cold and miserable. We had been out for hours in incessant rain and low clinging clag. We saw nothing but wet heather, wet grass, wet ferns and wet rocks. A typical 'character building' west coast day. A good-going fire, some food and a refreshment or two – perhaps three – soon put the memory of the misery to bed, as it did us.

Next part of our excursion would involve another couple of nights staying in the Loch Quoich area, at the Tomdoun Hotel bunkhouse. So in a fresh, dry morning, our spirits were high as we vacated A'Chuil and meandered through the forest to Strathan, the small hamlet at the west end of Loch Arkaig, where we had left the car. We made good time on the drive round to the Tomdoun Inn, where we spent the day drying out our gear, eating and checking out the map for our sojourn in this area. First thing I noticed, depending where I looked, was the triple spelling of Quoich. You could stick with that, or perhaps the Gaelic, *Chuaich*. If however one searches for it on the internet, you will find *Cuaich*. Take your pick. It means the Loch of the Cup or Quaich, whatever spelling one chooses. It was dammed at the east end in 1955 as part of the national Hydro scheme. That action raised its level by 100 feet, submerging several dwellings. It also increased the surface area from 3 to 7 square miles. It was our intention to head up the 919 metres of Gairich by going over the dam and following the stalker's track up the east shoulder. It was not amongst the biggest of hills days, but that suited as we were not planning a big day.

Whilst relaxing in the bar that night we met Allan Donald, an angler from Cumbria. Allan was here to catch ferox. He had a boat, and his plan was to motor to the west end of the loch and fish his way back to the east. As we chatted, a different plan was formulating in my head. About four miles further west of Gairich, on the same side of the loch, lies Sgurr Mor – a 1,003 metre Munro. It is an out-of-the-way mountain. Perhaps this was the perfect opportunity to get to it. The plan was simple. Blag a lift to the far end of the loch, get dropped off, climb up to the ridge and get over the two Munros. We broached our idea. He agreed. Not only would he drop us off – he would stay out fishing all day and then pick us up at a convenient spot. A quick map check, some working out of timings... all sorted.

So next day, Brian and I set out on one of the most enjoyable mountain excursions we have had the pleasure to participate in, thanks in the main to Allan the ferox hunter. An early rise, some breakfast, and – by the time we got to the loch – Allan was already raring to go. We got aboard and set sail on what was one of the best loch sailings I had ever enjoyed. Quoich is a beautiful loch in an awesome setting, surrounded by spectacular, jagged peaks as it intrudes into the east side of the rough bounds of Knoydart. It is simply breathtaking. In wild, wet, misty weather, as I have experienced, it can have a foreboding appearance. However, it is no less beautiful or breathtaking. It is also mysterious and surrounded in myth. Not just because of the three name spellings or the ferox. I refer to the horse-headed monster that calls the loch its home. A rival to the Loch Ness monster, by all accounts. Well, perhaps not a lot of accounts. The mystery gained traction many years ago when an anonymous Lord and his two ghillies spotted a serpentine-shaped beast, complete with what appeared to be a horse's head, sunning on the shore. The ghillies were sworn to silence. It was feared the sighting might bring charges of an excess of *uisge beatha*. About the same time, a second group of fisher folk on the loch claimed to have spotted a strange creature swimming in the depths. I am not aware of any more sightings of the cryptid creature. Whatever the truth, or otherwise, of the mysterious 'snake-like' loch creature, ferox was the only creature our ferryman was interested in this day. On our way down the loch, we got a lesson on trout and ferox fishing. We were also got a demonstration of his 'on-board' fish detection and recognition radar, a device he was particularly proud of. Ferox are described as a long-lived, late-maturing piscivorous brown trout. (Piscivorous means that it eats fish. Does that make it a cannibal?) The ferox is surrounded in myth and legend in the fishing world. It was once classified as of the salmon species, Salmo Ferox; however, some are not so minded and it may in fact be a genetic diversity of brown trout, Salmo Trutta. Whether pure salmon or pure brown trout, one thing is clear: it is a big fish. One of them, caught by rod and line in 2012, weighed in at just over 30 pounds.

After a delightful and interesting 'hurl doon the wat-
ter', we alighted on a lonely shore just where the Allt a'
Choire Bhuidhe enters the loch. Our link to civilisation and
safety glided off into the deep loch, leaving a trail of silver
bubbles, foam and agitated water. Then it was up to us. We
set off up the two miles or more of ever-steepening Coire
Bhidhe to an even steeper snow-covered end wall at Braigh a'
Choire Bhuidhe. We had no ice axes, and the end wall looked
pretty steep. However, as one neared, the optical illusion of
vertical proved wrong – as it often does. It was pretty steep
and did require care in the snow, but it was far from vertical
– well within our capabilities, and actually good sport.

We came out on the ridge just east of Sgurr Mor. We
were soon up the steep shoulder and on the summit, on a
grey, overcast day. The cloud ceiling was about four thousand
feet, above these Munros, so visibility was fine and navigation
was a doddle. We retraced our steps and continued past the
point where we had emerged onto the ridge. Soon we were
heading up the equally steep west ridge of the Corbett, Sgurr
an Fhuarain, 901 metres. Our bonus top for that day. Once
over, we descend the east ridge into Allt a' Choire Ghlais. at
250 metres, followed by an even longer drag up steep ground
onto Gairich Beag – the western outlier of the 919 metre
Munro, Gairich. A stalker's path made the early part of the
ascent easy, and we were soon on the summit and on schedule. We spent time on our last summit of the day, dining and
trying to spot our ferry. Oh, we were also on the lookout for
a creature with a horse-like head. I was convinced we would
be more likely to find it in the bar of the Tomdoun. As we
chomped the last of our fruitcake and continued to scan the
loch, a gust of wind snatched our map and deposited it
amongst boulders a few yards to the north. I scooted over to

grab it and save it from further exploration. It was then I saw it: the monster of Loch Quoich, plain as day. It was a thero- pod dinosaur, a bipedal Giganotoraurus – or as it is known locally, The Glengarry Kelpie. Why I had not seen it before evidences my lack of attention to detail. By chance, the gust of wind had not only snatched the map away but had turned it on its axis, so I was looking at it upside-down – from the north, the top of the map. Try it; look at the loch on the map from the north. Do you see it?

Then we spied a boat, way below us on the loch. Argh! Our lift. We sped off down the north shoulder to our rendezvous in the bay below, Coire Liath, near a small island; a perfect navigation point. As we dropped down, we moved through a lot of red deer, a regular feature of spending as many days in Scottish mountains as Brian and I have. Our ferox-hunting ferry was turning lazy circles on the loch, near our agreed pick up point, patiently awaiting our arrival. Then we were aboard and soon back at the dam. Allan did catch some trout, but missed the object of the trip: the elusive ferox. Something I was secretly glad about. That did not, however, interfere with tall tales in the bar of the Tomdoun a while later – featuring not only ferox, but their own very special monster, the Glengarry Kelpie. Thank you, Allan, for one of my most interesting outings in the Scottish mountains.

Not all the creatures one encounters are particularly mysterious. Sheep and border collies probably fit into that category. David Sadler and I spent many happy hours in mountains areas, occasionally on wheels but mostly with boots on. I recall a 'boots on' day that took place one winter. We were exiting another snow clad glen, having spent a few hours on a remote mountain area in the depths of another glorious winter day. Not a cloud in the sky, temperature well below zero; it does not get any better. We were down and heading back to the car and negotiating a well-worn, narrow part of the track, enclosed on either side by steep snow-covered banking. Suddenly our way was completely blocked by a large flock of sheep heading our way. Nowhere to go. So as not to panic the sheep and have them turn back, we quickly exited stage left and got out their way by scrambling to the top of the banking on one side. We sat on our rucksacks and waited till they had passed. Then five sheep dogs, border collies, appeared, followed by the shepherd. We were a few feet above him. He stopped, leaned on his crook and thanked us for not spooking the flock. Well, I think that's what he said. We then commenced to chatter for a few minutes. Meanwhile, his faithful dogs run about hither and yon. Each in turn skipping up to our position to examine the newcomers in their glen. A lovely mountain scene. I became aware of my right shoulder and back getting very warm and, on turning my head to check the sudden source of heat, I nearly had my eye taken out by a dog's hind leg projecting over my shoulder. I had been urine marked; I was now officially part of that dog's territory. Dave and the shepherd also nearly peed, but for a different reason. They suggested it was good luck. Not sure about that. Perhaps I should consider myself privileged?

Chapter 11

A S I move towards the end of my recollections, my reminiscences, I would like to take you briefly into the world of mountain rescue. For the majority of the 1980s I served in the Ochils Mountain Rescue Team. During that time I had spells as Training Co-ordinator and then Team Secretary. During my short discourse on this subject, I will concentrate mostly on training. In that regard, the incidents I describe will involve some humour, and I include them to show how team interaction and how regular training is crucial in developing trust and team spirit. Serious incidents I will keep to a minimum.

Prior to being accepted into the ranks, however, I had to participate in a few 'trials'. Mostly that meant simply participating in training days, though there was another quaint trial – perhaps 'initiation' might describe it better. I refer to it as the Dumyat rubbish clearance trip. That involved me accompanying the Team Leader and his Deputy to the top of Dumyat, every Tuesday night for a few weeks during winter – yes, in the pitch black. In these days, the summit was adorned by an open-topped, heavy-duty metal basket, or perhaps one should call it a brazier. Its principal purpose, certainly in modern times as far as I was ever aware, was as a signal

beacon in a relay process to signal the celebration of some national event. For example, to mark The Queen's Diamond
Jubilee in 2012. In this case, the first beacon was lit by the
Queen at Buckingham Palace, which was the signal to ignite
beacons all over the Commonwealth. The Dumyat beacon
was one of hundreds lit all over Britain that night. While that
was what might be described as its noble purpose, it had a
secondary purpose; that of a litter bin for many slovenly hill
users. Hence my Tuesday night trip to remove the rubbish
from said basket. It is my recollection that the weather was
usually foul. Tripping down into Menstrie carrying two or
three black bags filled with rubbish, I think, was a check on
my commitment and my hill fitness. By the way, we eventually filled the brazier with large stones and had a lid affixed to
the top. So no need for the bin run after that.

Once accepted as a member, I participated in the regular training programme. That consisted of a variety of disci-
plines and skills including search techniques, rope work, navigation, first aid, stretcher work, gorge rescues, cliff rescues and
– when the weather was suitable – winter skills. That was
pulled together by the occasional use of live 'victims', sent out
to go missing in order that we could swing our well-honed
search skills into action. We also kept up to date by training
on new techniques. Being members of the Mountain Rescue
Committee of Scotland was an important element in our
learning and profile, as it kept us in touch with the other
teams in Scotland and national developments. An important
element in all this was our close liaison and joint training with
the RAF Mountain Rescue Teams, including helicopter
awareness sessions, by way of regular familiarisation flights
and on-board lectures. In latter years, the Royal Navy Sea
Kings got more involved; mind you, they were so filled with

sonar search equipment we could hardly get a stretcher inside. At one national meeting, held at Glenmore Lodge, I was in attendance with our team chairman, John, when he got caught up in this simple but amusing conversation with the Flight Sergeant of the RAF Rescue team, who had travelled north from RAF Leuchars in a Wessex helicopter. During the well-attended meeting, John shouted across to the Flight Sergeant, 'Any chance of getting dropped off in Alloa on your way back to Leuchars?' The response was immediate, as though scripted: 'Yes, John; it will be my pleasure. What height will you be wanting dropped off from?' The next few minutes, and John's answer, was drowned out by laughter.

Annually we held a joint winter exercise with the other two teams that covered the Central Scotland Police area, the Killin and the Lomond teams. These exercise weekends were usually based in Killin where we billeted in some hall or other, sleeping on the floor. The Saturday element was usually winter skills, stretcher lowering, ice axe and rope work on steep ice or snow, somewhere on the Ben Lawers group. Getting to the location could sometimes be riskier than the actual exercise. On one memorable occasion there were ten or more of us packed into a minibus, travelling up the minor, unclassified road that runs from Edramucky, on the Killin to Aberfeldy A827 road, over to Glen Lyon, past the Ben Lawers Visitor Centre. It was a particularly cold winter and, in addition to shed loads of snow on the mountain, the minor road was ice bound – particularly the one we were on. As we chugged up, the wheels of our vehicle started to spin on the ice-bound road surface, then they lost traction completely and no matter how we all bounced about inside, and no matter what the driver did to gain traction, we started to slide back down the hill – slowly, almost imperceptibly at first, then faster and faster. The vehicle was carrying a lot of weight, as not only did it have a full contingent of well-clad and equipped mountain rescue personnel, it also had a fair number of ropes, a metal stretcher and other bits and pieces of heavy kit. In no time it was hurtling backward, toboggan like, to the noise of us in the back yelling at the driver to stand on the brakes – which he was anyway – then to pull on the handbrake and turn the wheel as far to one side as it would go, so it would somehow veer into the ditch at the side of the road and stop. The problem lay with the poor driver's conscience. You see, it was the Killin Community Bus and he did not want to damage it, so he was trying desperately to keep it upright and bring it to a halt, undamaged, on the road. Meanwhile, his ungrateful and selfish passengers were less interested in the fate of the minibus than they were about themselves. I was one of the ungrateful wretches. All we could envisage was the bus hurtling backwards, straight out onto the main road, at high speed and – if not 'written off' by some innocent, passing cattle float – crashing over the road, through the farm fence then hurtling towards Edramucky and (if we got that far) perhaps careering on into Loch Tay. Well, maybe not that far, but one's imagination does stretch in times of stress. Our directives to veer into the ditch got through to the driver eventually, and that is exactly what happened – at speed. We bounced about a bit, then came to rest at a crazy angle. Our next danger was being pierced by ice axes. In the event we avoided all but some minor bumps. The transport was a bit dented. But the show had to go on, so – after extricating ourselves – we (well, the majority) grabbed our kit and what other equipment we could tote and headed out on foot. It was treacherous, and visions of *Bambi on Ice* would not have been too out of place. We finally made it to Ben Lawers and got on with our day of joint training. Meanwhile, the driver and two others stayed by the bent minibus and waited for help, which came in the guise of a Lix Toll breakdown recovery vehicle.

The Sunday was usually reserved for showing off. Well, to put another way – it was reserved for a visit by senior police officers to see us in action. Often that took the form of a staged rescue scenario in Glen Ogle, the mountain rescue theatre I mentioned much earlier. The officers sat in their warm transport in a layby on the east of the glen, armed with binoculars and flasks of warm liquid of one beverage or another. Meanwhile, the joint teams were deployed on the 'railway' side of the glen, carrying out a search for some 'lost' soul. The casualty was always in a really awkward position, because that is where they put themselves, but in a spot where the spectators would get a good view of the action. The extraction and the grunt work was always by stretcher to the road where the viewers were situated. The fun bit was the actual manoeuvring of the casualty onto the precariously-positioned stretcher. Such joint training was always well attended, enjoyed, and an important part of our education and team building.

We did, on occasion, put our regular hours of practice into use. One Sunday a couple, armed with a torn page from a well-known and loved Sunday newspaper, set out from Menstrie to ascend Dumyat at the west end of the Ochil Hills. The south-facing flank of Dumyat is kind of steep, with a few vertical rock bands interspersed with steep sloping grass. The Sunday paper had a weekly feature on easy walks, and included a route marked by a line on a sketch of the mountain that vaguely indicated a route and showing a convenient car park and not a lot else. We arrived at the foot of the hill to see two people high on the steep south side, sitting on one of the horizontal grass ramps. The woman was waving a jacket to attract attention. When we got to the pair, the male was crag fast. The woman was fine, and acknowledged they were just out for a Sunday afternoon walk and were now well out of their depth, neither being mountaineers. Her husband would not even stand up. It eventually took six of us to get them down. We fitted both with a climbing harness, each with a rope 'tail' attached. The woman walked down with a single team member walking beside her, securing her by holding the short length of 'security' rope we had attached to the harness. The man, however – tail or no tail – was not for moving. So, in addition to the tail, firmly in the grasp of a team member, we secured a full length of climbing rope to the front of his harness. Four of us then spaced out along the rope, walked it to its full length and stopped. The man, still in his original spot and refusing to move, was then persuaded to walk, with his escort firmly gripping his short length of security rope and the rest of us firmly securing our bit of the extended climbing rope. Even if he jumped, he was going nowhere. As they reached each rescue team member in turn, that team member also walked, then the next, and the next – concertina fashion – until all five of us were clustered together. He stood still once more, and the four rescue team members stretched the rope out again. The man and his close protection then walked again, and we repeated that process all the way down. We did not go directly down the hill, so we had to zig-zag back and forward along the grass ramps, getting lower and lower. He was really terrified and, by the time we got him safely down, he was exhausted. He was a tall man, over six feet in height, whereas his wife was quite small. That really has no bearing on how one might be on a hill; however, it was – if I can be cruel for a moment – quite amusing. I think he was not the one making the dinner that night.

Calls out could be anytime. Midwinter blizzard, scorching hot summer afternoon... it made no difference. I recall forcing my way through waist-deep wet snow as I tried to find a route into the mountain on steep ground around midnight one winter night, snowflakes dazzling me as they reflected from the beam of my head torch. My thoughts were on the real possibility of an avalanche. The source of the light which had been reported flashing somewhere on the hill was never found. Another day I was the 'casualty' in a practice gorge rescue. The method being practised was a quaintly named technique called a Tyrolean Traverse. I was never convinced we would ever use the technique, but it was a seriously good method to engender technical skills and encourage working as a team. I was strapped into a stretcher, precariously perched on a rocky outcrop at the edge of a vertical drop into a ravine. If I thought getting lifted and strapped into the stretcher was a bit interesting, I had not experienced what was to follow. I trust my life to the team as they teeter on the edge of the cliff, grunting and heaving as they fix the stretcher to a pulley and then onto the single rope that had been strung across the gorge. Once they were happy they had secured the stretcher and that the pulley wheels were properly in place on the rope, all carried out amidst shouts of: 'Have you got that belay tied up? Is it tight enough? Are you sure the wheels are on straight? Are you ready on the far side?' Meanwhile, I just lie there and offer some verbal encouragement. Then I was off and being dragged out over the abyss, snuggled inside in my comfy stretcher. Disconcertingly, the first sensation is that of falling. The stretcher – once clear of the rocks it had rested on – drops alarmingly, then bounces back up and down and up before settling. We are moving and making progress. I am soon one hundred feet in the air over the roaring river in the gorge. As I lay looking up at the single rope – the umbilical cord to which I owed my survival – the stretcher is moving slowly along, being pulled from the far side, the rate being controlled from the 'launch' side. So far, so good. Then it all went 'tits up', to use a military term. One of the pulley wheels jumped off the rope and jammed, in front of my eyes. Helpless and strapped in the unbudgeable stretcher, I can do nothing except sway, spin and bounce up and down and back and forward, for what seemed an eternity. Meanwhile, my team mates are shouting back and forth to each other across the gorge as they desperately seek a solution. I gaze up at the dis-lodged pulley wheel, wondering how long it would take for the rope to snap. It is funny how shouting, swearing and tell-ing me to lie still and not panic seems to be the universal method for sorting out these situations. I did not panic; no reason to, for there was absolutely nothing I could do. In fact, I could not get my arms free anyway. They never managed to get the rope back on the pulley, and resorted to brute strength and a lot of heaving – controlled by even louder shouted in-structions. Half an hour later I was unceremoniously dumped on the far banking, released from my 'mummy' outfit and all was well. The rope was destined to be consigned to the dam-aged cupboard. Tall tales in a Tillicoultry pub later was all that was left of the day.

A mountain rescue incident, when I was actually in uniform and on police duty, got me into a bit of trouble. A school teacher called at Tillicoultry office in a panic. He had been taking a group of schoolchildren hillwalking in the Och-ils. One fell down a steep slope into a rough rocky section of the Daiglen Burn near where it joins the Gannel Burn, just into the hills above Tillicoultry Quarry. The teacher had run from the hill and, by luck, got a lift in a quarry lorry. The incident happened less than half an hour before. According to the teacher, the boy had suffered a compound fracture of his leg, above the knee, was bleeding profusely and was losing a lot of blood. He even suggested that if quick action was not taken the boy could die. We marked the location on the map and agreed a mountain rescue call out would take too long. I telephoned the RAF Search and Rescue at Leuchars in Fife, got straight through to the Flight Sergeant and explained the problem and the urgency. I gave him the grid reference of the incident, and we arranged to rendezvous at the rugby ground in the village. He said he was going to get airborne immediately, ostensibly to do some wet rope training – whatever that meant – but that I needed to contact RAF Pitreavie who had responsibility for allocating assets for such tasks. I duly contacted them, and the already-airborne Leuchars helicopter was dispatched. I summoned an ambulance and the police surgeon. The latter was my downfall; not his fault. That call alerted Police HQ to my situation. They despatched a uniform Inspector to take control. He was at the office within a few minutes. Taking control meant going over it all again with the ever-more frustrated teacher and deciding, over the protests of the teacher, to call out the mountain rescue team. He instructed I do that. I informed him there was not enough time and, in any case, I had called a rescue helicopter. 'No you haven't,' he said, 'only a police Superintendent has the authority to do that.' I agreed that would normally be the case; however, because of the urgency I had circumnavigated that route and called it myself. He was adamant: I could not do that. I assured him I had, and said if he put his head out the window he would hear the helicopter. He did, and he did. We rushed to the rendezvous point as the Yellow Wessex Search and Rescue Helicopter swung overhead. The Inspector – taking charge, I assume – dashed into the middle of the rugby field and held a handkerchief in the air. I guess his intention was to give the pilot the wind direction. I looked on in disbelief as a flare from the helicopter nearly brained him as it bounced and rolled across the rugby field, spewing out its bright orange smoke. He was obviously unaware that the waving handkerchief method of showing wind direction had gone out of fashion sometime before the Battle of Britain.

The 'chopper' swing round and landed. I quickly briefed the pilot and winchman of the situation, and confirmed the position of the casualty. The police surgeon got aboard and, as I was just about to get do the same, a voice on my radio asked for a media update. I declined to get involved, turned my radio off and got into the helicopter. In the event I was not winched down to the casualty; the doctor was. He and the casualty were soon back on board, and in jig time we were back at the rugby field and getting the young ten year old into the waiting ambulance. From falling to getting to the hospital had taken about two hours. He was badly hurt and needed in excess of forty stitches to heal his gashes.

The ambulance was no sooner away than my deconstruction began. First it was about the media. Headquarters said they were inundated with calls from the media and it was my responsibility to give them information. I asked when the media started running the police service and whether saving the casualty was a lower priority than feeding the press. We moved on from the media angle to the *who is responsible for calling out a helicopter* issue. I was duly summoned to meet senior management, and was left in no doubt it was not a Constable's place to contact the RAF and seek assistance.

Even reasoning with them about the urgency made no difference; I had stepped over a line, and it would be noted in my
record. I have no idea if it was. My point was, and has always
been, that there are systems and without doubt they are a
necessary requirement. However they are not a strait jacket
and, on occasion, there can and will be circumstances that require one to detour from the path. Such an action will require
to be justified, that is reasonable. The young boy recovered
well and, a couple of years later when I had been promoted to
the town where he lived, I made a point of visiting him at his
home.

During my years of Rescue Service, I encountered many
incidents; several pretty routine, some with an element of
light relief, and some involving an element of risk – or as one
of my more experienced colleagues used to say, 'moments of
objective danger'. Falling out of a flying aeroplane without a
parachute – and living to tell the tale – probably straddled the
latter two categories. Unfortunately for me, I was the 'faller':
the injured party. Perhaps my pride took the biggest hit. The
main question in the aftermath centred around the vexed
question of 'how did it happen?' and, in particular, 'was he
pushed or did he fall?' Was it not Sir Nicholas Fairbairn QC
and Solicitor General, when asked if he had been pushed or
did he jump – relating to his resignation at the time of the
Miss X case, a rape case he declined to prosecute – replied,
'neither: I fell'. Enough of Scottish legal history. The 'fall' incident I refer to was another mountain rescue situation. I was
team leader of a group toiling up to an injured person high on
a mountain. We were the stretcher party. Luckily an RAF
Wessex Search and Rescue helicopter was free to attend and
take us to the locus. Due to the steepness of the ground it
could not land, and we were individually winched in to the

helicopter. I was last, and there was not a seat for me. I simply sat at the door edge, still attached to the winch, with my feet dangling outside. We swung into the hill. Because of the gusty wind – coupled with the uneven, boulder-strewn slope – the helicopter could not land. They had no time to winch us all out, so a stark choice was offered. Go back down the hill, with the prospect of walking back up, or jump out. We chose the latter. We hovered about eight feet up. Technique: sit on the edge, push yourself forward, and drop feet first into the heather. A doddle.

I was first to take the plunge under the swirling, noisy and buffeting blades. I had not factored in the fact that I was sitting on the edge of a big, well-used metal box with an engine. The metal door edge was a bit frayed and, as I pushed forward, the seat of my trousers became snagged. I was stuck and swayed forward, secured to the helicopter by the seat of my pants, my upper body pulling me out to pitch me headfirst onto the boulders. The alert winch-man saved me from more

Wessex RAF Search and Rescue helicopter in the Ochils

injury by quickly and firmly pushing on the small of my back, thus breaking the helicopter's grasp on me and allowing me to stay relatively upright. It was still not controlled, and I fell on my side. I suffered minor bruising and major embarrassment, to say nothing of a draught in my nether regions as the arse was ripped out of my trousers. The others evacuated without incident and avoided the stretcher that followed. Then we were left in a helicopter-induced blizzard of grass, small stones and bits of heather. So, you have the answer: I tried to jump but finished up being pushed.

Another aeroplane incident. It was the 5th of April 1990, and I was on duty as a police sergeant when I got a call to grab my mountaineering kit and head for the village of Fintry. Just before nine o'clock that morning, a Cessna 210 plane, PH-EYE, had crashed into Dunbrach Hill, just over two kilometres directly south of the village. The plane caught fire, and the two occupants were killed instantly. While the general angle of the hill was 45%, the part they hit was a vertical rock outcrop and the site was in a difficult place to access. The pilot and co-pilot had flown over from the Netherlands in the early morning. They were fishing boat owners from the north of Netherlands, heading to a conference in Scotland. The weather was not good; low cloud, visibility problems and cold sleet. The plane had suffered icing problems, and was lower than it should have been as it set up to land at Glasgow. Unfortunately it never got to the correct height, and flew straight into the cliff. At the rendezvous I was met by the police officer in charge of the incident. My task was to secure the crash site by staying beside it overnight and not letting anyone approach. I was accompanied by a civilian member of the Killin Mountain Rescue Team. We were briefed, then supplied with food and a flask as well as waterproof bivouac bags. The last couple of hundred feet or so to the site were steep, slippy and bloody treacherous. The bodies were being removed when we arrived on site. Then we were on our own. In the pitch black, we scrabbled and slithered about on the steep wet hillside trying to find a suitable place near the wreckage to bed down. It was not easy. In the end we settled for a sheep scrape. Not the best, but as near to horizontal as we could find. It was not a comfortable night. There were freezing sleet showers all night, and lying in such a precarious position with your arms zipped inside the bag was disconcerting. I felt like I was sliding and all night had a vision of tobogganing to the bottom of the hill in the bivouac bag, adding a third casualty to the list. It was a sobering night as we looked onto the wreckage and contemplated the tragedy for two families.

But life goes on, and nature has a way of bringing us back. As dawn broke we were awakened by the sound of a blackcock lek, coming from a gap in the forest below us to our right. We drank the last of our cool tea as we watched in fascination as the lek came into sight. Something I was hardly likely to witness again. Wonderful. It was not long after that when the investigators arrived and we were allowed to stand down and head home for a warming bath.

Two things happened in the years that followed. Ten years after the crash, a daughter of one of the plane occupants contacted Central Scotland Police to ask if she could be taken to the site. A colleague had a brass commemorative plaque made and we affixed it to the cliff at the crash site. A few days later, we took the daughter to the site. It was a moving experience, and I hoped it helped her come to terms with her dad's death in some way. In 2016, I flew in the opposite direction in a small four-seater plane. We landed at Lelystad in the

Netherlands and stayed in Amersfoort. At dinner one night I was sitting beside a lady and gentleman. Most of those in attendance were connected with small planes – pilots or owners. I was neither. However, many of the conversations were about flying and planes. Because we were in the Netherlands and because of the connection to that crash, I related the tragic incident of all these years before in Scotland involving the death of two fishermen from the north of their country. They looked astounded and informed me they were from the same place and knew both the people who had been killed – and, in fact, he had been speaking to a relative of one of the deceased only a few days before the dinner. They were amazed that I had been so involved. It is an increasingly small world.

* * *

One of our team was off with a group of his friends to do some climbing in the Atlas Mountains in North Africa; the section that runs through Morocco. They did not have a lot of winter mountain experience and would be crossing a snow-covered mountain range that topped 13,000 feet in height at some parts. Some exposure to ice axe and rope work in snow conditions would be essential. I was 'roped' in, along with another team member, to help with said training – or 'familiarisation' might explain the day better. The day was spent in the Ochils and we were set up on a suitable, north-facing steep slope. It was well covered in deep snow and was about ninety to a hundred feet high, with a safe run out at the foot into more deep snow: perfect. At least we got that bit right, thankfully. We had tramped about on the steep slope, cutting steps, getting familiar with walking in crampons, arresting falls, using the ice axe. Stuff like that. All good fun, and with much laughter. Then we were at the top of the steep slope and one of the intrepid Mountain Rescue trio – the one heading with the group to the Atlas – set up an ice axe belay. Its purpose is to provide safety and security for climbers descending through steep ground and, in the case of a fall, arresting that fall. Our plan is to instil a bit of confidence in such techniques. Method as follows: dig trench horizontally across the slope, then dig a second deep channel at right angles to the horizontal trench, midway along and on the downside, creating a T shape. Embed one – or sometimes two – ice axes into the cross trench. We were using a single ice axe. Tie the rope to shaft of ice axe. Lay axe along the deep horizontal channel, with rope running down the vertical channel. Fill the trench and channel with snow and stamp it all down. That is the belay. Tie the other end of the rope to the back of the harness worn by the person providing security for the climber. Like a tail. I will call that person the anchor. The anchor then fashions a bollard seat in the snow and sits, at the ready. All set; ice axe belay is bombproof and the anchor, who is going nowhere, is ready to manage the rope. First victim – sorry, volunteer – is now at top of the slope ready to demonstrate the effectiveness of this technique in preventing a full-length fall. He has a rope tied to the carabiner at the front of his climbing harness. The person acting as the anchor has that rope around his body; he is also wearing stout gloves and holding the rope. Remember, he is also tied into the ice axe belay. As the person who has fallen approaches his position, the anchor – employing perfect timing and co-ordination – slowly wraps the rope around his body and, by pulling his arms together and crossing them over in front of him, creates enough friction between the rope and his body to arrest the fall and bring the faller to a safe and uneventful halt.

So we are set up and ready for the demonstration. The first to 'fall' will be the biggest and heaviest in the party. He had taken the extra precaution of donning his full waterproofs, leggings and all. He wanted to get speed up, he said. To aid that wish, as he set off he jumped into the air, shouted *Geronimo!* and hurtled into the abyss. So far, so good. His preparation to gain speed was certainly effective; so much so I wondered if he was a physicist or perhaps a Formula 1 aerodynamics engineer. Whatever, he was soon hurtling. Anchor man looked ready. As the 'faller' hurtled past the belay point, I was thinking, *maybe the waterproofs were a bit of a gamble... or was it the leap?* No matter; it was too late for such thoughts. We were past the event horizon, and our guinea-pig faller was travelling at around Mach 1 speed, I reckoned. *This will really convince them*, I mused, as Geronimo flew past the wide-eyed anchor man. 'Take the strain!' I heard from somewhere. And he obviously did. The big pull came on, the arms were crossed, the rope was tight around his body and he was pulled forward – all textbook so far.

The first clue to the success, or otherwise, of our demonstration was the burst of snow just behind anchor man. At the same instant an ice axe exploded out of the 'burst of snow' – and I mean exploded. Anchor man seemed also to explode; well perhaps not explode, but he certainly deserted his post at breakneck speed and off he went, like a rat up a drainpipe. Well, in this case down a drainpipe. He dutifully held onto the rope and, in a kind of surreal formation – Geronimo leading, on his back, loosely facing back up the slope and anchor man, on his front, facing down the slope, with his ice axe tail flailing about behind him, like some kind of Red Arrows stunt – they were gone. The team member who set up the belay stood transfixed for a nanosecond, then he was off, running down the same slope – no ice axe, no belay, nope... just running. *This was not in the script*, I thought. Although, to be honest, I am not too clear what I actually thought as I was lying on my back, rolling about, consumed by uncontrollable laughter.

But not all our planning had been in vain. Remember the long run out of deep snow? Well, our intrepid pair were half-buried in it. The flailing ice axe did not come into contact with flesh or bone, thankfully. Once we got them extricated, we headed back up and did it all again. This time digging the channel from the ice axe to the anchorman a tad deeper, so the rope ran straight and not over a bump in the snow. It worked perfectly the second time around, and confidence was restored. It was all a matter of engineering and angles.

Then there were the snow holes and real winter. It was another of our annual 'away weekend' training gigs. It was usually in late January or perhaps early February, and we would decant from the Ochils for a weekend of winter training in Lochaber with our friend and instructor, Mick Tighe. Just such a weekend in January 1989 saw a group of us with Mick, heading for the 1,130 metres that is Creag Meagaidh. A big lump of mountain with complicated topography, sited between Spean Bridge and Newtonmore. It was a lovely day, and early when we set out. Strands of wispy mist in the valleys with a bright winter sun negotiating with the clouds over who should reign supreme that day. The cloud won that day's argument, although the compromise left us with a bright glow for a time. A last-minute decision saw us attack the mountain from the south-west, across Moy Forest. We parked near Moy Lodge and loaded up with our gear. The plan is to spend the night sleeping near the summit. Because of that we are carrying some extra gear – in particular, food, sleeping bags and large snow saws. The latter will be used to slice into the snow and fashion our rooms for the night. We head onto the hill and move slowly east across the south ridge of Meall Coire Choille-rais heading for Moy Corrie, a beautiful bowl of 200 metre-high cliffs, surrounding and protecting the lovely Lochan Coire Choille-rais, nestling cosily and secretly at about 800 metres. The lochan shelters under the crook of the south shoulder of Meall Coire Choille-rais. It stays hidden from the gaze of all but soaring eagles until one enters the amphitheatre of cliffs and snow from its secret door on the south-east corner of the corrie at the outfall of Allt Coire Choille-rais, just where it commences its twisting, tumbling, bubbling cascade down the flank of the mountain as it rushes to replenish the waters of Loch Laggan, hundreds of feet below. The coire was so quiet, so still and completely devoid of colour. It is like a scene from an old black and white movie. There is something surreal about it. It is actually beautiful and, for the umpteenth time in my stravaiging of mountains, I have once more struck

Moy Corrie

lucky and stumbled on natural beauty. The monochrome view and the eerie stillness is down to a trick of the light, brought about by the sun's rays being diffused through the cloud filter, onto snow-plastered black, beetling cliffs. The only colour is from our clothing and gear. We felt we were in a special place and we spoke almost in whispers.

After a break and some fuel, we carefully pick our way over ice-covered rocks to the far side of the lochan to seek an escape route up into the cloud and onto the summit plateau. There followed a slow trudge up a very steep, nameless snow and ice-filled gulley in single file, into the cloud, hoping the route we had chosen would lead where we needed it to. After about forty minutes or so we reached an overhanging cornice, and our brave leader was given the task of breaking through. We followed like lemmings onto a cloud-covered summit plateau. Another study of the map and taking care with our bearing, we move out in a north-westerly direction through the grey, featureless, flattish world that is the summit plateau of Creag Meagaidh. Our destination is the steep northern flank of the mountain, about two hundred metres east of the summit cairn. When we get there, we are immediately split up into teams of three and told to pick a spot on the steep ground just off the plateau, just a few feet down. Way below our spot was Lochan Uaine. I am sure it is not well frequented.

We set about digging their five star snow-hole accommodation for the night. So for the next couple of hours, racing to get them finished before darkness, we dug and sawed and excavated. The saw allowed us to fashion large rectangular blocks, to be re-used for building a wall over the front of the excavated cave. Inside the snow hole, we had a wide shelf around two sides and the back. These were for sleeping on. The entrance was very small and was placed at the lowest part of the 'cave', level with the floor we stood on. Colder air stays low, so we would habitate a bit higher in the warmer section. Well, that was the theory; not sure it actually made much difference, because we did spend a cool night even in good sleeping bags. A hole in the roof was essential to allow our exhaled carbon dioxide to escape the snow-hole. We also dug out small eye-level shelves for putting our candles on. A touch of class. Getting in and out was a bit of a struggle. The entrance/exit was low and small, requiring one to crawl in and out. Then it got dark, and each team retired to their respective cool-box for a cosy night. We partake of supper in our sleeping bags, by candle light – perched on our individual ice ledge – washed over with a dram, before coorying down into said sleeping bags for a chat. Oh, and another wee dram.

At midnight it was up and out into the inky blackness and a gale, for a group photograph at the summit of Creag Meagaidh. Sleeping in a snow-hole is not like being in your own bed under a duvet; it is cold but, with the correct gear, just about bearable. Then there is getting up in the middle of the night to answer nature's call; but hey, that is another story. Enjoy your duvet.

Sunday was spent on that steep north slope of the mountain, practicing various winter climbing techniques. Just to reiterate: it was seriously steep ground, all 200 metres of it. If I thought cutting steps to traverse across it was intimidating, I had not figured – on the exercise that followed – the ice axe breaking. This was no ordinary exercise. It is normal to sit down and hurtle down such slopes seated, then simply turn onto your front and deploy the ice axe to arrest your progress. In this 'reality' exercise, as Mick described it, he wanted to inject some realism. He reasoned that one does not normally fall seated, just in the correct position to roll over. So he fashioned himself a suitable platform on the steep ground. He then lined us up in single file and had us walk across the lower side of his platform, one at a time. He was standing on his secure ledge, ready for the exercise. I was first and, as I walked in front of him, he suddenly and without warning grabbed my ice axe, pulled me sharply toward him, then – almost instantaneously, and with a fair amount of violence – pushed me away, and at the same time he hooked his foot around my ankle. I did not fall down the slope; I was projected and tumbled head over heels, at speed. I remember bouncing, then sliding head first and on my back. Somehow I gained some measure of equilibrium, and my previous training fell into place. Arm out to one side, dig ice axe into the slope. That has the effect of spinning you round, still on your back – but now feet first, still travelling at speed. Simple now. Roll onto your front, get into breaking position and dig in ice axe. One soon comes to a stop in a flurry of snow. I got to my knees and looked up. I had travelled the best part of one hundred feet, perhaps more. I noticed two things immediately after that. My left cheek bone was sore and bleeding. Probably having come into contact with my ice axe. The second thing – Mick had applied a modicum of health and safety to the exercise. Another two hundred feet or more below he had deployed a member of the Lochaber Mountain Rescue Team to act as back stop, or perhaps wicket keeper.

I will say something about Mick Tighe at this point. He was previously a Marine and had a lifetime of experience on mountains, on rock faces, in snow, on ice cliffs, climbing and skiing. In the years we came across each other on these mountain escapades, I grew a huge liking and respect for him. He was a member of the Lochaber Mountain Rescue Team, and he had his own professional mountain guiding company.

His style of leadership and guidance was way out at the front end of his profession. I became a far more confident mountain person under his tutelage, and better able to not only look after myself but others. Mick was a supreme judge of people, and had that knack of allowing you to take yourself to limits you never dreamed you had. I spent many hours stretching myself on winter mountains in his company.

On one such winter mountain rescue training week in Lochaber, the group headed to Meall Garbh – a southerly outlier of Chno Dearg. The last part of the approach was a forty minute walk. It was February and it was a still, grey overcast day, several degrees below freezing. My vivid memory of that approach was being showered, so gently and so unobtrusively, by ice crystals. The real deal: the air was filled by thousands of hexagonal crystals, like delicate, fragile filigree petalons, gently, imperceptibly, landing on our cloth-ing, on our hair. They were everywhere. A myriad of small, white, perfectly-shaped crystal clusters, gently drifting in the still air, almost suspended; the building bricks of snow. Even the tough-edged mountain rescue stalwarts, each having seen their fair share of the grisly and unpleasant, were like chil-dren, holding out their arms to catch the drifting crystals and showing them to their colleagues. It was a wonderful, pre-cious, never-to-be-forgotten few minutes.

The buttress under Meall Garbh contains a handful of reasonably-graded winter climbing routes. Mick split the group into pairs and gave us a route each. It seems my partner and I had a grade three – or, in perfect conditions, a grade four. I have no idea what it was named, but I do have an idea about how difficult it was, certainly the first two pitches. I took the lead and proceeded to climb a nearly vertical pitch, maybe about fifty feet. I was directly above my belayed partner and had not yet put in a second belay. I was on my cramp pon points, on hard water ice between two ice-covered bulges. Placing my ice axe was difficult; each time I tried, a big chunk of ice – the size and shape of a dinner plate – broke away and clattered down towards my colleague, who was my life line, directly below me. After a couple of wasted minutes getting nowhere, and with my legs starting to shake and feeling as though I was on the verge of toppling back past my colleague, I shouted over to Mick that I was stuck. He replied in the way I suppose, deep down, I expected: 'Well, why are you wasting your energy shouting at me? Get sorted out and get through it.' At that he shimmied, like a spider, upward and out of my sight. I calmed down, assessed my position, changed my footing stance and attacked the awkward bit from a slightly different angle. Success; through and upward. I soon had a belay secured, and brought up my climbing companion to my position. He led the next pitch, up and out of sight, round a corner behind a bulging snow-covered buttress. I followed round the corner on a nearly-vertical pitch and joined him. He then headed off along a horizontal traverse, up through a vertical rock corner and out of sight. I was left alone with all the gear. The four groups had all passed up that same rock corner. I got there after the rest had gone through it. Alone on seriously steep ice; except there was little ice left. The previous sets of crampon-footed creatures had kicked it clean of ice and left exposed rock, which I cramponed through. Then I was over the difficulties, and all that was left was a long trudge up a steep-angled but straightforward snow ramp. On arrival, Mick met us with his usual greeting: 'So you made it, Mr 'Oh, I have never done anything this before' and his pal, 'Oh, I can't do this.' No hug, no 'well done'... in fact, his only other comment was: 'You shouldn't be in Mountain Rescue if you can't do this. Now let's get down.'

On the last day of that week, Mick teamed our Winter Mountain Rescue course with a parallel course he was running that week, 'An Introduction to Winter Hill Walking'. The weather had been foul, and the clients on that course had spent a week practicing navigation and hardly getting their feet on a hill. Friday weather forecast was excellent, and he hoped to finish their course on a high – a winter ascent of the Ben. The route planned was Number 4 gulley. I was teamed up with a really nice bloke from Kent, who confided in me that this was well beyond his capabilities and that he was really nervous. We gathered in Coire Leis, sorted ourselves into our allotted pairs and got roped up. I was to be at the cow's tail again. As we gained height I could detect a touch of nervousness in my charge. He had stopped asking questions and was silent. Maybe he was fed up with my answers? Then he said, 'what do I do if you fall?' I told him I wasn't going to fall. He was not too sure and asked me another twice. I assured him that Mick was watching everything and not to worry.

The ground was getting steeper, and I got closer to him and made a play of managing the rope that joined us. The gulley is just short of 900 feet. Just before the nearly-vertical last 80 or 90 feet, there is an indent on the right where the others had gathered and tied on to some 'dead men' snow anchor belays, while they waited their turn to go up the last vertical section and out of the gulley. By the time we got there, the last climber was already out and on the rope that led up and over the edge. I got my charge tied on and gave him some instruction, and he was off and soon out of sight and over the edge. I was now alone in the gulley. I retrieved the dead man belays, hooked them to my harness gear loop and headed out to rope up. I was jangling like an iron monger. When sorted, I shouted: 'ready, climbing'. I saw Mick looking over and I felt the rope go taut. I shouted that the rope was too tight and to loosen off a bit. It was on deaf ears and it got even tighter, dragged me out of my foot placements and, before I could protest further, dragged even faster and faster up through what remained of the cornice, over the edge, before being dumped unceremoniously on my front beside all the other gear. My rope was not belayed and they had slung it over their shoulders and run away from the edge, dragging me like a rag doll. Mick had a big grin on his face.

Once the gear was gathered and refreshments consumed, it was back over the edge and down the gulley we had just ascended and back to the pub. We had a great night, and I was plied with drink by a seriously happy Kentish man. We had not gone to the summit and, in fact – despite other climbs on the Ben – I had never bothered with the summit, until one day a year or two later. At that point I was with three of my mountain rescue team friends ascending the North East Buttress, one of the highest cliffs on Britain's mountains, and heading for the summit of the Ben for the first time. We set out up the Buttress after what had been a few weeks of really good weather. We had hardly got roped up when it started raining; gently at first, as though encouraging us to continue, which we did. By the time we got maybe a third the way up, it was sluicing down and water was fluming over us from the steep rocks above. Not only was it wet but, after weeks of dry weather, the wet rocks were treacherously slippy. We were finding it difficult to gain traction. Summit conference required (excuse the badly timed pun). Well not actually a summit conference: a part-way-up conference. Decision? Bail out. Getting back down into Coire Leis was a tad tricky. Once there we huddled by the CIC hut and decided on our next move. Decision made, we shared out the ropes and other gear, stowed them in our sacks and set off to climb the Ben by way of the abseil post on the Carn Mor Dearg arête. It was hard, and not made any easier by our earlier failed attempt on the North East Buttress. Heading up to the abseil post from the CIC hut was bloody torture on horrible ground; certainly the last steep section. For every four steps gained we slid back a couple. Not made any easier with the weight we were carrying. What a relief to get onto the arête, then the Little Brenva Face – which was steep, a bit jumbled, but easy – and then we were out onto the summit, and for the first time I touched the top of the highest mountain in Britain. Down the tourist path seemed like an eternity, and I was limping by the time the hostelry was reached. My right leg and hip again playing up. What a hard, but what a great day.

The foregoing section was largely about mountain rescue. I deliberately kept most of it a bit light-hearted, and away from some of the less light-hearted moments. But Mountain Rescue is not a light-hearted business; it is a serious and often a very dangerous activity. Team members, all over the UK, give freely of their time and go about their business, willingly and with dignity. The danger came home to us all on February 1st 1987. A climber was reported missing on Ben More. The Killin and Lomond Teams were involved in the rescue attempt. Police constable Ian Ramsey and Sergeant Harry Lawrie, members of the Killin Team – police colleagues and friends of mine – were in an RAF Wessex Search and Rescue helicopter from Leuchars, heading towards the top of the mountain. As they were getting ready to alight, part of the aircraft struck the mountain and it crashed. Harry was killed and Ian received severe injuries, as did the helicopter winch-man, Mick Anderson. Three rescue personnel, Billy Stitt, Stewart Ingles and Hugh Pearce, the helicopter pilot, were awarded Queen's Commendations for their actions that night. Unfortunately, the person they were trying to rescue died. A cross was erected on Ben Ledi in memory of Harry.

Mountain Rescue goes on, and volunteers continue to risk their lives to help other mountaineers. They love the hills and they just want to put something back, without fear or favour. Long may they continue. Team building is all about trust and little to do with contrived high fives or huddles. It is about working at the sharp end and placing your trust, some-times your life, in the hands of your colleagues, with no blame or recriminations.

* * *

Postscript: Ian Ramsey died in hospital on 2nd January 2020. His funeral service took place in Killin Parish Church on Monday 13th January that year. Over 200 people crushed into the church to pay their respects.

While physically Ian never fully recovered from the crash, his spirit and bravery did not diminish.

Epilogue

I T is the nineteenth day of October 2002. I am a smidgen older, a bit slower, and I am facing 'The Horns'. William Arthur Poucher, in his book *The Scottish Peaks* – the book gifted to me by Frank, the book I so treasure and the book that awoke in me the initial stirrings of mountains and mountaineering – describes the ascent of Beinn Alligin as a sporting course, and the only problems one will encounter are the Horns. He talks about taking great care and about using pressure holds on the first of the Horns. He obviously was traversing the mountain clockwise and, by the sound of it, on a dry day.

Well, as it happens, my small group – three of us – were tackling the mountain anti-clockwise, and not on a dry day. This day, my day, was dreich, blizzardy and 'super dangereux', with wet, fresh snow clinging to every ledge. Pressure holds were not available and, as we were descending that part – not ascending – things were a tad tricky, to say the least. In case you are wondering, no, we did not have a rope – nor did we have crampons. It was challenging and I savoured every moment, and – like so many days before – being on the edge, pushing on, braving the storm, brings its rewards. We are through the tricky part; we are over the Horns, the black

Beinn Alligin, with the Horns on the right

clouds part, and stunning views emerge. I stand on the summit of my last Munro.

My head spins with thoughts; with memories, people I have climbed with, special people: Alex, Dave, Brian, Tom, Mick, Roger, Frances, Ben, my family who supported me; my son Stuart, who followed in my footsteps, and my other two sons, Douglas and Alasdair, who displayed more sense, but still supported me, and so many more. I remember why I do this, and why I will always do it. It does not need explaining; explanations can devalue. Our mountains do not need explaining. They can speak for themselves; just get out and listen to them. I think of Mackem sitting there and of two simple words he uttered – words of inspiration, 'being alive' – and I remember these two old friends living out their dreams on the terraces of Brockville Park, Falkirk, all these years ago. Both long since dead. Without them this privilege may never have been possible. I place my last stone on the summit, I kiss it, and I thank every one of them.

Frank, I kept my promise.

'Let us endeavour to live so that when we come to die even the undertaker will be sorry.'

Mark Twain (1835-1910)

About the Author

Ian McNeish was born in 1946, in Falkirk. That not only made him a Bairn, but also a Bulge Baby. His formative years in the post-War period were spent in Bonnybridge then Balloch. His early employment was with Carron Ironworks in Falkirk and then Ferranti Limited in Edinburgh, before heading south for a time to Cosser Electronics where he worked as an Organisation and Methods Officer in the electronic manufacturing sector. He then came back home to a job with Aberdeenshire County Council where, in addition to examining work methods and producing detailed project management reports, he also liaised with staff, unions and management.

In 1974 Ian joined Ross and Sutherland Constabulary, and in seven months was trusted to police in a single station officer role within a rural area of Scotland with a population of six thousand people. In 1978 Ian transferred to Central Scotland Police where he rose to the rank of Chief Inspector, before retiring in 2004.

In the police service Ian gained a Higher National Certificate in police studies, as well as a certificate on Strategic Investigation and a certificate on Structured Debriefing. He is a trained Emergencies Planning officer and successfully completed his Strategic Chief Inspector's course at the Scottish Police College. He trained at the Home Office Crime Prevention Centre, and gained certificates in Crime Prevention and Community Safety as well as Architectural Liaison and Designing Out Crime.

In 1992 Ian was seconded to work within the Policy Unit of Central Regional Council to develop a strategy on community safety, the first officer to take on that role within a Regional Council in Scotland. The strategy, entitled 'Switched on to Safety', was successful and recognised by the Secretary of State for Scotland's Advisory Group on Sustainable Development. It was highlighted in the white paper 'This Common Inheritance, 1996'. The strategy was further recognised by the UK National Council for the United Nations Conference on Human Settlements as one of the top Best Practice examples in the UK and presented at the Habitat ll, United Nations City Summit Conference in Istanbul in June 1996.

On returning to the force, Ian continued his career in Falkirk and then as Local Unit Commander based in Bo'ness. He was promoted to Officer in Charge of Community Safety at Police Headquarters, and took charge of the force's Safety in Communities strategy with particular responsibility for Youth Crime, Safety in Communities, Diversity, Drug Education and liaison with partner agencies, Victims of Crime, and general Crime Prevention issues.

In that role, Ian acted as senior police advisor to the Scottish Office Environment Department when they put together and published their Planning Advice Note 46, entitled 'Planning For Crime Prevention'. He was also responsible for planning and writing the booklet on women's safety entitled *Talking Sense/Seeing Sense*, and advising the Scottish Office on production of the video of the same name. 300,000 copies of the booklet were printed, as well as scores of the video, for use throughout Scotland.

On leaving the police service, Ian set up his own company advising small businesses on policy issues as well as carrying out investigations on employment disputes and preparing reports. Ian has also chaired several internal discipline hearings and produced written judgements. He also was Chairman of the board of Signpost Recovery, and for about eighteen months managed the project.

As a consequence of the foregoing he has amassed a wealth of experience carrying out investigations and producing reports for the criminal justice system and the internal police discipline system, as well as strategic reports and latterly reports and judgements of disputes in the employment arena. Ian has also carried several in-depth investigations involving employment disputes and reported his findings to an employment lawyer.

His spare time is taken up with mountaineering, for a time being in Mountain Rescue. He has found time to ascend Mont Blanc and climb all the Munros. He also cycles and has some long distance treks to his name, including cycling from Edinburgh to Paris. He plays competitive curling and also coaches beginners. He did play golf, but cut back on that as he could not spare the time. He has a family: three boys and six grandchildren. When he is not employed with any or all of the above, he writes. Ian's first book, *The Fearn Bobby: Reflections from a Life in Scottish Policing*, was published by Extremis Publishing in 2018.

Ian was elected a Fellow of the Royal Society of Arts in 2019.

The Heart 200 Book

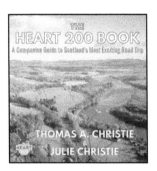

A Companion Guide to Scotland's Most Exciting Road Trip

By Thomas A. Christie and Julie Christie

The Heart 200 route is a unique road trip around some of the most beautiful locations in Central Scotland. Two hundred miles running through Stirlingshire and Perthshire, Heart 200 takes its visitors on an epic adventure to suit every taste—whether you are an outdoors enthusiast, an aficionado of history, or simply looking to enjoy yourself in some of the most stunning natural surroundings in the world.

Written with the full approval and co-operation of the Heart 200 team, *The Heart 200 Book* is a guide to the very best that the route has to offer. You will discover the history and culture of this remarkable region, from antiquity to the modern day, with more than a few unexpected insights along the way. Over the millennia, this amazing land has made its mark on world history thanks to famous figures ranging from the ancient Celts and the Roman Empire to King Robert the Bruce and Mary Queen of Scots, by way of Bonnie Prince Charlie, Rob Roy MacGregor, Robert Burns, Sir Walter Scott, Queen Victoria and even The Beatles!

So whether you're travelling by foot, car, motorhome or bike, get ready for a journey like no other as the Heart 200 invites you to encounter standing stones and steamships, castles and chocolatiers, watersports and whisky distilleries... and surprising secrets aplenty! Illustrated with full-colour photography and complete with Internet hyperlinks to accompany the attractions, *The Heart 200 Book* will introduce you to some of the most remarkable places in all of Scotland and encourage you to experience each and every one for yourself. It really will be a tour that you'll never forget.

The Fearn Bobby
Reflections from a Life in Scottish Policing

By Ian McNeish

'It's all about the community', the words of Kenneth Ross, Chief Constable of Ross and Sutherland Constabulary, guided Ian McNeish through thirty years of police service. They were true then, back in 1974, and they are true now.

Ian held a police warrant card for three decades, serving communities across Scotland. In that time, his work saw him moving from the northerly constabulary where he policed the rural Hill of Fearn to the social challenges that presented themselves amongst the urban landscape of Central Scotland.

From his formative years in post-War Scotland through to his application to join the police service, Ian has led a rich and varied professional life that ranged from working in iron foundries to building electronic parts for the Kestrel Jump Jet and legendary Concorde aircraft. But once he had joined the police service, he found himself faced with a whole new range of life-changing experiences – some of them surprising, a few even shocking, but all of them memorable.

Leading the reader through his involvement in front line situations, Ian explains the effects of anti-social behaviour and attending criminal court appearances, in addition to dealing with death and the responsibilities of informing those left behind. He considers topics such as ethics, public interest, police and firearms, drug issues, causes of crime, and a lot more besides.

In a career where his duties ranged from policing national strikes to providing comfort and support through personal tragedies, Ian advanced through the ranks and saw first-hand the vital importance of effective management and good teamwork. Whether as the 'Fearn Bobby', policing a remote countryside outpost, as a seconded officer working for the Chief Executive of a Regional Council, or as a Local Unit Commander in Bo'ness, Ian always knew the importance of putting the community first. Comparing to-day's policing techniques with his own professional experi-ences and examining both the good times and the harrow-ing pitfalls of the job, his account of life in the force is heartfelt, entertaining, and always completely honest.

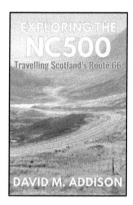

Exploring the NC500
Travelling Scotland's Route 66

By David M. Addison

Travelling anti-clockwise, David M. Addison seeks his kicks on Scotland's equivalent of Route 66. Otherwise known as NC500, the route takes you through five hundred miles of some of Scotland's most spectacular scenery. No wonder it has been voted as one of the world's five most scenic road journeys.

There are many ways of exploring the NC500. You can drive it, cycle it, motorbike it or even walk it, even if you are not one of The Proclaimers! And there are as many activities, places of interest and sights to be seen along the way as there are miles.

This is a personal account of the author's exploration of the NC500 as well as some detours from it, such as to the Black Isle, Strathpeffer and Dingwall. Whatever your reason or reasons for exploring the NC500 may be, you should read this book before you go, or take it with you as a *vade mecum*. It will enhance your appreciation of the NC500 as you learn about the history behind the turbulent past of the many castles; hear folk tales, myths and legends connected with the area; become acquainted with the ancient peoples who once lived in this timeless landscape, and read about the lives of more recent heroes such as the good Hugh Miller who met a tragic end and villains such as the notorious Duke of Sutherland, who died in his bed (and may not be quite as bad as he is painted). There are a good number of other characters too of whom you may have never heard: some colourful, some eccentric, some *very* eccentric.

You may not necessarily wish to follow in the author's footsteps in all that he did, but if you read this book you will certainly see the landscape through more informed eyes as you do whatever you want to do *en route* NC500.

Sit in your car and enjoy the scenery for its own sake (and remember you get a different perspective from a different direction, so you may want to come back and do it again to get an alternative point of view!), or get out and explore it at closer quarters – the choice is yours, but this book will complement your experience, whatever you decide.

Also Available from Extremis Publishing

Digging into Stirling's Past
Uncovering the Secrets of Scotland's Smallest City

By Murray Cook

Stirling is Scotland's smallest city and one of its newest. But, strangely, it's also the ancient capital and one of the most important locations in all of Scottish history. If you wanted to invade or to resist invasion, you did it at Stirling. It has witnessed Celts, Romans, Britons, Picts, Scots, Angles, Vikings, Edward I, William Wallace, Robert the Bruce, Edward II, Oliver Cromwell, Bonnie Prince Charlie, the Duke of Cumberland, and even played a decisive role in D-Day.

This huge history has left its mark all over this tiny place. Stirling is Scotland's best preserved medieval city, boasting one of Europe's finest Renaissance palaces, the world's oldest football, Mary Queen of Scots' coronation, James III's grave and murder scene, the site of a successful 16th century assassination of Scotland's head of state, Scotland's first powered and unpowered flights, Scotland's biggest royal rubbish dump, one of Scotland's earliest churches, Scotland's two most important battles, vitrified forts, Scotland's oldest and best preserved Royal Park, connections to King Arthur and the Vikings, Britain's last beheading, Scotland's largest pyramid – and its oldest resident is 4000 years old!

This book tells Stirling's story through its secret nooks and crannies; the spots the tourists overlook and those that the locals have forgotten or never visited. Join Stirling's Burgh Archaeologist, Dr Murray Cook, as he takes you on a tour of a fascinating city's history which is full of heroes and battles, grave robbing, witch trials, bloody beheadings, violent sieges, Jacobite plots, assassins, villains, plagues, Kings and Queens... and much, much more besides.

For details of new and forthcoming books
from Extremis Publishing, including our
podcast, please visit our official website at:

www.extremispublishing.com

or follow us on social media at:

www.facebook.com/extremispublishing

www.linkedin.com/company/extremis-publishing-ltd-/